THE CLASSICAL THEATRE OF CHINA

by A. C. Scott

THE KABUKI THEATRE OF JAPAN

The Ghost in the play *Huo Cho Chang San-lang*

THE CLASSICAL THEATRE OF CHINA

by

A. C. SCOTT

*With illustrations by
the author*

GREENWOOD PRESS, PUBLISHERS
WESTPORT, CONNECTICUT

Library of Congress Cataloging in Publication Data

Scott, Adolphe Clarence, 1909-
    The classical theatre of China.

    Reprint of the 1957 ed. published by Macmillan,
New York.
    Bibliography: p.
    Includes indexes.
    1. Theater--China.   2. Chinese drama--History and
criticism.   I. Title.
[PN2871.S4 1978]   792'.0951   77-16447
ISBN 0-313-20022-X

First published in 1957.

Reprinted with the permission of George Allen & Unwin, Ltd.

Reprinted in 1978 by Greenwood Press, Inc.,
51 Riverside Avenue, Westport, CT. 06880

Printed in the United States of America

THE CLASSICAL THEATRE OF CHINA

by

A. C. SCOTT

With *illustrations by*
the author

NEW YORK

THE MACMILLAN COMPANY

PREFACE

THIS volume is intended as a practical handbook on the classical theatre of China. I am very conscious of its limitations in Chinese eyes. My only excuse for adding to the existent mountain of literature on China, is that there is relatively little first hand information on the theatre in English.

I have considered it necessary to describe the actor's technique at such length because that, after all, is the basis of the symbolism which it is important to follow. Apart from this, it forms a record of a theatrical process which will almost inevitably undergo many changes if it is not already doing so. The material is so arranged that the most technical descriptions impinge as little as possible on the general information. It is impossible to avoid a great number of special terms in a work of this nature, but these I have tried to explain as fully as possible. The romanization used throughout is that of the Wade system with the exception of place names which use the old Post Office spelling. Dynastic dates follow those of the Handbook of Oriental History compiled by the Royal Historical Society, London.

A. C. S.

ACKNOWLEDGMENTS

I AM indebted to a great number of people for their generous assistance and advice over the years in which this book has been in preparation. In the first place, its inspiration has been due to the art of the Chinese actor and actress and to them I pay homage. Mr. Yü Chen-fei by his friendship and counsel, as well as the genius of his talents, has been a source of encouragement in my work on the Chinese drama. Mr. Chang Chun-ch'iu gave me a great deal of assistance and extended me many privileges when his troupe was in Hong Kong. I am also grateful to a young actor of his company at that time, Mr. Wang Te-k'un, who provided me with much information concerning the *ch'ou* roles as well as posing for me in costume on a number of occasions.

I owe a special debt of gratitude to the actresses Miss Li Hui-fang of Shanghai and Miss Wang Hsi-yün of the Ch'ing Lo Yüan, Nanking. During the early days of my studies they gave me the free run of their dressing rooms, loaned me their costumes and Miss Li placed the services of her *pao t'ou ti* at my disposal. From her I learned much concerning technical matters of make-up and costume.

Mr. Boyen Li, one-time member of the administrative staff of the Hsi Ch'ü Hsüeh Hsiao, Peking, has helped me in a number of ways on matters connected with the drama and has willingly given me the benefits of his connections with the theatre. Mrs. Li T'ien Shu-hsiu of Peking has been a most useful aid as a language instructor always ready to don theatrical make-up the better to get facts right.

I acknowledge the facilities extended to me by the Institute of Oriental Studies of the University of Hong Kong together with the personal help of a member of the language school staff, Mrs. Wu Yü-lan.

Professor Ma Chien, of Hong Kong, and Mr. Chiang Yee, of Oxford, have helped me with bibliographical material. The photographs on plate IV were given to me specially by Mr. Liu Tsun-yan of the Education Department, Hong Kong, from his private collection.

My wife in her capacity of Librarian of the University of Hong Kong has assisted with bibliographical requirements as well as patiently checking drafts and proofs. Finally, I must thank Mrs. Anne Chang of Hong Kong for her efficient and painstaking preparation of the typescript and for writing the Chinese characters on page 52.

A. C. S.

Nanking/Hong Kong, 1947-55

SELECT
BIBLIOGRAPHY

LI YÜAN YING SHIH, by Hsü Mu-yün. (Chung Hua Yin Shua Kung Szu. Shanghai 1933.)

CHING HSI ERH PAI NIEN LI SHIH, compiled by Lu Yuan. (T'ai P'ing Yang Yin Shua Kung Szu. Shanghai 1928.)

HUAN YU P'U, by Lu Kao-i. (Shih Chieh Shu Chü. Shanghai 1939.)

CHUNG KUO CHÜ CHIH TSU CHIH, by Ch'i Ju-shan. (Peking (circa 1925).)

K'OUEN K'IU. Le Theatre Chinois Ancien, par Tsiang Un-kai. (Paris. Librairie Ernest Leroux 1932.)

FAMOUS CHINESE PLAYS, by L. C. Arlington and Harold Acton. (Henri Vetch, Peiping 1937.)

SECRETS OF THE CHINESE DRAMA. Cecilia S. L. Zung. (Kelly and Walsh, Shanghai 1937.)

CONTENTS

ILLUSTRATIONS

LINE DRAWINGS IN TEXT

Original photographs prepared by Mr. Yung Chin-t'ai

CHAPTER I

INTRODUCTION

᠁

THE description Classical Theatre of China could be used to mean a variety of dramatic forms and developments, but in this book it refers to the *ching hsi*, or Peking drama. *Hsi* is a generic term for theatricals in general, while *ching* is capital, meaning the drama of the capital, i.e. Peking. Within recent years when Peking was referred to as Peip'ing for a time, the term *p'ing hsi* was often used as a description. This should not be confused with *p'ing chü*, an entertainment which originally came from country districts and was developed in the cities, where it is now being encouraged under the new government. *Ching hsi* is the older and more commonly used name for the Peking theatre.

The history of a true Chinese theatre has been one of many changes since the time of the Mongol invasion and the commencement of the Yuan dynasty in 1280. Local dramatic techniques developed, prospered for a time and then fused with each other, first one and then the other taking pride of place in public esteem. Eventually, what could be called a national drama came into being. The *ching hsi* evolved about the middle of the nineteenth century and became so popular that it replaced the *k'un ch'ü*, which had remained supreme as a national entertainment since the middle of the Ming dynasty (1368–1644). The new theatre flourished from the beginning, it received Imperial patronage and rapidly became the favourite of the ordinary people as well, a position which it continued to retain in the twentieth century. During this period, there were many developments and, in later days, some aberrations. The latter could be related with declining standards of appreciation in a public affected by newer and more realistic forms of entertainment. In spite of this, the *ching hsi* has commanded a popularity greater in proportion than any of its rivals; it continues today but here we are concerned only with its history until 1949. It is impossible at present to form a correct and unbiased opinion on its more recent developments.

The Chinese drama is often called opera in English. It is true that there are certain similarities, song is all important and the actor in a *ching hsi* play must sing a large proportion of his parts. However, there are so many other factors to be taken into equal consideration with vocal accomplishment that it is not possible to judge a performance only by the kind of standards required for the appreciation of Western style opera. A Chinese play aims at a harmony of effect which is attained by a strict formality applied rigorously to every aspect of the actor's performance. Song, speech, movement, costume and make up, as well as the musical accompaniment, are alike bound by this formality. Ideally, not one of these may be sacrificed in the interests of the others. Western opera depends primarily on aural values, song is the only reason of its being. Supreme vocal talents in the West are not necessarily consistent with the most suitable physical appearance demanded by opera costume; personal eccentricities and sometimes a ludicrous figure may be forgiven, or forgotten, for the quality of the singing. In the Chinese theatre, any slight deviation from the visual pattern, either in the physical appearance of the actor, his movements and costume, or in the stage ensemble, detracts from the completeness of the entertainment to jar upon the sensibilities of the experienced playgoer with the imperfections produced. The key to a true understanding of the *ching hsi* therefore, is best found by considering its early origins and the reasons of its being, rather than trying to tabulate it under a comparison with Western forms.

It is of paramount importance to understand two things when studying the early origins of the Chinese, and indeed, Japanese drama. First, dancing in ancient days was always combined with spoken verse or song and second, instrumental music was invariably composed to accompany chanted verse or narrative rather than to perform any solo function as playing. These factors are at the bottom of a great deal of the basic construction of Chinese theatrical entertainment of which a drama like the *ching hsi* is the ultimate expression. Old writings record that from the earliest times dance, song and poetry were used to celebrate public, private or religious ceremonies and festivities, dancing methods enlarged the expression of words on these occasions. An extension of this is seen in the *ching hsi* actor who, with the variations of his movements and symbolic gestures, completes the meaning contained within song and narrative. Song, speech and movement cannot be considered as separate activities, they are units which combine to form the main pattern of expression. In order to understand this more perfectly, the technique of the *ching hsi* stage may be briefly described in its various aspects.

The stage itself is devoid of all scenic aids, it looks what it is, a bare platform from which the actor declaims his part. A hanging curtain at the rear, a single carpet on the floor, two plain wooden chairs and a small table are the basic requirements for a typical stage, however large. The audience do not require any external trappings, their interest is focused on the person of the actor who is telling them a story by word and gesture and the symbolism of his technique dispenses with time, place and atmosphere in any material fashion, these are created in the imaginations of the onlookers.

The actor's technique is the crux of the whole entertainment, the play itself is a vehicle which uses a hallowed theme presented in a fashion best calculated to create situations in which the virtuoso qualities of the actor may be used to the maximum advantage, it is around his skill and talent that the whole thing revolves. The audience comes to see the actor rather than the play, they do not tire when they are confronted with stories which, although they may have been rearranged, are the dramatic inheritance of generations before them. They are thoroughly conversant with the conventions and symbolism of the actor's performance which, in their critical eyes, must not deviate in any way from the standards set by a line of master players before him and yet contain that intangible quality which springs from personality, the hallmark of any actor worth his salt.

In the *ching hsi*, the actor's roles are divided under four main headings, *sheng*, *tan*, *ching* and *ch'ou*, or male, female, painted face and comic. These symbolize the characters and qualities of certain standardized personalities and pay no attention to normal variations in human appearance. In addition, each type of role has its own gestures, way of walking, and particular vocal technique. The audience expects and is familiar with this rigid and unchanging presentation. If the *ching hsi* stage itself lacks ornamental qualities, the costumes of the actors more than make up for it and their brilliance, fine materials and decorative effect, make it appear as though a plain deal box had been opened to reveal a collection of sparkling jewels and brilliants. It is part of the device to concentrate the attention of the playgoer on the person of the actor, regardless of any other factors.

Since the reign of the Emperor Ch'ien Lung (1735–96), women's parts on the stage have always been acted by men and to this day the most distinguished and talented player of feminine roles is a man, Mei Lan-fang, who epitomizes the tradition. Within recent years women have taken to the *ching hsi* stage and the actress has become more and more common. More will be said about this in a later chapter.

When an actor makes an entry or an exit he obeys a certain procedure in his speech and movements which never varies and is governed by the particular role he plays. This formality is extended throughout the play, the actors use certain movements of their heads, hands and feet to accompany their narration and singing as the plot of the play is unfolded both visually and vocally to an audience primed and fully conversant with dramatic symbolism. Costume, make up and even the more realistic forms of movement such as fighting or sword play, all follow similar strict rules of procedure which is also applied to the position and placing of the actors on the stage and its compositions in general. Realism is dispensed with from every point of view, unless one excepts the byplay of the *ch'ou*, or clown, and the mime in some of the lighter feminine roles, but even in such cases there is present a certain deference to conventions which mark it apart from realism in any literal interpretation of the word. The dialogue of the plays does not imitate ordinary speech except again in the case of the *ch'ou*, who speaks his part in the *pai hua* or everyday talk of Peking, and even he sometimes relapses into more conventional phraseology. Honorific and polite terms mark the *ch'ang pai*, or actor's vocal technique apart from everyday speech, but it is not only there that the difference lies. The effect aimed at is a rhythmic pattern vocally, to gain this the actor adapts his words to special modulations of the voice which rises and falls or draws out certain syllables in accordance with this attention to rhythm, regardless of literal conversational state-ment. The timbre of the actor's voice is also adapted to the particular type of role he is playing, for, as already stated, each type has its own particular vocal technique. The rhythm of his speech and song is counterbalanced by the rhythm of his move-ments, while he is singing and speaking he may be walking, sitting, riding or gesturing and his actions are controlled in accordance with the principles already described. It is on these occasions that the ancient method of combining song with dance is seen developed, if through many processes, in the present stage technique.

Pure dancing as such is rarely seen on the *ching hsi* stage as it is in the Japanese kabuki for instance. It is true that there are certain plays which contain dance pieces, the actor Mei Lan-fang has introduced many based on old Court dances into his repertoire, but it is in the action, gestures and fighting of the *ching hsi* that the dancing element is really preserved. As in the kabuki, a pictorial effect is often achieved during a performance of a play, when the actors remain posed in a tableau for a few moments, particularly in the fighting scenes, but these tableaux are to be observed in the middle of a play rather than the end. While kabuki plays like to conclude with a pictorial composition over which the curtain is drawn, in the Chinese equivalent it is necessary for everyone to leave the stage immediately the last scene ends, for the next scene or play must follow immediately with no curtain and only an orchestral prelude to announce it.

While the strictest formality controls the actor's performance in the Chinese theatre, the reverse is true of the orchestra and the stage assistants who look after the actor's needs during the course of a performance. The orchestra is placed on the stage, generally to the right of the audience, the members sitting in a certain arrangement according to the instrument they play, but here any attempt at formality ends and the ceremony and costume which is seen on the Japanese stage is absent altogether in the case of Chinese theatre musicians. They come and go as they please between scenes, show a catholic taste in the costume they wear and in general display a nonchalant attitude to their whereabouts. This attitude is deceptive however and in no way interferes with the precision of their playing. So too with the stage assistants, who leisurely perform their duties in full view of the audience while the play is proceeding and remain on the stage throughout. Their attire is often quite informal, particularly in the hot weather. It emphasizes a sharp difference between the theatres of China and Japan. In the latter, everyone from the actors down to stage hands obey conventions which add to the pattern of movement and stage design as an entity. In the

Chinese theatre nothing matters beyond the actors, their brilliant figures and precise movements are the only things that concern the audience, beyond them the utmost latitude is granted to everything and everybody connected with the performance. Indeed, to the outsider this latitude is emphasized to an extent at times which makes one feel that the Chinese actor must have the hardest task of players anywhere.

The plays of the *ching hsi* are customarily divided into *wen hsi* and *wu hsi*. The former deal in general with aspects of social or domestic life while the latter contain more martial elements and deal with wars, military encounters, the adventures of brigands and so on. The characteristics of both styles are often intermingled in the plays, whose plots are drawn from historical sources both real and imaginary, mythology and folk lore. Again, facts from any of these sources may be mixed freely in order to make a good dramatic story.

For the uninitiated a better appreciation of the *ching hsi* may be obtained with some knowledge of stage technique and symbolism and a general understanding of the Chinese background. Stage technique is explained at length in a later chapter, what follows here is a brief account of certain features of Chinese life which are useful as a basis of knowledge when considering the plays of the *ching hsi* theatre.

The government of old China was a monarchial one, the nation being ruled by the Emperor as the father of the people, so appointed by the will of Heaven. He was also commander in chief of all the armies, nominal head of religious and ceremonial affairs and dispenser of justice to the state. Society was broadly divided into four classes *shih*, scholars, under which classification also came *ch'en*, officials, and *shen shih* or landed gentry. *Nung* were the farmers or agriculturists, *kung* the artisans and *shang* the merchants. The Emperor administered justice from the capital, the seat of government, where also resided the hierarchy of officials and scholars. The country was divided into provinces which were each administered by a governor who was directly responsible to the Court for the affairs of that province and the other officials and nobles under him. The governors were vested with powers of punishment and reward. Revenue was derived by the state from land tithes and various forms of taxation imposed on the provinces from the capital, a system which required

Su San wearing the cangue

a widespread body of officials of varying degrees. Appointment to official posts was by means of the famous competitive literary examinations held triennially in Peking, to which candidates flocked from every part of the country. The examinations were open to all suitably qualified candidates, rich and poor alike, and it was the ambition of every young scholar to succeed and so make a career for himself. Certain classes considered as outcasts in society were not allowed to compete in the examinations however, this included all actors. The young scholar journeying to the examinations at Peking as a theme colours a number of plays. The unit of provincial administration was the local magistracy to which came senior magistrates on circuit. The background of government with its scholar officials and magistrates is seen portrayed time and time again on the *ching hsi* stage. Criminal offenders were punished for their more serious faults with decapitation or flogging, often symbolically represented in the theatre. Women prisoners were marched to the courts with a *cangue* round their necks. This was a kind of wooden collar through which their hands were also secured in front of their face, a wooden tablet fixed on the back of the prisoner was inscribed *nu fan*, women criminal, followed by her name. This practice may be seen enacted on the stage in plays like *Chin So Chi* or *Yü T'ang Ch'un*, in both of which the heroine is a prisoner falsely accused.

Marriage was prearranged by parents in old China, celibacy being in general discouraged. The principal aim of marriage was the continuance of the family line and the provision of heirs to carry on devotions to the ancestral spirits. Romantic love was never taken into consideration as a reason for marriage. Betrothals were arranged by parents through the intervention of a matchmaker, a role which provides great scope for the *ch'ou* actor. A marriage concluded with the progress of the bride from her home to that of her parents-in-law where she took up residence as a member of her husband's family. Concubinage was an established practice, originally sanctioned as a further means of securing male heirs. Concubines became members of a family being subject to the supervision of the wife, in theory at any rate. Concubines of the Imperial house have on more than one occasion exerted considerable influence on state affairs besides being famed in story and legend for their beauty and charm. Yang Kuei Fei, the favourite of the Emperor Ming Huang (A.D. 712–54) and Yü Chi, mistress of Hsiang Yü, the King of Ch'u (B.C. 232–201) are two who may be named, for their exploits are perpetuated in plays which rank among some of the most popular in the *ching hsi* repertoire. Women in general, however, occupied a secondary position in society, a woman was expected to be modest, chaste and loyal to her husband while conducting his household affairs and these qualities are symbolized in the type of heroine's role called *ch'ing i*, a sub-division of the *tan* role. No wife could divorce her husband and it was considered a disgrace if he exercised his legal powers to divorce her. A widow rarely remarried as it was considered an act of chastity to remain faithful to a dead husband to whom she still belonged. Few women cared to defy this social convention, so deeply was it regarded in the eyes of society. A man, of course, could remarry

or take a concubine, for in his case he was adding a new member
to the clan and therefore strengthening the family line. The
family was the keystone of Chinese society and filial piety was
a virtue to which everything else was subordinate, a son's prime
allegiance was to his parents and through them the spirits of his
ancestors. As might be expected, the theatre drew largely on the
pattern of life described above and found rich material for its
plays.

The courtesan has inspired important roles on the stage for in
a society where marriage was so rigidly controlled she was at
one time a significant figure in social life. Courtesans were professional women trained from an early age in singing and playing
musical instruments, composing poetry, practising calligraphy
and being skilled in the art of entertainment generally. Young
men and scholars paid court at the houses where they resided and
the plots of several plays are concerned with the 'singsong' girls
of other days. *Yü T'ang Ch'un* is a good example, its heroine
Su San, the singsong girl, being one of the best known characters
on the stage.

A fashion of the women of former times might be mentioned
here, i.e. the practice of foot binding which has given rise to a
special stage technique requiring great acrobatic skill on the part
of the actor. Accounts differ as to the origin of foot binding as a
custom, one authority relates it as being due to women trying to
imitate the small feet of the favourite concubine of an Emperor
of ancient times, another that it was initiated as a safeguard to
prevent women straying too far afield. Whatever the true ex-
planation it became a fashionable cult with women who vied with
each other in the smallness of their 'golden lily' feet as they were
termed. The practice long ago died out although occasionally an
ancient woman may still be seen with the pinched feet resulting
from this custom. The method by which *ching hsi* actors simulate
bound feet on the stage is described in detail in Chapter V.

The segregated state of women in China had the effect of
developing a strong sense of comradeship in the male sex and a
young man would esteem it a privilege to acquire a 'sworn'
brother who would share his pleasures and stand by him in time
of need. This type of relationship is often emphasized in the
drama where the loyalty of pledged friendships offers great scope
for the actor.

In the past, the Chinese have laid great stress on ceremony and the punctilious observance of an etiquette created to cover all aspects of daily living. Ranks of society were distinguished by certain styles of clothing and types of weapons or objects for everyday use. There were standard forms of address between superiors and inferiors, or vice versa, greetings, the reception and seating of guests and a host of other matters were all bound by formal rules. Disregard of these codes of behaviour was looked upon as the mark of ill breeding, or a barbarian. This regard for ceremonial is clearly expressed in the *ching hsi* where the etiquette of former times is crystallized in the yet more formal speech and gesture of the actor and the costumes he wears.

China's history has been a long series of wars, armed revolts and civil strife. Her dynastic periods have succeeded each other with the rise to power of some new military conqueror and her legends are full of the prowess of the warriors of ancient times. In spite of this, the soldier has always been looked down upon in Confucian society. The drama is full of the feats of arms of the warriors and generals of early times, especially the plays that deal with the Three Kingdoms period (A.D. 220–265) but it is perhaps significant that strategy and ruse are as often shown as the attributes of a great warrior as mere physical feats of arms. A good example is seen in the famous play *K'ung Ch'eng Chi* or the strategy of the Empty City. In this, an unguarded city is prevented from falling into the hands of enemy forces by a ruse which would make any military historian smile, but on the stage it provides first class material for the technique of the actor, particularly his singing!

Religion, in so far as it affects the stage, may be briefly mentioned. The Chinese have always been extremely tolerant in religious matters and Confucianism, Buddhism and Taoism have flourished side by side as the three principal faiths of China. Confucianism was not a religion in the strict sense of the word but a system of ethics for the conduct of living. The moral principles of Confucianism had their foundation in ancestor worship, as a faith it was agnostic and set the whole pattern of family life and through that the conduct of the state. Confucianism was perhaps dominant among religious beliefs although the majority of Chinese people were eclectic and subscribed to all three faiths quite impartially. Buddhism, which came to China

Chu Pa Chieh

from India, was a religion which appealed through its spiritual conceptions of life after death. Its influence was shown outwardly by the great number of monastaries built all over the country, often in the most commanding positions. Taoism, originally a philosophy evolved by Lao Tze about the end of the the fifth century B.C., became a form of spirit worship which took a good deal of its religious formula from Buddhism. The moral reasoning embodied in numbers of plays in the *ching hsi* is based on the principles upheld by Confucianism. Buddhism, on the whole, receives scant treatment at the hands of the playwrights and the Buddhist priest is more often than not a figure of fun, the butt of the dramatist. In passing, it is interesting to note *Hsi Yu Chi*, a record of a journey to the Western paradise to secure the Buddhist scriptures for the Chinese Emperor. The work is a dramatization of the introduction of Buddhism into China and has produced some colourful stage material, including that pair of strange characters Sun Wu K'ung, the monkey god, and Chu Pa Chieh, a spirit who was banished from Heaven and in earthly exile became half human and half pig. The chief contribution of Taoism to the theatre is a number of gods and spirits from its gallery of the supernatural. Elements from Buddhism, Taoism and Confucianism are mixed where necessary, as indeed they have been in the religious life of the Chinese people. The *ching hsi* is chiefly concerned with religion from the point of view of making dramatic entertainment, its function is not to spread spiritual propaganda.

In the *ching hsi*, the stark symbolism of stage properties and lack of settings do nothing to create a visual representation as provided say on the kabuki stage of Japan. Such effects as there are only serve to stimulate the workings of the playgoer's imagination, he must conjure it all up for himself. In concluding this chapter, it is worth while considering a few more details useful to the layman whose imagination is not already coloured by the background knowledge which is the prerogative of the Chinese playgoer. Old Chinese cities were built within walls whose gates were closed at nightfall. Streets were unlit and pedestrians walked abroad accompanied by an attendant carrying a lantern, the stage utilises this old custom to suggest night time in a play. Houses, at any rate the larger ones, were built within a system of courtyards reached through entrances whose double doors opened right and left and were bolted horizontally with a lock in the centre. In addition, they were built with a threshold several inches high which necessitated lifting the feet when entering or departing, facts which are all symbolized in the mime and gestures of the actor. The latticed window panes were not made of glass but opaque paper, as an actor playing the part of an inquisitive old woman will indicate by poking an expressive finger through an imaginary pane, and applying an even more expressive eye to an equally imaginary hole. Travel in the past was by means of horses, closed palanquins or two wheeled horse drawn chariots. Warriors and officials rode horseback but women never, they travelled by palanquin or chariot. Oar and sail propelled junks and sampans conveyed travellers by water and ferried them across rivers. All these forms of transport are represented in original fashion on the stage and are described in detail later.

Every aspect of Chinese life and sentiment has been drawn upon by the *ching hsi*, and it has translated what it has borrowed into dramatic situations which are a part of a formal theatrical art unique in its symbolism, within which are consummated principles found in all Chinese art. One does not go to the Chinese theatre in search of great literature, it is, as already stated, first and foremost contrived as a setting for the art of the actor; this outline is intended as a useful starting point towards an understanding of that art.

CHAPTER II

A SHORT
HISTORICAL SURVEY

⨭⨭

THE *ching hsi* drama traces its origins back to the song and dance which accompanied festivals and religious or public ceremonies of ancient times. These are regarded as the basis of all dramatic expression in China. From such a beginning, the drama evolved against a shifting background of social and political changes which contributed to what, eventually, became a national theatre. There are records of dance entertainments which go back to the Chou dynasty (1050–249 B.C.), but the distinguished scholar of the theatre, Ch'i Ju-shan, has pointed out the importance of developments in T'ang times (A.D. 618–906) in their relationship to the *ching hsi*. His researches show that descriptions of T'ang dances, as given in early writings, indicate a remarkable similarity between certain of the dance movements and various aspects of the *ching hsi* actor's technique for instance.

A great deal of our knowledge of the early Chinese drama must remain as a matter for conjecture only, but it seems certain that the T'ang period was one of great developments in dramatic art. During this period the Emperor Ming Huang (A.D. 712–54) became a patron of the theatre and established the celebrated 'Academy of the Pear Orchard' for training young singers and actors to perform at Court. The title 'Leader of the Pear Orchard' was one which later became conferred on China's supreme actors. Imperial patrons encouraged the drama throughout its history and often took an active part in it as amateurs, a position which continued until the death of the Empress Dowager in 1908. It is curious to reflect that, in spite of such exalted esteem and close connection with the Court, the theatre was also frowned upon by scholars and moralists alike in Confucian society and the actor was regarded as an outcast until quite recent times.

The Yüan dynasty (1280–1368) is looked upon as the period which prepared the ground for the growth of the drama and

Sleeve movement

built foundations which were to remain as the basis of all future development; it is from then that we shall trace the history of the *ching hsi*. Until the Yüan dynasty, Chinese drama was not created to any set rules, it was what were called the *tsa chü* of Yüan times which first provided a model for play construction. *Tsa* literally means miscellany and *chü* a play. *Tsa chü* were devised with song and dialogue or declamation woven into a play which was always divided into four acts and they are considered as the oldest form of complete drama in China. The term Yüan drama is not used in the strictest sense of the political dynasty for it includes developments which had their beginning in the Sung dynasty (A.D. 960–1279) and reached their zenith in the Ming dynasty (A.D. 1368–1644). The Yüan drama was marked by a division of styles which are important in tracing the history of the *ching hsi*.

It must be realised that the whole question of the development
of various styles of drama through the centuries, as well as their
influence on each other, is a complex one on which a great deal of
research still remains to be done by Chinese experts. It was never
considered worth while keeping records of the drama in former
days, the theatre at the best of times is an art of the moment and
the passing years quickly obscure stage trends in a vast country
like China. Elderly people of today, for instance, can remember
ching hsi performances of forty years ago which, while staging
plays seen now, included acrobatic and humorous numbers that
were no doubt bequeathed to the *ching hsi* from various local
dramatic entertainments. This is but a minor example, but it
indicates the difficulty of analysing the many influences and
developments which have waxed and waned throughout even
quite a short period of time. However, during recent decades
Chinese students have formed a fairly consistent picture of the
main stream of developments which led to the rise of the *ching
hsi* as the national drama of China.

The division of styles in Yüan times already mentioned is
usually referred to under two schools, Northern and Southern, or
pei ch'ü and *nan ch'ü*. *Ch'ü* literally means song and plays and *pei*
and *nan* North and South respectively. Within each of the two
schools there were many different dramatic forms however and
when describing the characteristics of each of the schools it must
be accepted as a somewhat arbitrary naming of general basic
points, rather than detailed fact about the many individual styles
contained within them. The important difference in the
Northern and Southern schools lay in the construction of plays,
i.e. the music, dialogue and procedure which differed with the
locality of inspiration. The Southern style paid strict attention
to certain rules of prosody and the length of its measures while
embodying the use of scholarly and literary expressions. The
Northern style took some liberties with rules and incorporated
the use of terms from everyday speech. The Southern style used
a musical scale of five notes and no semitones where the Northern
style had seven notes, i.e. five tones and two semitones. String
instruments accompanied the singing of the Northern style but
the Southern style only used these in a secondary capacity, the
chief instrument being the flute. The songs of the Northern
school were lively and vigorous in keeping with the bolder spirit

of its region, those of the Southern school were softer in melody and feeling.

The two schools continued to thrive, each in their own fashion, until about the beginning of the Ming dynasty (A.D. 1368–1644) when a development of the Southern school of drama, the *ch'uan ch'i*, began to exert a powerful influence on public interest at the expense of the Northern school whose popularity waned. *Ch'uan* means to announce or transmit, while *ch'i* means wonderful or rare, hence the combination of the two words came to mean a play or drama. The term had been used earlier of certain technical developments in Yüan drama but finally came to be associated with Southern school developments. The *ch'uan ch'i* was largely based on the technique of the Southern school but also borrowed from the Northern particularly in matters connected with the roles of both comic and serious characters as well as in the simplification of certain plots. The *ch'uan ch'i* were generally arranged in about thirty or more acts each of which had their own title and were to some extent complete in themselves, thus allowing plays to be shortened at will by the exclusion of certain acts if desired. Each act was composed of a part for singing and a part for dialogue. The first act commenced with a secondary actor named the *fu mo* appearing on the stage, the two terms literally mean assistant and insignificant. The *fu mo* did not take part in the rest of the play, his task was to recite and sing a summary of the plot to the audience so that they understood the main outline of the piece. The plot of a *ch'uan ch'i* play would begin to unfold in the second act and become more complicated as it was interwoven among numerous episodes which were finally disentangled in the finale. As in the Chinese theatre today, there were no intervals between acts which followed in quick succession. There were six principal role divisions *sheng*, *tan*, *ching*, *ch'ou*, *mo* and *wai*. *Sheng* were the male roles, the heroes of the piece, who were generally young lovers or scholars and known as *hsiao sheng* or *kuan sheng*. When the *sheng* actor played older men they were known as *lao sheng* and these roles were not so important as the first named. This is different in the *ching hsi* where the *lao sheng* is one of the most important roles. *Tan* were the female roles which had different names according to the type portrayed. These were *cheng tan*, generally a fairly old woman though sometimes young, but always a good if serious character. *Tz'u sha* was a talkative lively woman and *tso tan* a role full of action and movement. *Kuei men tan* was a yoing girl, *lao tan* an old woman and *t'ieh tan* a secondary character. *Mo* and *wai* might be either young or old, men or women, but they were always secondary roles. Principal parts were called *chu chiao* and secondary parts *p'ei chiao*. A *chu chiao* part was invariably a *sheng* or *tan* role.

The *ch'uan ch'i* of the Southern style drama, i.e. *nan ch'ü*, attained such popularity that they eclipsed the rival Northern style plays completely and eventually brought about a dramatic style called the *k'un ch'ü* which was to remain supreme in the theatres of China for three hundred years. At the beginning of the Ming dynasty, the Southern style drama, which outstripped the rival Northern style in popularity, was divided into several small schools named *yu yao*, *hai yen* and *yi yang*, which had their origin in different provinces and which, while deriving from the main dramatic stream of the times, adapted themselves to local needs including dialect. This state of affairs continued until the middle of the Ming dynasty when the collaboration of a famous dramatist Liang Po-lung and an equally famous musician Wei Liang-fu brought about developments which were to have a far reaching effect on the course of the Chinese theatre in general.

Liang Po-lung was a scholar who came from K'un Shan in the province of Kiangsu and was unusually gifted in the art of dramatic composition. He was considered a master poet and his work was known everywhere. A Chinese writer has recorded that he was a handsome and elegant man with a magnificent beard, who sat facing West at a large table when instructing the theatre people and singing girls who flocked to him for instruction. Wei Liang-fu came from Kiangsu also, being a native of T'ai Ts'ang, a neighbouring town of K'un Shan, the birthplace of his colleague. He was a highly skilled musician and composer and is said to have spent twenty years on the creation of a musical style called *shui mo tiao*, before he became a professor of music at Soochow. Liang Po-lung went to consult him on theatrical matters with the result that Wei Liang-fu composed the music for the dramatist's newest play. It had such a great reception from the public that it became the forerunner of a new school of drama, adopting, at first, the name *shui mo tiao*. After this, the work of the two men acquired them a brilliant reputation and a number of scholars and musicians went to work under them, while the other schools of drama all began to be influenced by these new developments in the theatre. Eventually, the new school of drama took the name *k'un ch'ü* which was henceforth to designate the principal form of theatrical art in China for centuries to come.

Certain factors assisted the rise to popularity of the *k'un ch'ü* drama. During the Ming dynasty Soochow became the cultural centre of China, scholars and poets settled there and began to extend their patronage to the theatre. Composing and writing for the drama were regarded as accomplishments. The best actors and singers went to Soochow to participate in an art which was beginning to receive such intellectual favour. It was not only the literati who helped to make the *k'un ch'ü* so popular but also the singsong girls and public entertainers, their renderings of *k'un ch'ü* airs were quickly responsible for their being on the lips of high and low alike. Soochow at this time was a centre of fashion which became a model for the rest of China, its singsong girls were emulated by their sisters elsewhere even down to their accents. Besides this, Soochow remained the most prosperous commercial centre in China until its fall in the T'ai P'ing rebellion and the conquest of Kiangsu province in 1853. The *k'un ch'ü* thus also received financial as well as intellectual encouragement and it can readily be seen how a combination of circumstances established this drama as a first favourite among the Chinese people.

The *k'un ch'ü*, as dramatic art, passed through several stages of development and enjoyed Imperial patronage which reached its climax in the reigns of the Emperors K'ang Hsi (1661–1722) and Ch'ien Lung (1735–96). The increasing interest of courtier and dilettante was responsible in some measure for the decline of the *k'un ch'ü* after this, the ordinary public found the theatre was acquiring qualities too rare for their appreciation. On the other hand, during the period 1821–1850 the scholars began to neglect the *k'un ch'ü* in favour of other literary tendencies and the contents of the drama began to deteriorate in the eyes of the connoisseurs. The conquest of Kiangsu by the T'ai P'ing rebels in 1853 rang the death knell of the *k'un ch'ü* theatre. Soochow, the heart of the theatrical world, was thrown into complete disorder by the civil war which threatened the whole nation and the

B

training of singers and actors had to be abandoned. The Soochow companies resident in Peking left the capital for their native place under the stress of events and the *k'un ch'ü* drama fell into a decline from which it never recovered.

During the long reign of the *k'un ch'ü* drama, local dramas continued to exist to a greater or lesser degree. The *k'un ch'ü* itself had drawn upon many of these for its ultimate inspiration, a process of intermingling which had characterized the whole history of the Chinese theatre and was to continue to do so. The dramatic styles of Anhui, Hupeh and Shensi came into prominence with the decline of the *k'un ch'ü* and were drawn upon to create a new and single drama. When the *k'un ch'ü* disappeared so quickly from the scene another form took its place for a brief period in Peking, this was the *yi yang* style mentioned earlier as one of the three schools in existence prior to the emergence of the *k'un ch'ü*. Its new popularity soon waned before that of the *hu tiao* which came from Hupeh province. This local drama was adapted and perfected by actors of Anhui province and so it became called the *hu tiao* of the Anhui school, a school which was to play a prominent part in the development of the new *ching hsi* drama. The *hu tiao* style drama had already made an appearance in Peking during the later years of the *k'un ch'ü* when *hu pan*, or Anhui troupes, were established in the capital alongside the *su pan* or Soochow troupes. The first occasion of their appearance is recorded as on the occasion of the birthday celebrations of the Emperor Ch'ien Lung in 1790. The Anhui troupes quickly multiplied in the capital with the disappearance of the Soochow troupes at the time of the T'ai P'ing rebellion and gained an increasing popularity among Peking audiences. The Anhui style drama soon eclipsed all other forms and went from strength to strength. Peking became the centre of development, which eventually led to the creation of the *ching hsi*, or theatre of the capital. At the time these developments were going on, another dramatic style had a short run of popularity in Peking, this was the *pang tzu* school which originated in Shensi province. Its style was inferior and it was soon overshadowed but it too made some contribution to the new drama for the *ching hsi* drew upon it as upon other forms although to a much lesser degree.

The decline of the *k'un ch'ü* therefore brought a wider public to the other forms of drama, some of which had already begun to have a greater attraction for the ordinary playgoer. The fusing of certain techniques from these various styles created a pattern which formed the basis of the *ching hsi* drama and the Anhui school of actors were largely responsible for this. The *hsi p'i* and *erh huang* styles, which form the basis of the *ching hsi's* musical construction today, originally came from Hupeh through the Anhui school. The two names are now telescoped to give *p'i huang* as a general term for a musical style. *Hsi p'i* literally means Western skins, the origin of the term is obscure but it is presumed to refer to the skins or hides used in the construction of the instruments. *Erh huang* is explained in two different ways. Some writers say that it derives from two districts in Anhui both bearing the name Huang, while others declare that it means 'two flute airs' and refers to the fact that formerly two instruments were used in the accompaniment. *Erh* means two so there can be no argument on the numerical score, *huang* is also a name for a reed which is used in a certain kind of ancient musical instrument, but it was not a flute and the latter instrument has no reed anyway, so that the true origin of the name *erh huang* would still seem to be a matter of opinion.

It may be useful at this point to make a brief comparison between the fundamental characteristics of the *k'un ch'ü* drama and the *ching hsi* which replaced it. There have been several movements to revive the *k'un ch'ü* during the present century but with no widespread success. It has remained the prerogative of the connoisseur or amateur singer. A number of its plays are still performed and Mei Lan-fang has incorporated some of its more popular qualities in his personal plays, the scholars and playgoers of an older generation remember it with admiration but it is a form which finds no place in the general standards of dramatic appreciation in modern China. The greatest living exponent of *k'un ch'ü* is the famous actor Yü Chen-fei, one of the most distinguished players of the *hsiao sheng* role in the *ching hsi* theatre. He is the son of a leading *k'un ch'ü* scholar of Soochow and was literally cradled in this theatre, for he tells how his father sang the airs of the drama to him as a lullaby when a small child. In addition to being a master actor, Yü Chen-fei is also an accomplished performer on the *ti tzu* or flute, and he has also collected and revised the important plays of the repertoire many of which had become bowdlerized. Yü Chen-fei has been living in semi-retirement in Hong Kong for the last four years. He has managed to give an occasional performance but the lack of theatres and supporting casts have presented insuperable difficulties. He has eked out an existence with film work and teaching *k'un ch'ü* music. To listen to Yü Chen-fei playing his flute on a quiet evening, as this writer has often been privileged to do, is a never to be forgotten experience and one which brings the fervent hope that such art may never disappear from the Orient. At the time of writing this, Yü Chen-fei has just left for the mainland and rumour has it that he has been invited to become head of a school for *k'un ch'ü* which the authorities wish to open in order to preserve this old dramatic art.

The chief differences between the *k'un ch'ü* and the *ching hsi* may be said to lie in the musical accompaniment and the structure of the plays. The *ching hsi* uses string instruments for song accompaniment where the *k'un ch'ü* uses the flute, so that there is immediately a marked contrast in the quality of the music, that of the older drama being softer and possibly more romantic. There is more variation in the musical phraseology of the *k'un ch'ü* than in the *ching hsi* which possesses a limited range of airs to be used again and again, and which are transposed to suit the particular dramatic situation. This is a device which makes it easier for a wide public to familiarize themselves with the music of the theatre. *K'un ch'ü* music makes use of a more subtle technique and embodies a far greater number of musical styles in its accompaniment than does the more rigidly defined *p'i huang* of the *ching hsi*.

Although in both theatres the sung parts of the actors are written in verse those of the *k'un ch'ü* have a greater value as pure literature. The dramatists were men of letters who employed their talents in writing for the theatre, and their work is full of metaphors and allusions expressing their sentiment and philosophy in elegant style. The *ching hsi*, on the other hand, drew its plots from popular historical novels and romances whose characters were familiar to everyone and therefore admirable subjects for the actors to portray. The plays of the *ching hsi* were devised by actors rather than literary men and the repertoire as a whole was conceived from their standpoint first, the stories were simply vehicles for the technique of the actor and there was no attempt to create independent literary works of art. The *ching hsi* was intended to appeal to the theatregoer only but the *k'un ch'ü* aimed at satisfying the reader as well as the spectator. It is because of this that the vigorous, colourful and swift moving combat scenes which characterize the *ching hsi* are not found in the *k'un ch'ü*. They are conceived purely in terms of visual values.

K'un ch'ü plays divided into *ch'ih*, or acts, follow in detail the events of the various episodes and the actions of all the characters in the plot: *ching hsi* plays by comparison are short and often only briefly indicate the origin of the plot or even its conclusion, concentrating on the developments between these events as related to certain characters. An entire *ching hsi* play may often be no longer than one or two acts of a corresponding *k'un ch'ü* drama. The fact that each act of a *k'un ch'ü* play was more or less an independent dramatic unit of its own made it possible to utilize such acts in the *ching hsi* drama and it is this kind of process which has provided such *k'un ch'ü* elements as are incorporated in the newer theatre.

The rise to supremacy of the *ching hsi* might rudely be described as the triumph of the art of the boards over the art of the book and, as described, was due in great part to the many great actors who lived during the Ch'ing dynasty (1616–1912). Prominent among them was Ch'eng Chang-keng of Anhui, a man who had a profound influence on the theatre of his time and who is commonly regarded as the father of the *ching hsi*. He is said to have been primarily responsible for the emergence of its finished technique. His teaching benefited many who followed him. Another celebrated name was that of T'an Hsin-p'ei; he had a magnificent voice and developed the bearded *sheng* roles to new heights. His contribution to the drama was also a far reaching one, his acting and teaching benefited a long line of actors who followed him. There were many other outstanding actors besides these two men who both received the favours of the Court. The Empress Dowager (1835–1908) last of a long line of Imperial patrons and herself an enthusiastic amateur actress, played a part in encouraging the *ching hsi* theatre and the work of actors like the two named above.

Both these men were masters of the *sheng* role which was regarded then as the supreme one for an actor to play but in 1913 there appeared like a meteor out of the sky a young actor who was to shed lustre on the *tan* or female roles to an extent never known before. This phenomenon was Mei Lan-fang (1894–), grandson of Mei Ch'iao-ling (1841–1881), a noted actor of his time. Since he made his debut at the age of nineteen in Shanghai, Mei Lan-fang has remained the stage idol of China and his individual contribution to the drama has been a distinguished one. Trained in the rigid discipline of the old school of acting from childhood, he has remained unrivalled as a female impersonator throughout his long career. It is through him that the *tan* roles have assumed an artistic importance on the stage that they never had previously. In addition to his peerless acting Mei has been responsible for producing new plays in the classical tradition, reviving ancient dances as well as modifying and designing traditional theatrical costume. A school of acting has grown up within recent decades bearing the hall mark of his individual genius and many of the actresses who now grace the *ching hsi* stage derive their main inspiration from him. Hsueh Yen-chin, a talented actress who was one of the first to be accepted in orthodox stage circles, was a pupil of Mei Lan-fang, who will always be remembered as one of the great forces in his country's theatre.

The Japanese war interrupted developments in the *ching hsi* theatre as in all other artistic fields, but it carried on in one form or another in both free and occupied areas. The Japanese, a race with a long theatrical tradition of their own tried, not always successfully, to encourage the *ching hsi* during their occupation. Many well known actors refused to perform in occupied China as a patriotic protest. Mei Lan-fang was among them and, according to report, grew a moustache during this period to emphasize his decision the more effectively. One noted actor became *persona non grata* with the Nationalist Government after the war because he continued to act in occupied territory: it is perhaps significant that he was eventually invited back to China by a Communist government.

The post war years saw the theatre suffer from the nation's common ills. Inflation, plus the lack of effort on the part of apathetic authority to assist, brought hardship to theatre people in general. While lip service was paid to cultural traditions nothing was done to extend practical aid to an impoverished national art and its training schools. With the barrier that now exists between China and the outer world it is impossible to form an accurate and unprejudiced appraisal of the *ching hsi* theatre today. Propaganda utterances made it clear at the beginning of the Communist regime that the old drama would have to be changed to suit new ideology and if the long list of revised or banned plays published in the press is accepted, it is clear that this process is being carried out. All other available evidence points to the fact that the *ching hsi* is still an immensely popular dramatic entertainment which, when it does not impinge on the dictates of new thinking, has been encouraged to continue. The fact that it does come under political pressure is of course another question. Certainly if we penetrate beneath the propaganda verbiage which cloaks all statements about art in the new China, it would appear that the *ching hsi* theatre is in a healthier physical state than it was. It would be strange indeed if the Communists had not managed to make capital out of the depressing conditions in which actors found themselves prior to 1949.

After the Communist government came to power and during the period 1950–51, three leading actors from the mainland, Ma Lien-lang, Chang Chün-ch'iu and Yü Chen-fei, each distinguished in their own particular field of acting, gave a regular weekly *ching hsi* performance with a company in Hong Kong, the first occasion on which this colony had had the opportunity of acquiring a standing *ching hsi* company. Unfortunately the actors were compelled to abandon their performance in less than two years. There were several reasons, the chief ones being the difficulty of making financial ends meet and the lack of interest on the part of local Chinese people in the Northern drama. The Cantonese drama, an exceedingly debased and vulgar but none the less popular form, occupies the few leading theatres in Hong Kong and the managers refused to make any financial concessions to the Northern actors while at the same time allowing them only the worst bookings. Cantonese audiences have little appreciation of *ching hsi* drama, so that the Northern actors, depended solely on their compatriots, of whom by this time there was no inconsiderable number, for their patronage. It was unfortunate that some of the Shanghai people, with the help of others, did not do something towards establishing the company on a firm basis, it could have been achieved with a little public spirit and imagination. As it was, the actors were in perpetually low straits from the beginning and eventually Ma Lien-liang, together with Chang Chün-ch'iu, returned to China at the invitation of the Communist government and they are now acting on the mainland again. The chance of building up a first class *ching hsi* company in Hong Kong has gone for ever. Some years later Yü Chen-fei has followed the example of his colleagues and returned to the mainland. All the great actors are now in China and one can hardly expect them not to remain there. What the eventual future of the *ching hsi* actor will be it is difficult for anyone outside China to surmise, it would seem that his theatre is still a vigorous entity, if a controlled one.

CHAPTER III

THE MUSIC OF THE
CHING HSI THEATRE

༈

THE history of Chinese music is a long and obscure one and the earliest records of it are very scanty or have been lost altogether. There have been many developments due either to the various alien races who invaded China during her long history or her own conquests of foreign territory and relations with other Asian people. Music in China has at all times been associated with ritual and ceremonial observances besides being regarded a necessary factor in the education of the community. The *I li*, or Book of Etiquette, describes music as one of the six arts necessary in the accomplishments of the scholar. It is not the purpose of this chapter to deal with musical history in any detail, but only with the practical aspect of it in its relation to the *ching hsi* stage. An important thing to bear in mind is that verse and declamation have always been closely related with Chinese music, whose instruments have in general been conceived to accompany the spoken word rather than to perform solo functions.

It has been said in the last chapter that two musical styles, *hsi p'i* and *erh huang*, known collectively as *p'i huang*, have contributed a great deal to the musical construction of the *ching hsi* drama. A further style was mentioned called *pang tzu*. This form is generally considered to have originated in Shensi; it first became popular in Peking theatrical circles about the time of the disintegration of the *k'un ch'ü* theatre and had a great vogue for a period. It was soon eclipsed by the *p'i huang* styles which were in future to become supreme as theatre music. They incorporated some characteristics from *pang tzu* which were retained for certain plays. This style took its name from the *pang tzu*, an instrument which consists of two pieces of redwood about $7\frac{1}{4}$ inches long, one piece being $1\frac{1}{4}$ inches wide and 1 inch thick. This is held in the hollow of the left hand and struck with the other piece which is round and about $\frac{3}{4}$ inch in diameter. It acts as a time beater. The music of the *k'un ch'ü*, called *k'un ch'iang*, has made a contribution to *ching hsi* music in so far as it is used for plays of *k'un ch'ü* origin. It will be remembered that the former uses the flute as a principal instrument, unlike the *p'i huang* which uses the *hu ch'in*.

What it really amounts to is that *ching hsi* music has become a mingling of styles whose differences lie in the use of various airs together with their tuning, combination and timing. It is necessary to remember that the *ching hsi* is largely the creation of actors who consider music in relation to its stage effect. To achieve their ends they have collaborated with the theatre musicians and then drawn what they require from several musical sources in order to create melodic formulae for the atmosphere and emotional effect of different stage situations. More will be said about musical construction, but first it is of interest to consider the different types of instruments used in the theatre.

The instruments used in the stage orchestra, or *ch'ang mien*, are sometimes classified by Chinese writers under the headings metal, skin and wood. They include string, percussion and wind types and with the exception of the *ti zu*, or flute, used in *k'un ch'iang*, only the string instruments are used for vocal accompaniment and these will be described first. The influence of other races on the Chinese people is well shown in their musical instruments many of which were introduced from outside, later being modified to suit the requirements of indigenous music.

The Hu Ch'in

The *hu ch'in* is the principal instrument for song accompaniment used in the *ching hsi* theatre. It is considered to have been brought into China by invading tribes from the North and some authorities record it as having been first used during the Ming dynasty (1368–1644). Whatever the exact facts about its origin, the high shrill pitch of this instrument has a wildness which certainly calls to mind its alleged background. *Hu ch'in* is really a generic term for a whole family of instruments constructed on similar principals, i.e. stringed and played with a bow. In China today, *hu ch'in* commonly refers to the instrument used in the *ching hsi* theatre, where it is also called *ching hu*.

The *hu ch'in* is an extremely difficult instrument to play well and most of the leading actors employ their own *hu ch'in* player

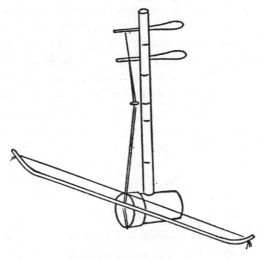

The Hu Ch'in

who accompanies them wherever they go. The actor's *hu ch'in* player taking over from the routine member of the stage orchestra is a characteristic sight in the theatre. Naturally, such a musician is a skilled artist whose reputation in his own field is sometimes as great as that of the actor he accompanies and he often receives applause from the audience for some well rendered passage. In passing, it might be added that there are no women players, the instrument is the exclusive prerogative of male musicians.

The *hu ch'in* has two silk strings and is played with a bow of horsehair. The illustration shows the construction of the instrument. The body, *t'ung*, is cylindrical, being made of a piece of hollow bamboo 4½ inches long and 2¼ inches diameter. It is open at the rear but the face is covered with skin, *p'i tzu*, secured with a band of blue cloth, *pao bu*, bound round the end of the *t'ung*. The neck, or *tan* of the instrument consists of a piece of bamboo 18 inches long and 1 inch diameter which passes right through the body. Two fluted wooden tuning pegs six inches long are fixed in the top of the *tan* from the rear. The strings are called *li hsien* and *wai hsien*, or inner and outer string, the inner being the thicker of the two. The strings are attached to the two pegs, *li hsien* to the upper one, and pass through a brass hook, fixed in the centre of the neck, over a small bamboo bridge, *ch'in ma*, placed in the centre of the *p'i tzu* and are finally attached to the base of the neck where it protrudes underneath the *t'ung*, or body. A bow, *hu kung*, is attached to the base of the strings and cannot be removed from the instrument. The arm of the bow, *hu kung kung kan*, is of thin bamboo cane 25 inches long bent over at both ends which support the bow hair, *hu kung kung mao*. The bow passes in between the two strings so that when it is drawn across, the underside of one string is played and the upper side of the other. Rosin, *sung hsiang*, is smeared on the top of the body between the strings and the arm where the path of the bow lies while playing. The diagrams show the methods of tuning the *hu ch'in*.

The Erh Hu

The *erh hu* belongs to the same family as the *hu ch'in* with which it is sometimes used as a secondary accompanying instrument on the stage. It has a hexagonal shaped body $4\frac{3}{4}$ inches long which measures $3\frac{1}{4}$ inches from point to point across the face. It also uses snake skin but the body and neck are made of redwood and not bamboo. The neck is 22 inches long and curves back at the top, the tuning pegs are similar in style to the *hu ch'in's* and also the bow which however is 28 inches long. It has a lower pitch than the *hu ch'in* and is much softer in tone.

The Yüeh Ch'in

Yüeh means moon and *ch'in* is a generic term used for instruments of the lute and harp family. This instrument is so named because of its large circular body which has an exceedingly decorative appearance. It is said by some authorities to have had its early origins in Central and Eastern Asia, there is a similar instrument in Japan called the *gekkin*. The moon guitar, as it is often named in English, has a circular body 14 inches in diameter and about $1\frac{3}{4}$ inches deep, is of rosewood, but the disks facing it are made of *wu t'ung* wood. The short neck is of redwood being 10 inches long, scroll shaped and bent sharply back to curve up again. It has four silk strings, ten frets and four tuning pegs. The strings are attached to a wooden holder at the bottom of the sound box in similar fashion to that of the European guitar. The *yüeh ch'in* is used to assist the *hu ch'in* in song accompaniment and again is much softer in tone than the previously mentioned instruments. It is also used in *k'ün ch'iang*.

The San Hsien

The *san hsien* is three stringed and played with a plectrum. It has
a flattened oval shaped sound box of redwood faced on both sides
with snake skin and measuring $6\frac{3}{4}$ by 6 inches and $2\frac{5}{8}$ inches in
depth. The neck is of redwood 30 inches long with three tuning
pegs. It passes through the body of the instrument, the strings
being attached to the projecting portion as in the *hu ch'in*, the
top of the neck is scrolled and turns back. This instrument is of
interest as being the prototype of the Japanese *jamisen* which
later became the celebrated *samisen*.

Like the *yüeh ch'in* and the *erh hu* it is used as a secondary
accompaniment to the *hu ch'in* on occasions.

P'i P'a

This instrument perhaps holds one of the most distinguished
places in the history of Chinese music. It is thought to have had its
origins in Western Asia but there are records showing it in use in
China as early as the sixth century A.D. It belongs to the lute
family and there have been many different versions of it in the
course of its long history. It is the prototype of the Japanese
biwa. If any Chinese instrument could be described as a solo one
it is the *p'i p'a* and there has been a great deal of descriptive
music written for it. Court ladies performed upon it in the past
and it was also played by the singsong girls.

It has a long graceful pear shaped body with a shallow curved
section. The neck is of redwood with an ornate scroll at the top
curved back nearly at a right angle. On the neck are four large
rounded ridges of ivory or wood which are used as frets on
occasion. There are four fluted tuning pegs set in pairs at either
side of the scroll at the top of the neck. Frets are placed on the
face on the sound board—their number varies between six and
thirteen: four silk strings are attached from the pegs to a cross
piece on the lower face of the soundbox. The strings are stopped
with the first, second and third fingers of the left hand and the
melody played with the thumb and first finger of the right hand,
the instrument being held upright on the thigh. It is used
occasionally for solos in the theatre and secondary accompaniment.

These constitute the principal instruments of accompaniment
on the stage with the exception of the flute. In view of its special

functions it will be described here instead of with the other wind instruments to be listed.

The Ti Tzu

The *ti tzu*, leading instrument of the *k'un ch'ü* theatre is a bamboo flute which is played transversely. It is just over 26 inches long and not quite 1 inch in diameter. The blow hole is situated 10 inches from the left hand end, a second hole after this one is covered with a membrane, followed by six more holes used for stopping. Two more holes at the end perform the function of expelling air. The *ti tzu* is one of the most popular Chinese instruments and understandably so, for its clear sweet notes have a superb quality. As it is the commonest instrument of fixed pitch, it is used, in addition to accompaniment, for setting the tuning for strings and voice on the stage. Different keys are registered according to the position of the note on the *ti tzu* which corresponds to the outer string of the *hu ch'in*.

Besides the instruments mentioned above, there are others whose function is to lead the orchestra, beat time and obtain special effects. The drums, cymbals, gongs and an instrument called the *pan* are important for timing and leading the orchestra. These will be described next.

The Tan P'i Ku or Hsiao Ku

This drum is very important for it is played by the leader of the musicians who uses it to beat out time for the other players in general and to accentuate the very quick rhythm of a beat in particular. It stands on a tripod and is beaten with two light bamboo sticks without heads. The drum itself is made of hardwood with a hole $2\frac{1}{4}$ inches bored through the centre. It is $10\frac{1}{4}$ inches in diameter and 3 inches in depth. The upper surface, which is convex, is covered with hide stretched rigid and fixed to the body of the drum by iron nails. In musical timing the drum is used for indicating the *yen* described later in the chapter. It has a sharp, clear almost metallic sound. The stage opposite the position of the player of the *tan p'i ku* is referred to in theatrical circles as *chiu lung k'ou*, literally 'nine dragon's mouth'. There are various theories about the origin of this name but none seem to agree. The term is used technically now to indicate a position on the stage where an actor stands to sing in certain circumstances, often when agitated or excited or making an entry.

There is another drum rather similar to the *tan p'i ku* in construction but smaller in size. It is played with a single stick and known as the *huai ku*. Somewhat lower in tone than the larger instrument, it is not used in *p'i huang* music but to accompany the flute in the *k'un ch'ü* theatre.

T'ang Ku or Ta Ku

This drum is seldom used in the ordinary plays but is heard in military plays and it is used to accompany the *hu ch'in* in some of Mei Lan-fang's dance pieces. It is heard on certain occasions when the musical form termed *fan erh huang*, used in tragic scenes, is being played. In the play *Chi Ku Ma Ts'ao*, the *t'ang ku* is required in the course of the action on the stage, for the principal actor in the role of Mi Heng must actually play this large drum (see the chapter on the plays of the *ching hsi*). This drum is barrel shaped and suspended by rings attached to a frame consisting of three curved uprights joined by cross pieces below. It varies in size but the height is customarily about equal to the greatest diameter, the heads are of ox hide and it is played with two headless bamboo sticks. The sides of the drum are lacquered in black and often ornamented with a gold dragon pattern.

The Pan

The *pan*, not to be confused with the *pang tzu* although they both serve a similar purpose, is peculiar to the Chinese stage orchestra. It is a time beater which might be said to act as the conductor's baton. It is held in the left hand of the *t'an p'i ku* player, i.e. drummer, who uses it to mark the pan, a unit of timing, explained later on in the section on musical construction. It is made of three pieces of hard redwood, $10\frac{3}{8}$ inches long, in the shape of a broad spatula which tapers convexly from a width of $2\frac{1}{8}$ inches at the top to $2\frac{1}{2}$ inches at the bottom. Two of these pieces, respectively $\frac{3}{8}$ of an inch and $\frac{3}{16}$ of an inch thick, are bound tightly together by fine cord at the top and bottom to make a single piece. Holes are bored through this and the other piece, also $\frac{3}{16}$ of an inch thick, and a double tape $3\frac{3}{4}$ inches long knotted through to join what are now the two single pieces together. The outer surface of the thick piece and the inner surface of the thin piece are slightly convex with a straight ridge down the centre of

The Pan

each. The thin piece is held aloft in the left hand of the drummer with the tape holding the thick piece hanging loosely over his thumb. A subtle turn of the wrist brings the surfaces of the two pieces of wood together with a clear, sharp sound. The diagram and illustration will give a clearer idea of the *pan*.

The Ta Lo
The *ta lo*, or large gong, made of brass, is 1 foot in diameter, with a slight cone in the centre of the surface. It is suspended from a grip with which to hold it and beaten with a headed stick.

The Hsiao Lo
The *Hsiao lo*, or small gong, is similar to the larger version but about 6 or 7 inches in diameter and beaten with a short wedge-shaped piece of wood. It is always used to herald the appearance of a *tan* actor on the stage and in sequence with the *ta lo*. The

gongs are rarely used while singing is going on except sometimes to mark the timing. They are mainly employed for certain effects, timing and stopping movement, particularly in the vigorous combat of the military plays. They suggest anger and the clash of arms as well as being used prominently in the *ta san t'ung*, that brassy pulsation of sound which is heard before the play commences, notifying the audience the performance is about to begin and warning the actors to be ready for their calls. They also feature prominently in the special preludes played on the entry and exit of the actors.

The Hsing

This instrument consists of two small brass cups connected by a cord which allows them to be held in an inverted position and struck against each other to produce the sound. The *hsing* is an accessory which is only used on occasion, it is sometimes heard during *pei tiao*, i.e. sad or tragic airs, in sequence with the drum. It is said to be Buddhist in origin.

The Yün Lo

The *yün lo* is another accessory which is not often used. It is never heard with singing but sometimes accompanies other instruments during ceremonial scenes in certain plays. It consists of ten small gongs about $2\frac{1}{2}$ inches in diameter suspended in a wooden framework with a handle, the tenth being fixed on the top of the framework. Each gong is of different thickness producing different tones in gradated series, a wooden striker being used to produce the sounds.

The Po

The *po*, or small cymbals, are similar to their western counterpart being made of brass, they are used in conjunction with the gongs though not in time with them. They are heard particularly in military plays and ceremonial scenes such as a marriage or the entry of an Emperor.

The So Na

The *so na* is a wind instrument which consists of a conical pipe of redwood fitted with a brass mouthpiece to which a loose disc is attached with a small chain. The opening of the instrument consists of a sliding, brass, bell-mouthed funnel. A small straw-reed is bound in the mouthpiece with a piece of wire. There are seven finger holes in the upper side of the pipe and one on the lower. The overall length is about $17\frac{1}{4}$ inches, the mouthpiece being about 2 inches and the pipe 10 inches. The diameter of the pipe ranges between $\frac{1}{2}$ to 1 inch and that of the funnel opening is just over 5 inches. The instrument has a most piercing note which is often heard during wedding or festive occasions on the stage or at the beginning of an act.

The general placing of the musicians in the orchestra is as follows. Normally they are seated on the stage to the right of the audience with the leader, the *tan p'i ku* player, or drummer, in their centre. He also manipulates the *pan*. At his left sits the *erh hu* player and to his right the *po*. In front of him to the left is the *hu ch'in* player and to the right the *hsiao lo*. In the immediate rear of the drummer and leader the *san hsien* player is seated with *ta lo* to the right and *yueh ch'in* to the left. This arrangement provides the basis for the accompaniment and timing of the actors.

Musical Construction

The scales used in Chinese music have undergone many changes in the course of the centuries but the relation between those of ancient times and that in modern use is very little understood by scholars. The scale used by Chinese theatre musicians is based on one introduced by the Mongols in the eleventh century while the system of notation used is a hieroglyphic one which is shown in the diagram. Known as the *kung ch'ih* system, it is used for musical notation rather in the way that the West uses the stave. The Chinese practice of writing characters from top to bottom of the page did not allow the adoption of anything like the stave from a practical point of view though and the notation, being hieroglyphic, indicates the pitch as well as the name of the written note. Timing, known as *ban yen*, is signified by two marks, o for *yen* and x for *pan*.

The *ban* gives the accented note and the *yen* the unaccented note approximating to the beats in bars in Western music. The first is beaten out with the instrument called the *ban* already described, and the second on the drum called *tan p'i ku*. The principal forms of timing are *man ban*, *ku'ai ban*, *yuan ban*, which can be analysed as one *ban* three *yen*, one *ban* no *yen*, and one *ban* one *yen*. The first is slow time, the second quick, and the third moderate. When there are three *yen* they are named *t'ou yen*, *chung yen*, *wei yen*, literally 'head', 'middle' and 'not yet' *yen*. For instance if a song is said to commence on *chung yen* it means the middle unaccented note or beat in the bar. There is another timing called *erh liu*, two six, though no Chinese authority seems to be able to explain the origin of this numerical title, *erh liu* is actually played in one *ban* one *yen* time. When the actor is singing *erh liu*, the *huo men*, or preliminary tune played on the *hu ch'in*, contains twelve *ban* and on the thirteenth *ban* the singing commences. There are also *yao ban*, *san ban*, *tao ban* and *to ban*. These four have no fixed numerical beat and are used by the actor on specific stage occasions, *tao ban* for instance when the actor sings a prelude in a loud voice behind the scenes before making an entry.

The two principal forms of the *p'i huang* style, i.e. *hsi p'i* and *erh huang*, incorporate different tunes whose names indicate the particular emotional function they serve as well as their timing according to the *ban yen* system. These are mastered in all their combinations by every theatre musician. Many different plays make use of the same tunes for the main repertoire of theatre music is built up by using passages which occur in constant repetition and therefore quickly become familiar to the ears of the audience. In this way they are provided with a musical key to the emotional atmosphere of the action on the stage. The *erh huang* and *hsi p'i* styles are each divided into two principal types of airs, *cheng tiao* for general purposes and *fan tiao* the sad and tragic ones. Both styles contain variations based on different *ban yen* timing methods. The names of these follow.
Erh Huang.
Cheng erh huang, ssu p'ing tiao, fan erh huang, fan ssu p'ing.
Hsi P'i.
Cheng hsi p'i, nan pang tzu, fan hsi p'i.

Making a working generalization, *cheng erh huang* is used for more serious occasions in plays while *cheng hsi p'i* is, on the whole, happy and spirited in feeling. *Fan hsi p'i* and *fan erh huang* are used for sad and tragic occasions or during a kind of lament which is a feature of some roles. *Ssu p'ing tiao* suggest leisure and play time while *nan pang tzu* is melancholy and pensive. The latter style was devised in the Yangtze valley area but has a connection with the old *pang tze* style mentioned earlier. The use of picturesque terms like *liu shui ban*, flowing water tune, may be noted and *hui lung ch'iang*, the turning of the dragon tune. The first a quick timing and the second gaining its name from its drawn out style which is likened to the swaying motion of the dragon.

The *kung ch'ih* system of notation, shown below, is far more arbitrary in its original form than Western notation, as may be gathered. Although sounds are indicated at a certain height there is no indication of their values and the paucity of symbols makes it impossible to learn a tune by reading the music. The most skilful musician could only surmise the general form of a piece seen for the first time in writing, in order to decipher it he would have to hear it played. Tradition therefore compels the theatre musician to learn the whole of his repertoire by ear. Within recent years, systems have been devised to overcome these difficulties and there are popular tune books of theatre music published in which the notation is arranged with symbols and Roman numerals which serve the purpose of the Western sol fa, but no *ching hsi* musician troubles about developments like these.

The Kung Ch'ih System of Notation

ACTUAL NAMES OF NOTES			WESTERN EQUIVALENT			CHINESE CHARACTER		
Ho.	Ssu.	Yi.	Shang.	Ch'ih.	Kung.	Fan.	Liu.	Wu.
C.	D.	E.	F.	G.	A.	B.	C.	D.
合	四	乙	上	尺	工	凡	六	五

The actor's singing voice is described as being one of five different styles which are named from the *kung ch'ih* scale. They are *liu tzu tiao, cheng kung tiao, yi tzu tiao, shang tzu tiao, ch'ih tzu tiao*. The first requires deep and low singing, the last two, high notes. The keys of the *p'i huang* styles differ so that if an actor's singing voice was *liu tzu tiao* he would sing *cheng kung* in *hsi p'i*. An actor who only sang *liu tzu tiao* would have great difficulty in singing *hsi p'i* airs at all. A particular style of singing is called *p'ai*. For instance in the *sheng* role an actor may be said to sing *t'an p'ai* which originated with the actor T'an Hsin-p'ei from whom it derives its name. A little more may be said about this as a good example of the complexities inherent in the development of musical technique.

The *sheng* actor's *p'ai* is broadly classed as *ch'eng p'ai*, which was developed by the actor Ch'eng Chang-keng (1812–80). This again is now divided into three *t'an p'ai*, *wang p'ai* and *sun p'ai*, which originated with the actors T'an Hsin-p'ei (1846–1917), Wang Kuei-fen (1860–1905), and Sun Chu-hsien respectively. Of these *t'an p'ai* is the prevailing singing style adopted by *sheng* actors today. Formerly, besides *ch'eng p'ai* there were *k'uei p'ai* and *yü p'ai*, styles devised by the actors Chang Erh-k'uei and Yü San-sheng. The *k'uei* used purely ancient styles of enunciation and its speech forms were in *wen li*, literary style, so that it became difficult for the more ordinary listeners to follow. As it paid no heed to modern developments it gradually died out. *Yü p'ai* was again the invention of another actor, Yü San-sheng, who had a great vogue. When the present *t'an p'ai* was devised both *yü p'ai* and *k'uei p'ai* were drawn upon to create a new style of singing. This intermingling is typical of so much that has gone on within the content of the Chinese theatre.

Song is used by an actor to express every kind of emotion: his monologues or dialogues are both followed by and interspersed with sung passages. When an actor is about to commence singing he will indicate the fact to the orchestra by raising his voice at the end of his speech, stamping his foot or making a special movement with his sleeves. He never looks at the orchestra while singing; if he does so it indicates that the musicians have made a mistake. He breaks into song if he is expressing surprise, for instance if someone is unexpectedly heard approaching, or if he is worried at his inability to pursue a course of action. Singing expresses his sighs of regret, melancholy for the past or grieving for the present. If he is bewailing the character of his associates or waiting for someone who does not come he expresses his feelings before the audience in song. Anger, hate, happiness, love or fear are all interpreted in the same way, as are the satisfaction of work well done or mere carefree idling.

The entry of an actor or actors is called the *shang ch'ang* and exit *hsia ch'ang*. Both are accompanied by special speech forms and movements, either the one or both, but always by special orchestral passages which are mostly rendered on the gongs and drum, though occasionally other instruments are included. It is these accompaniments which give rise to so much of the brassy clang on the stage that many writers have deplored as over-powering in din. Certainly it takes time for the layman to adjust his perceptions in the case of the percussion music used on the Chinese stage, which probably at first impinges loudly on his un-trained ear. In spite of this, it serves a very special purpose and however bizarre it sounds there is a precision about it which marks a pattern of bold rhythm, serving a very practical purpose in addition to often being a powerful stimulus.

Besides the entry and exit accompaniments mention must be made of the passages for string instruments called *kuo men*, literally 'through the entrance'. These are a series of musical phrases played on the strings either before or in between the actor's song. They give him time to rest or else provide a back-ground for such action as is going on in between periods of singing. There are *kuo men* peculiar to the two main styles of music and their various timings, a seasoned playgoer can tell by hearing a particular *kuo men* the styles of singing or events that are to follow.

Obviously no real impression of Chinese theatre music can be conveyed in writing. This analysis is provided to illustrate the basis of its technical construction and the practical purpose it serves in accompanying the actor's singing, controlling the timing of his movements and providing an atmospheric back-ground to the different kinds of plays. In short, the position of music as a fundamental part of stage technique. In conclusion, a list of the names for the *shang ch'ang* and *hsia ch'ang* orchest-ral accompaniments follow with their meaning and a diagram showing the tunings of the *hu ch'in* for song accompaniment.

Shang ch'ang.
Ta ch'ao shang: Used before an Emperor makes an appearance or high court officials.
Fa tien shang: This is used before the opening of a military court.
Hsiao lo man erh t'ou shang: This is used when persons of dignity make an entry.
Hsiao lo ta shang: This is used when persons of dignity are in their homes or offices.

Hsiao lo k'uai ch'ou t'ou shang: This is heard when a refined and scholarly person appears on the stage, generally coming from another place. It is always directly followed by singing.

Hsiao lo man ch'ou t'ou shang: This is used when a character appears coming from another place and continuing the singing from a preceding scene.

Hsiao lo shui ti yü shang: This is used for characters in their hours of leisure.

Hsiao lo ch'ang szu t'ou shang: This is heard when a character comes running quickly from another place.

Hsiao lo tzu lang shang: This is heard when ordinary, quiet and peaceful characters appear.

Hsiao lo liu ling shang: This is used if four eunuchs appear or a low rank official, or for walking along outside.

Hsiao lo ch'i san ch'ang shang: This is used to express business, a person entering in a great hurry.

Hsiao lo tso ts'ai shang: This is heard when a low grade official is seen at home or in office.

Hsiao lo yuan pan to t'ou shang: This indicates a gentleman of good character and must be immediately followed by singing.

Hsiao lo man pan to t'ou shang: This is used when a woman of good character and high virtue is at home or occupied.

Cha shang: This is used for a bad character such as a thief and some of the comic roles.

Ta lo ssu chi t'ou shang: This is played when, as often happens in military plays, four generals appear on the stage together.

Ta lo yuan ch'ang shang: This is heard when a very high official is at home or in his office.

Ta lo ta shang: This is similar to *ta ch'ao shang*.

Ta lo hui ts'ao shang: This accompanies the appearance of several military characters who have previously left the stage.

Ta lo ssu pien ching shang: This expresses the desire of a group of military characters to go into combat.

Ta lo man ch'ang ch'ui shang: It is often used when good characters and officials of high rank are portrayed at leisure, singing must always follow.

Ta lo k'uai ch'ang ch'ui: This is similar to the above.

Ta lo shui tu yü shang: This is used for travelling and moving along swiftly; it also expresses a state of worry.

Ta lo fan ch'ang ch'ui shang: This is heard when a good or important character is coming from another place.

Ta lo ch'ou t'ou shang: This is used for an important official or a good character.

Ta lo yin lo shang: This is used for fairies, spirits or animals.

Ta lo niu ssu shang: This indicates ordinary people coming and going quickly from one place to another.

Ta lo chi chi feng shang. This is used for the appearance of painted face characters and in military plays.

Ta lo luan ch'ui shang: This is used in a fighting scene where one character is defeated and leaves the stage.

Ta lo tao pan shang: This indicates a character has arrived from a far distance or else indicates the leading personage in a play.

Ta lo ch'ang chien shang: This is used when high officials make an entry and is followed immediately by actors speaking and not by singing.

Ta lo ch'ung t'ou shang: This indicates the arrival of a messenger, or that someone is going to appear shortly.

Ta lo ssu pien shang: This is used when a character in a military play, either a comic personage or otherwise, is walking in a stealthy fashion indicating that he is unobserved by anyone else.

Hsiao kuo men shang: A musical interlude in the main action of a play, e.g. as in *The Strategy of an Unguarded City*, this being played while two soldiers are sweeping the entry to the city gates.

Shih san p'eng lo shang: This is used for an important person out of doors and coming from a far distance.

Ka pa shang: A drum passage used for a comic or bad character.

Pa ta ts'ang shang: The same as above except that the characters have come from a far place.

Ta lo chin ch'ien hua shang: This indicates leisure time or out of doors.

Feng ju sung shang: This indicates soldiers practising combat and returning to headquarters.

Ch'ui ta shang: This is used when a message is given by the Emperor to someone, often a high official.

Nan lo shang: This is used when a comic male or female character is shown out of doors or for a bad character.

P'ing ban to t'ou shang: This indicates an ordinary person at leisure or out of doors.

Hsiao lo feng ju sung ho t'ou shang: This is used when a non-military official appears and it is not his first entry.

Chi ku shang: A drum passage used in fighting plays when arrows are used.

Ta ching shang: This is used when watchmen appear on the stage, they themselves carrying a gong or wooden striker which have no other accompaniment.

Chiu ch'ui pan shang: This is used when painted face characters who are unimportant or evil appear.

Ch'u tui tzu shang: This is used when an important character accompanied by *pao lung t'ao*, standard bearers, is at leisure.

Hsia ch'ang or exit: The following are special musical passages used in *hsia ch'ang*, or the exits of the actors.

Chi chi feng hsia: This is used in fighting plays to express swift running.

Sao t'ou hsia: This expresses the indecision of one who does not know whether to proceed but eventually decides to do so.

Feng ju sung hsia: This is used when a general orders his men to battle.

Chi san ch'iang hsia: This is heard when a prisoner is being taken to execution.

Chu nu erh hsia: This indicates many soldiers going into battle.

Hsiao chu erh hsia: This indicates a small group of soldiers being led to combat by an officer of secondary rank.

Ch'i yen hui hsia: This is used when a large body of men are going to battle.

Pei ch'i yen hui hsia: The same as above but indicating an even larger force of men.

Wu ma chiang erh shui hsia: This is used when a victorious general comes from afar to visit the Emperor.

Chao yuan ling hsia: This is as above although in this case it may be a statesman as well as a general.

I Fan chiang erh shui hsia: This suggests naval combat or fighting over water.

I chiang feng hsia: This is heard when the Emperor is going out at leisure and accompanied by the Court.

Ch'ing chiang yin hsia: This is used for spirits and Gods.

Shen chang erh hsia: This is used for less important spirits and deities.

Liu yao ling hsia: This is used for civilian officials of low rank or eunuchs.

Ch'ui ta hsia: This is heard when important personages appear, returning from some destination.

Ta hsia: This is used to notify the audience that the second scene will quickly follow.

Wei sheng hsia: This announces the play is over.

The speech and gesture techniques used in *shang ch'ang* are described in Chapter V.

STRING TUNINGS FOR THE HU CH'IN

Erh Huang		*Hsi P'i*		*Fan Erh Huang*	
Inner	Outer	Inner	Outer	Inner	Outer
C. HO	CH'IH G.	D. SSU	KUNG A.	F. SHANG	LIU C.
D. SSU	KUNG A.	E. YI	FAN B.	G. CH'IH	WU D.
E. YI	FAN B.	F. SHANG	LIU C.	A. KUNG	YI E.
F. SHANG	LIU C.	G. CH'IH	WU D.	B. FAN	
	WU D.				

CHAPTER IV

THE ACTOR AND
HIS ROLES

꒦ꙩ꒦

THE Chinese actor must submit himself to a long training which is probably unequalled in the severity of its discipline and in the past was noted for the harsh demands made upon youthful pupils. When he has mastered his craft he must face an audience whose critical fastidiousness is carried to a point which would probably drive his Western colleague to exasperation. Not only that, the Chinese . theatre audience must be among the most unconventional of such gatherings anywhere and the onlooker might be forgiven if at times he thought the last thing it was interested in was the actors on the stage. The young actor making his debut will receive no encouragement from the onlookers, he must stand trial before their seeming indifference; if he proves his mettle he will eventually be accepted, but it takes time. No concessions are made in front of the footlights. There are no overnight cuts to stardom and even if, as was the case with Mei Lan-fang, the actor makes a brilliant debut, it will take many years of hard work and hard living to establish himself as an artist capable of carrying on the great traditions of his predecessors. The *ching hsi* actor must play to an audience which is primarily interested in the technique of interpretation of accepted forms, and he is judged from the beginning in the light of masters who have already set the standards for these forms. The newcomer must re-create a stage character in a way which fulfils all the conventional requirements and yet possess the talent to give it new life and spirit with his personality and mark it apart from soul-less imitation. Depending on his ability to do this he will be started on the road to success or dismissed to failure. These at any rate were the standards that applied even of late years, though probably more strictly to the letter in Peking than in other cities. The Peking theatregoer has always been the most uncompromising critic as well as the most ardent stage devotee. Within recent times the standards of appreciation have changed in audiences. A younger generation, in a modern world of all kinds of new entertainments, has not the same regard for the old drama as its forefathers and consequently cares less about the finer points of classical acting.

The training of the actor commences in childhood between the age of seven and twelve when he becomes a pupil of one of the schools whose function it is to produce the stars of the future. Once enrolled, he must live a life of monastic seclusion, for he is seldom if ever allowed outside the walls of his school unless under close supervision, while inside he is submitted to a barrack room discipline during the whole period of his training, which takes six years. Many stories are told of the implacable rule of the old instructors and the punishment meted out to those pupils who failed to meet his demands. Things have changed somewhat since the earliest days and the treatment of students is kinder if still very strict. The actor pupil now undergoes a general education together with his professional training, but in the early years of the present century the actor was still regarded as a social pariah, descendants of an actor to the third generation were forbidden to compete in the public examinations, and no stage apprentice was considered worthy of education in anything other than the technique he required for his profession. This did not alter the fact that there were actors who were men of education and standing, several of the great actors of last century might be named as examples, although in their cases it was due to the fact that they had taken to the stage later in life or first been amateurs. The professional actor trained from childhood was sometimes illiterate. Tradition dies hard and as in most countries, there are still people in China who regard the stage and its inhabitants as beyond the social pale, but by normal standards the status of the actor has undergone a complete change during the last forty years and he is now a respected member of the community like anybody else.

The amateur has always held a unique position in the *ching hsi* and all through its history there have been many examples of amateurs taking to the professional stage and achieving distinction. Professional actors in fact may be divided into two classes, those who graduated from the *k'o pan* or training schools and those who commenced their theatrical life as *p'iao yu*, or amateurs. In the latter case however it must not be thought that they succeed without any training; it will be found that the amateurs who arrive as professionals have generally been connected in some way with the theatre since their earliest days, either through family connections or sheer enthusiasm, and have studied under the most famous teachers. The actor Yü Chen-fei is a good case in point.

At the end of the last war there were three training schools in Peking, two operated by celebrated actors and the third, a very famous one, the Fu Lien Ch'eng, by a member of a well-known acting family. The post war years were not propitious for running establishments like these and they all fell on evil times if they did not actually close their doors. No accurate information is available as to the state of training schools in Peking today, but one has now been organized on new lines with Mei Lan-fang at the head. In 1930 a training school was opened in Peking which was intended to be a model of its kind. This was the Hsi Ch'ü Hsüeh Hsiao, a co-educational establishment, for its purpose was to train actresses as well as actors, a new departure in keeping with the spirit of the times. It was intended at first to train people for the Western style drama as well as the Chinese classical stage, but this was never very successful and finally the school concentrated on producing actors and actresses for the *ching hsi* stage only. The Japanese war brought an end to its career and the school never reopened, but it is of interest to consider the way it was run as giving a fair idea of the training of an actor for the classical stage under more modern conditions.

An aspirant for stage training is judged by his future instructors in rather the same way that ballet dancers are now judged in the West, that is to say an expert teacher on seeing a pupil for the first time can assess his general aptitude for the profession quite irrespective of the fact that he has yet no particular technical ability. In many ways the training of a Chinese actor may be compared to that of the Western ballet dancer, for both must start their training while they are yet in a formative state of physical development and can be gradually prepared for the stern demands which will be made on their physical powers later. In the case of the Chinese pupil his instructors will decide straight away, after noting his particular physique and demeanour, as to which type of role he is best fitted to play, i.e. *sheng, tan, ching* or *ch'ou.* The quality of his voice, facial appearance and stature are

Ch'ou actor wearing Chan mao

important factors which decide the choice as well as the general aptitude already mentioned. Physical appearance is not the least important of the qualities to be taken into consideration; a student who has the face suitable for playing the *ch'ou*, or comic, roles for instance, would never under any circumstances be considered for *tan* or female roles. Once the pupil's suitability for a certain role has been decided, he will then be directed into a course of training which will equip him to become adept in all techniques pertaining to his particular role. It sometimes happens of course that a student once embarked on his training may be found more suitable for another role in which case he will be switched over, but it is rare that his tutors misjudge his suitability in the first place. Naturally there is a good deal of basic training which is necessary for all students in spite of the fact that everyone is specializing from the very beginning.

The Hsi Ch'ü Hsüeh Hsiao was built to accommodate a little

over three hundred pupils, a large number when one considers that the ordinary training schools generally would have about a hundred students. Once accepted, board, lodging and uniform were provided by the school and the student was bound to remain there for six years. The only contact allowed with the outside world during this time was the weekly visits of parents and relations permitted on Sundays: vacations were spent in the school. At the end of the six years' training the student was bound to give his professional services to the school for one year more and during this period he had to act as and when directed by the school. The school, in addition to giving regular performances in its own theatre, provided senior students for professional performances in all the Peking theatres, there being a special rotation system operated by the Peking National Drama Association. If after two or three years training a pupil did not justify his early promise he would be turned over to become a useful member in some other capacity; a theatre musician, or even a stage hand. He was liable to expulsion for severe misconduct, whatever his talents, at any time.

When a pupil applied for admission to the school, provided he had a satisfactory family background and was between the ages of seven and twelve, he was submitted to a preliminary examination. If he was considered generally suitable for acting, his voice was tested against a *hu ch'in* accompaniment and he was then passed through groups of examiners sitting at different tables, each table being devoted to the different roles. Once accepted by one of these groups he was enrolled as a first year pupil. The school time table was a strict and arduous one. Students were called at six a.m. summer and winter. If they had begun to study singing they were marched out by a supervisor and spent an hour being made to sing at the top of their voices against the city walls which were used as 'sounding boards': in this fashion their voices acquired the necessary power and strength. A drastic method but one that apparently works and has been used from time immemorial in the training of Peking actors. In this exercise breathing is abdominal, the emission of the breath must be slow and to assist this no food must be taken beforehand. This was a prelude to every day's work whatever the season of the year. Breakfast followed the return from the city walls and classes commenced promptly at eight thirty a.m. The whole morning was spent in basic dramatic training which included a great deal of physical exercise and special gymnastics. In the same way that a ballet dancer practises at the bar, *ching hsi* pupils were required to spend a certain amount of time every day lifting their legs high to acquire correct balance and stance. Tumbling, standing on the hands and methods of walking were also a part of the routine. It was necessary for pupil *tan* actors to learn to walk on the *ts'ai ch'iao*, described in the next chapter, an exceedingly difficult art. At first the budding actor learns to do five minutes daily, gradually increasing the time until he can walk freely and skilfully for two hours: he is then considered competent (see photograph, pl. III). The use of weapons, manipulation of *shui hsiu*, the water sleeves, and various other techniques all formed part of the morning's general training. Students were allotted in groups to individual teachers, all actors renowned in their particular fields. There were between thirty and forty of them employed as instructors in the school. Each student would probably receive something over one hour's individual instruction during the course of the morning, the rest of the time being spent in watching the teacher with the other members of the group. During this time special super-visors wandered round and woe betide any pupil whose interest was flagging. This principle of supervision was applied to the students at all times, in their classrooms, dormitories, the theatre, and out in the streets. Vigilance was never relaxed on their deportment and behaviour. At the end of the morning's classes the various groups would line up under their respective tutors and co-ordinate their lessons learnt as a group. Lunch was at twelve-thirty and the rest of the afternoon until four-thirty was occupied by general education classes. The evening, both before and after dinner, was devoted to individual practice on the part of the students themselves, though again under super-vision. Everybody retired at nine p.m. unless, as was the case with many of the senior students, they were required to be at the theatre.

Once the various groups had advanced with their basic training the teachers would be instructed by the school's administrative board to do a complete play with their pupils, the title being named and a time limit set for completion of studies. The study completed, there would be a rehearsal on the school stage to correct mistakes and co-ordinate matters in general. Another fortnight would be spent on polishing the play and then a full dress rehearsal would be given at which actors and critics were asked to attend and pass comment. After this, the particular drama was considered ready for public performance by the students. A special committee met every month in the school to consider the texts of old plays infrequently performed or considered unsuitable for contemporary times. There were many hundreds of such texts in existence which the committee dealt with during the school's existence. If a play was considered to have possibilities, suggested alterations or modifications were made and the drama was then recommended for study in the school.

This, then, gives some idea of life in a *ching hsi* training school. A one-time official of the Hsi Ch'u Hsüeh Hsiao told the writer that the monthly cost of running the school was in the region of several thousand pounds sterling. It was privately owned, as indeed were the others mentioned earlier, their basic training methods being more or less the same except on a smaller scale. In the last century it was customary for pupils to be sold to schools, the children literally became the property of the owners until such times as they could repay them with their earnings, a process which might take long years. Many an old actor has related the hard life he led in schools of this description. No one will regret the passing of the more evil elements of the old theatrical training, but when one considers how the men at the top of the acting tree today gained their position, it is difficult not to feel that the old style *ching hsi* actor is a dying race. The demands of the State on a new generation will surely not permit the same type of training described here.

The principal roles of the *ching hsi* actor were described in the first chapter as being divided under four main headings, *sheng*, *tan*, *ching*, *ch'ou*, a classification which, in theatrical circles, is always given in that order and formerly signified the relative importance attached to the roles by theatregoers. In actual fact each role is indispensable to the construction of the plays, but formerly the *sheng* roles included the greater number of principal parts and were therefore more often the prerogative of the leading actors. Each of these four roles is subdivided into variations of the type and these will be described in detail.

Wen sheng actor

Sheng

The *sheng* are always male characters who represent scholars, statesmen, warrior patriots, faithful retainers and the like. They have no painted make-up and with the exception of the *hsiao sheng*, the conventional young men of the stage, they mostly wear beards. The *sheng* roles are described as *wu sheng* if the part requires stage fighting and acrobatics, and *wen sheng* if the part is one for singing and acting only. If a role includes both these elements it is sometimes referred to as *wen wu sheng*. The *wu sheng* class may again be divided into three types, *wu lao sheng*, *chang k'ao* and *tuan ta*. The *chang k'ao* are generals or high ranking warriors who wear the full regalia of stage armour with the four flags or pennants attached to the shoulders behind. The actor in this role must have a dignified bearing and be well versed in gymnastics and vigorous movement, including the swift but controlled movements used in stage fighting. Ideally he will have a good voice as well, but this is not so essential as his command of gesture and bold movement. The *wu lao sheng* is a similar type of role except in this the actor portrays an aged warrior who always wears a white beard and must give the dignity of old age, but is yet active in his movements. The *tuan ta* characters are different from the first two. They wear close fitting costumes which are generally black and they wear flat soled soft boots. They are skilful swordsmen and twirl and leap about with the lightfootedness of cats. The first two types, while swift in movement, must always preserve a dignity of poise and bearing in keeping with their characters. The *tuan ta* on the other hand is concerned only with his prowess with the sword or even his fists; he is not required to sing, and he portrays bandits, robber chiefs, or men of lower class who are skilled in fighting, or even committing crime.

The *wen sheng* class may be divided into two, *hsü sheng* and *lao sheng*. The actor who plays these parts must, before everything else, have an excellent voice, for all characters in these classes have long singing parts. The singing style of the *sheng* actor is marked by a rich almost baritone quality and at the same time he must maintain a delicate but perfect synchronization of gesture and pantomime with his song. The glance of an eye, the crook of a finger, all accord perfectly with the music and therefore the emotion of the occasion. The *hsu sheng* are chiefly middle aged scholars, statesmen, and so on, the *lao sheng* are aged men, often of the poorer classes, peasants or retainers. Their singing is noted for the great pathos of its style. The *fan tiao* described in the chapter on music is a notable feature of the singing of both the *hsü sheng* and *lao sheng* parts. The term *lao sheng* is sometimes used loosely to designate the whole range of the *sheng* singing roles as against its more specific meaning. The name *hung sheng* is given to those actors who specialize in the role of Kuan Kung.

The *hsiao sheng* are always young men, the princes, dandies, lovers and poor young scholars of the stage. They never wear beards. There are three principal types, *shan tzu sheng*, *chih wei sheng*, *ch'iung sheng*. The first named is noted for the play of his fan—he is generally a young man of good family or a man about town; the *ch'ih wei sheng* plays a young warrior or prince and wears the long pheasant feathers in his head dress; the *ch'iung sheng* is a poor scholar or young man in distress. The good *hsiao sheng* actor plays all these parts with equal skill, but in addition to the special qualities required for each type he must always have a good voice, singing is an important characteristic of the role. The *hsiao sheng* was an important role in the *k'un ch'ü* theatre but it is a limited and difficult one to play well on the *ching hsi* stage and there are few first class actors of the role today. The technique of the *hsiao sheng* actor is unusual for it mingles the vigour of the male roles with the softness of the female parts, the singing and speaking voice combines the *sheng* actor's vocal modulations with the falsetto quality of the *tan* actor. This is also the case with the movements and gestures, a glance at the section on technique will show how often the *hsiao sheng* and the *tan* use a similar method. The graceful movements of using the pheasant feathers are a particular feature of this role which is characterized by qualities that combine a little of everything from the other three. The greatest living master of the *hsiao sheng* role today is the actor Yü Chen-fei, who brings to it a grace and spirit unequalled by any other player.

Laughing is a very necessary part of the actor's vocal technique. This may sound strange to the layman but the ways of expressing various emotions by conventional laughter are important, indeed one old writer even said that laughter was the first qualification of a good actor. The *hsiao sheng* actor in particular has a special way of laughing, prolonged and high toned but rich in quality. Yü Chen-fei gains effects in his laughter which have caused Mei Lan-fang himself to say that no other actor has ever perfected this technique like Yü. Meeting him in private life one was always impressed by the vibrant tones of his voice and his infectious smile.

Tan

The *tan* actors play all the women's roles. There are six principal classifications within the main role but before going on to describe them in detail, it is perhaps necessary to say something about the position of the female impersonator on the Chinese stage and afterwards that of the actress.

It is common knowledge that male actors have, by long tradition, played all feminine roles on the *ching hsi* stage, until the early part of the present century women were frowned upon in the orthodox theatre. Early records show that the practice of employing youths of good voice and physical charm for the parts of women on the stage had long been common in China, as it was in the Elizabethan theatre, but this did not prevent the use of women also in the theatre where, until the Ch'ing dynasty (1616–1912), there seems to have been ample scope for both the sexes. During the Yüan period (1280–1368), the profession of actress was a flourishing one although considered to provide a freedom from moral restraint which was contrary to the precepts of Confucian society. As a result, the actress was officially classed with the courtesan in the social scale. It should be remembered that a great deal of the dramatic entertainment of other days was confined to the Imperial palace and to private residences, where the wealthy would invite companies of actors to entertain them. The latter practice continued until quite recent times in fact. The nature of this system laid it open to abuse in the past and in the reign of Ch'ien Lung (1735–96), the emperor, himself an enthusiast of the theatre, was prevailed upon to issue a decree forbidding the use of women in Court entertainments. After this the female impersonator became increasingly important and technique was developed more and more to meet the requirements of a stage from which women were banned. During the last century the female impersonator reigned supreme and so well has he done his work that even now he has not yet been ousted by the actress, who, strangest of all, must learn the conventional and symbolic interpretations of the male actor if she wishes to play her own sex. There are a great many talented actresses whom the theatre-going public accept without question, a new attitude in audiences as recently as the thirties of the present century. Even so, the greatest interpreters of women's roles are still the male actors and it is a fact that no actress yet has ever surpassed the leading impersonators in the highly developed technique of femininity which is none the less a product of the masculine mind. This may sound nonsense by Western standards but an examination of certain facts may help to clarify this statement.

When women were forbidden the stage, the theatre was faced with a serious crisis which had to be overcome if the drama was to survive as entertainment and the obvious solution was the female impersonator. At first, he was considered chiefly for his looks and a soft voice, the important thing was how feminine he could look in costume. In earlier days in China, the feminine roles were considered secondary in acting importance and voice pitch and appearance were the principal qualities to be emphasized by the actor playing the woman. They continued to remain important, naturally, but they had to be combined with a great many more qualities as the drama developed and with it the actor's technique. The old Chinese drama was non-realistic by any European standards; it depended on a formal symbolism which, in its essentials, has been retained to this day. The development of the *tan* actor's technique was all the time conditioned by this pattern of symbolism, within which it had to preserve a harmony while using other special devices. The task of the *tan* actor was to interpret feminine character and behaviour for audiences to whom symbolism presented no difficulty; they accepted it as a normal form of dramatic expression. The technique of the *tan* was based on a double symbolism; in addition to fulfilling the requirements of stage practice of the time it had to create the impression that it was a woman who was acting. To achieve this the actor had to appear more feminine than any woman; it was not by caricature that he achieved his end but by his skill in seizing upon the essential points which would convey the essence of all that typified woman in the eyes of his onlookers, using them to symbolize the qualities idealized, or deprecated, according to the standards of the time. There is no need for the female impersonator in modern style drama and the *tan* actors of the classical theatre are gradually disappearing. Since the 1912 Republic women have taken increasingly to the stage and within recent years it has become more and more common to find actresses replacing the male *tan* players. They have proved to be charming, skilful and at times brilliant exponents of the old acting traditions, but the fact remains that they provide the curious phenomenon of women imitating men imitating women and there is a difference. The strength of the old style actor lay in the fact that he was always in a position to develop and add to what was in the first place a creation of the male artist. Actresses are bound to fall back upon their natural qualities, they cannot sustain the intensity of the actor's symbolism and little by little realism creeps in. This is the reason why the old theatregoer deplores the presence of the actress in classical drama, although the younger generation, less appreciative of the austerity of symbolism, welcomes the intrusion of feminine glamour.

A few actresses began to appear in public some years before the Republic of 1912 and more and more after that date. There was a great deal of prejudice against them nevertheless; they were not accepted in orthodox stage circles nor were they allowed to appear in company with male actors. Their repertoire was limited, none of the best teachers or actors ever considered taking them as pupils and more often than not they had to fall back on roles best suited to the physical charms of their sex. Even when their numbers began to multiply, actresses were confined to single play-houses in the great theatrical cities both of Peking and Shanghai, the Ch'eng Nan I Yuan in the former and the Ching Wu T'ai in the latter. An actress who made a reputation for herself at this period was Pi Yün-hsia, a native of Soochow. She had a good voice, a graceful presence and was an accomplished artist who, according to Chinese writers, was more talented than many actors. She finally left the stage for marriage. The position of women on the stage first began to assume a notable importance with the appearance of the actress Hsüeh Yen-chin of Peking and a few others contemporary with her such as Hsin Yen-ch'iu and Chang O-yün. These actresses formed themselves into a talented group which eventually won recognition from the great *tan* actors and theatre managements, leading to the appearance of men and women on the stage together for the first time in 1928, at the Ta Hsi Yüan, Shanghai. Hsüeh Yen-chin first attracted the attention of Mei Lan-fang, of whom she became a pupil. The others of her group were also accepted as students of celebrated teachers and actors, their repertoire was increased and technique perfected, the public applauded them and their careers were made. They were the forerunners of many talented actresses who came after them, women like Meng Hsiao-tung, Wu Su-chü, Ho Yu-lan and T'ung Chih-ling, to name a few. When actresses first began to appear with actors, it was of course in the female roles such as *ch'ing i* and *lao tan*, but later there was a strange reversal of positions when several actresses became specialists in the male roles. In the days when women were segregated in companies composed solely of their own sex, naturally they had to play all the parts and it may be because of this that the male impersonator became a regular feature of the *ching hsi* theatre, even when the actress had become installed as a permanent partner with the actor. In later years there were several actresses who were noted for their interpretation of male parts. Meng Hsiao-tung was one of them; among other roles she played that of Chu Ko Liang with distinction, a part long hallowed as a supreme one for the *sheng* actor.

The actress first became really accepted in Shanghai therefore. Peking was slower in signifying a grudging approval: in the early thirties there was still one of the older theatres in Peking which even resolutely continued to ban women theatregoers, an indication of the strong anti-feminism lingering on in the stage circles of the capital. Today the actress is as popular in Peking as elsewhere; indeed it seems likely that within a few years she will have usurped the stage completely from her rival the *tan* actor. The only query raised by this hypothesis is whether or not by that time the traditional *ching hsi* theatre itself will not already be obsolete.

The *tan* role is divided under the six main variations of role whose names and descriptions follow. *Ch'ing i*, also known as *cheng tan*, *hua tan*, *wu tan*, *kuei men tan*, *tsai tan* and *lao tan*. The *ch'ing i* parts lay great importance on singing but require none of the more vigorous forms of movement like fighting and

Ch'ing i costume

gymnastics. The actor who plays this part must, before all else, have a first class singing voice suitable for the plaintive melodies typical of the *ch'ing i* repertoire. This role portrays types like the faithful wife, filial daughter or lover in distress. The movements are demure but graceful, the feet are kept close to the ground and the hands in an elegant position, often crossed on the waist. The eyes are kept lowered or directed straight in front; there is not the slightest hint of coquettishness or freedom of behaviour. The singing voice is high and clear, it is in fact a falsetto, and although it must have strength it is not robust. The *ch'ing i* symbolizes the good and virtuous woman as defined in the society of old China. The *hua tan* on the other hand represents the woman of bold, often questionable, character. In this role singing is not required but great stress is laid on the acting. The *hua tan* is full of charm and seduction, every movement is vibrant with expression from the coy tilt of her head to the fluttering of her scarlet handkerchief held in one hand. Her devastating smile captivates the audience and the actor who plays this role must be a master of facial expression as well as a good gymnast, for the part often calls for more vigorous action. The costume of the *hua tan* is gay and colourful as befitting her character. Formerly the *ch'ing i* and *hua tan* were distinct and separate roles played by actors who specialized in one or the other, but their particular characteristics have changed considerably since the early years of the century. This is largely due to the work of Mei Lan-fang who has brought a new interpretation to the two roles which is now accepted. It is usual in these days for the actor to play both *ch'ing i* and *hua tan* roles which have been modified and even at times borrow a little of each other's qualities. The old *ch'ing i* had a severity which is not seen now; the actor Wang Yao-ch'ing was responsible for first adapting the style to new forms but he lost his singing voice early and Mei Lan-fang studied his methods and developed them. The *hua tan* of earlier days was a little less restrained than now, her humour, like her stage character, was sometimes questionable. The amusing story is told of the famous *hua tan* who, in answer to some call from the gallery, retorted 'Pull down the blinds, can't you see what I'm about'. If the new *hua tan* is now more respectable she is not less graceful and mischievous. The *wu tan* represents a maiden skilled in fighting, riding and the more masculine accomplishments. Although not full of seductive graces like the *hua tan*, she is still beautiful and has feminine charm, but at the same time she is strong and accustomed to vigorous action. The role calls for great skill in gymnastics and in wielding swords and lances. A variation of the part is sometimes described as *tao ma tan*, literally horse and sword *tan*. It is now customary for the first class *tan* actor to be versed in the technique described here as well as *hua tan* and *ch'ing i* styles and this again is due to the influence of Mei Lan-fang who is a master of all three forms, although he is probably the only actor

who performs with such equal skill in them all. The *kuei men tan*
represents the young unmarried girl; she is attractive and graceful but with some of the demureness of the *ching i* whose style
of singing she follows. The *ts'ai tan* portrays a woman of evil
nature, a wicked maidservant or a scheming matchmaker,
although the latter type is more often played by the *ch'ou* actor in
these times and in fact there has been a tendency for him to act
all the *ts'ai tan* roles leaving the parts symbolizing the more
attractive qualities of the women on the stage to the straight *tan*
actor. The *ts'ai tan* combines qualities of being comic, lowly and
bad natured, though she was not always bad looking; the latter
virtue of course is ignored when the *ch'ou* steps into her shoes.
The *lao tan* is probably the most realistic of the female roles
portraying as it does the old women of the stage. The actor walks
with bent back and head lowered, supporting hesitant steps by
the aid of a long staff, *kuai chang*, without which he never
appears. The role is noted for its singing parts and plaintive
laments; the *lao tan* actor's voice combines qualities of both the
tan and *sheng* and must possess a vibrant power typifying the
dignity and pride as well as the sadness of old age. As in the
hsiao sheng role, good *lao tan* actors are scarce. Formerly the
lao tan parts were less important and in consequence a little
neglected. It was largely through the actor Kung Yün-fu
(1862–1932) that they assumed a prominence not known before.
At a time when there were no exponents of note, he mastered
the difficult vocal technique and his own excellent voice and
stage presence enabled him to bring many innovations to the
role. He introduced a number of songs into the limited repertoire
and developed a quality and expression which had been lacking
before. He in fact founded a new school of acting which set the
standards for all *lao tan* actors of the future.

Ching

A striking feature of Chinese stage technique is the practice of
painting the face and forehead with a bold and colourful pattern
in the case of the actors who play the *ching* roles. These portray
brave warriors, swashbuckling bandits, crafty and evil ministers,
upright judges and loyal statesmen and there are some who
represent gods and supernatural beings. These characters
symbolize strength and power in fighting, thinking or scheming,

and each movement or utterance that they make as they strut and swagger about the stage emphasizes these facts. Everything about them is emphasized to give an effect of towering grandeur and unbounded vitality. In addition to their bold make-up, they wear padded shoulder jackets beneath their outer costume to increase their bulk and very high soled boots to increase their height. The actors who play this role must have broad faces and foreheads suitable for the painted make-up patterns: they must also be tall and have a voice that is full and which has great carrying power. The *ching* actor is often referred to as *lien p'u*, literally a face that shows a record, or *hua lien* or *mien*, flower face. The principal behind the painted face make-up is the symbolizing of personal character through colour, although the proportions of colour on the face do not necessarily indicate an equal strength of the personal quality concerned and sometimes emphasis is laid on making a bizarre pattern for stage effect. More is said about this in the section on make-up. The vocal technique of the *ching* actor is quite extraordinary; his voice is robust and full, nasal, even raucous in quality, and characterized by protracted enunciations of tremendous volume. It is common for Chinese dramatic writers to say of their favourite *ching* actor that the walls of a theatre still echo three days after he has sung on the stage. The layman hearing a performance for the first time may well wonder how the human voice is capable of such effect and it is hardly surprising that there are comparatively few actors whose voice withstands the heavy strain put upon it in this role. Nevertheless there is an excitement and bizarre appeal about the technique once it is understood, the combination of sound, colour and swift movement when a *ching* actor takes the stage cannot fail to hold the spectator fascinated if a little breathless. The *ching* role is divided into three styles, *cheng ching*, *fu ching* and *wu ching*. The *cheng ching* portrays the great and important people of good character, the first qualification for this style is expert singing. The *fu ching* is often a bad character and there is not so much emphasis on singing as the technique of movement and robust speech. The eyes are important in the facial expression of the *ching* actor for he rolls them round and round with great effect. The *wu ching* concentrates chiefly on fighting and gymnastics. This is a division of styles used formerly although today it is customary to describe the role under two

Ch'ou actor as an innkeeper

headings, *ta hua lien* and *erh hua lien*. The *ta hua lien*, big flower -
face, include all parts in which singing is of prime importance,
while *erh hua lien*, two flower face, actors must be skilled chiefly
in their posturing, acrobatic turns and expert enunciation of
their spoken words. The term *t'ung ch'ui*, copper hammer, is also
used of the *ta hua lien* role.

Ch'ou

The *ch'ou* is the clown or comic of the Chinese stage. He is not
necessarily a fool and may portray a serious or evil character as
against a merely ribald one. He is the one character on the stage
who uses everyday speech, that is to say Peking colloquial. He is
at liberty to improvise as the mood strikes him, the spontaneous
quip and local jest are both a part of his technique and he takes

the audience into his confidence with a bat of the eyelids or a knowing leer. In all his interpretations there is combined the skill of the mimic and the acrobat. His make-up is always characterized by a white patch round the eyes and nose, sometimes various markings in black are superimposed. These vary according to the part played although each remains faithful to its own individual markings. The exact significance of them seems to have been lost in the past and no one has ever been able to enlighten the writer on the subject, not even the *ch'ou* actors themselves, but everyone may recognise the white patch as the universal trademark of the clown. To the Chinese audience this make-up is a convention that the actor must portray specified emotions in the different variations on his theme, but it does not always signify buffoonery or low comedy. In the play *Huo Chan San Lang*, for instance, the title role is one for a *ch'ou* actor, but the play is actually a weird tragedy powerful in its representation of the supernatural: here is no clowning in the accepted sense, rather there is a Goya-like quality about it. As a female impersonator the *ch'ou* invariably plays the part of a shrewish mother-in-law or rascally go-between, parts which bear some affinity with the dames of Western pantomime, although the caricature from life is often so telling that it goes far beyond Widow Twankey. The main role is divided into two styles, *wen ch'ou* and *wu ch'ou*. The former may be a character such as a woodcutter, a jailer, a watchman or a servant, while the latter is an armed character such as a minor military official who performs the acrobatics connected with fighting and horse riding. The *wu ch'ou* is also sometimes referred to as *hsiao hua lien* or *san hua lien*. The role of *ch'ou* is not an easy one to play well, the actor must be familiar with every kind of part for there is often a little of them all mixed into his own technique. Chinese theatre critics like to quote *ch'ou* as the first role in perverse contradiction of their hallowed order of *sheng*, *tan*, *ching*, *ch'ou*. There is a popular theory which has given rise to this: it is to the effect that the T'ang emperor himself used to play the part of *ch'ou*. This is also supposed to have been the reason for a tradition that was common backstage until quite recent times, decreeing that no actor should commence making up until the *ch'ou* had first smeared some of his white make-up on his own face. None of these facts ever seem to have been verified however. It may be true or it may be another of those apocryphal stories which tend to be numerous in writings on the Chinese theatre in both hemispheres.

Some Actors of Note

It is impossible in the space available here to give particulars about every actor of importance: that would naturally require a complete volume in itself. The men who are described therefore, are some of those who have made significant contributions to the history of the theatre during the last two hundred years, or have held, or still hold, a distinguished place on the contemporary stage. There needs must be a great number of names omitted which deserve inclusion under either heading: it is no detriment to their talents that they are absent from the list. It is a difficult task to obtain reliable data about actors long since dead and in fact about some who are still living. This is partly due to the fact that it was never considered worth while keeping authentic records of theatrical matters in China. So often when people do write about actors they content themselves with idle chatter and irrelevancies about their heroes and ignore the most elementary information such as dates. The reader, more often than not, is left with the vague statement that an artist died at such and such an age or was born about the middle of so and so period without any specific elaboration of their approximations. Even when dates are given they do not always agree in the case of different biographers. This, coupled with the fact that communication with Chinese sources is now so difficult, is responsible for the fact that a great many of the dates given here are queried as approximate as well as the notes about certain actors being scanty. The author has assumed that a few words of fact are better than the many unverified stories and poetic references with which a majority of accounts of Chinese actors are larded.

The Chinese actor is an artist with the virtues and idiosyncrasies of his kind the world over. The social seclusion which was enforced upon him in the past sometimes encouraged unorthodox living in a society that was then in many ways feudal. But there is no reason to suppose that every actor was a rogue who dwelt in a world of vice and immorality. The very nature of its being makes the professional world of the theatre a unique one: this is as true of any country as it is of China. The actor must work harder than most to rise in his profession and is subject to a physical strain few others could tolerate. The Chinese actor is no exception; he cannot afford to spare himself at any time and is bound to be admired for the consummate artistry he brings to his craft.

The biographies of actors which follow are given in order of *sheng, tan, ching, ch'ou.*

Sheng ACTORS

Ch'eng Chang-keng (1812–1880?)

Ch'eng Chang-keng was a native of Anhui province and is often referred to as one of the two great sons of Anhui, the other being the statesman Li Hung-chang. He was a student in his youth and received the normal education of his time only later taking to the stage, on which he first became an expert in the *k'un ch'ü* drama. He had an early success and was a very popular actor eventually assuming leadership of the famous San Ch'ing Pan, a theatrical company which had been in existence since 1789, during the reign of Ch'ien Lung. He was noted for the style and quality of his singing and brought many innovations to the *sheng* roles. Ch'eng is generally regarded as the 'father' of the *ching hsi* drama for he was responsible for co-ordinating elements from other dramas in the final form which became the new favourite of the theatre-going public. As a teacher he was widely respected and had a great influence on the younger actors: he was known everywhere by his nickname *Ta lao pan,* the head of the troupe. He used his magnificent voice to good effect to develop the style called *ch'eng p'ai,* the source from which developed the *sheng* actors' technique of the future. In this connection he is also said to have been responsible for populari- sing the use of the *hu ch'in* in the stage orchestra. Ch'eng Chang- keng received the favour of the Imperial court, where his acting was held in high esteem, but he was respected by all ranks of society for both his artistic and personal integrity.

Yü San-sheng

He was born in Peking but it is difficult to find any accurate dates for this actor. He was the son of a business man and received a good education. Chinese writers say that he first appeared on the stage in 1862 and died at the age of eighty. He was a gifted singer, particularly in *hsi p'i* and developed the vocal style for *sheng* roles called *yü p'ai*. One of the famous *sheng* actors of the present century, Yü Shu-yen, was his grandson and carried on his grandfather's tradition. His son was the *tan* actor Yü Tzu-yün.

Chang Erh-k'uei (?–1853)

This actor was an Anhui man and a contemporary of Ch'eng Chang-keng. He came of a wealthy family, received a good education and first took to the stage as an amateur. He developed the style of singing known as *k'uei p'ai* which was based on old literary forms and unaffected by new developments. He had no pupils and his technique fell into disuse, being one for the connoisseur rather than the ordinary theatregoer.

T'an Hsin-p'ei (1846–1917)

T'an Hsin-p'ei was born the son of an actor and came from Hupeh province. He rose to great heights in playing the *sheng* roles and his acting had a lasting influence on the generation which followed him. He possessed an excellent voice which early won him the title of 'little hailer to the heavens' from an admiring public. He developed the bearded *sheng* roles to a technical pitch which was new in the theatre and gave his name to the celebrated *t'an p'ai* style of singing incorporating something of the technique of the three actors named above, yet developing his own individual style, which is still followed by modern actors. T'an is a significant figure in the history of the *ching hsi* theatre and did a great deal to advance a new technique. He was apprenticed to the stage at the age of eleven. After experience in several troupes he attracted the notice of *Ch'eng Chang-keng* whose company, the San Ch'ing Pan, he joined. The older actor encouraged the younger and taught him a great deal which contributed to his development as an original artist of great distinction. T'an Hsin-p'ei became extremely popular at Court and was one of the Empress Dowager's favourite actors. He appears to have been a strict disciplinarian in the theatre and noted neither for his benevolence nor charity towards the faults of others. He had several sons all of whom took to the stage but only one, T'an Shao-p'ei, became at all successful although a grandson, T'an Fu-ying, became one of the idols of the Peking stage within recent decades. It is interesting to note that some early gramophone recordings of T'an Hsin-p'ei are still extant.

Yang Hsiao-lou (1876–1937)

Yang Hsiao-lou was the foremost *wu sheng* actor of the century, famous for his majestic bearing, skill and highly developed technique in the military roles. He first gained fame when he appeared before the Empress Dowager as a very young actor, after which occasion he never looked back. He came from that birthplace of so many great actors, Anhui province, and his skill, instead of diminishing, seemed to increase with the years. In 1928, when he was over fifty, he was voted a *chao teng*, or actor unsurpassed in his art, a distinction he shared with four others, all masters of different roles. He remained a first favourite with the theatregoing public until the end of his life. He was the first actor to appear on the stage with the actress Hsin Yen-ch'iu in Shanghai.

Yen Chu-p'eng (1890?–1942)

This actor first became interested in the stage as an amateur and only began as a professional very late in life. He was a keen follower of T'an Hsin-p'ei of whose style of singing he became an accomplished exponent.

Yü Shu-yen (1890–1943)

Yü Shu-yen was the grandson of Yü San-sheng and a popular exponent of that actor's style. He was a great favourite with Peking audiences. He was aged about fifty-three when he died but it is difficult to verify his exact dates.

Yang Pao-sen (1917–   )

Yang Pao-sen was the pupil of Yü Shu-yen whose tradition he carries on. He is a native of Anhui. He is said to resemble his teacher very strongly and was often called the little Yü Shu-yen. He is still acting.

Ma Lien-liang (1902–   )

Ma Lien-liang, who is a Mohammedan by birth, is still acting in China. He was a pupil of the famous Fu Lien Ch'eng school in Peking where he graduated as the best student of his period. He commenced his stage career in adolescent years and soon became extremely popular. He has always been a great favourite with Shanghai audiences. He is particularly noted for singing the pathetic and tragic roles of the *sheng* actor. His style is rather individual, belonging to no one school of acting. He went to Hong Kong after the war and remained there until 1951 when he was invited to return to the Mainland. After he went back a false report of his death was issued in the Taiwan press but was afterwards corrected by his family.

T'an Fu-ying (1906–   )
This actor is the grandson of the famous T'an Hsin-p'ei and has had a great vogue with Peking playgoers during his career in which he has continued to act the roles made famous by his grandfather.

Hsuü Hsiao-hsiang (1831–1882)
Hsü Hsiao-hsiang was the most distinguished actor of *hsiao sheng* roles at the end of last century. He was a native of Kiangsu province but was early taken to Soochow by his family where he basked in the *k'un ch'ü* tradition. Later he moved to Peking with his father. He was fond of the stage as a child and early became an enthusiastic amateur player and made quite a reputation for himself in private performances in Peking. After the death of his father he took to the stage as a professional and devoted himself to mastering his craft with a single minded devotion. After several years' study he joined the troupe of Ch'eng Chang-keng where he became that famous actor's *hsiao sheng* lead, becoming as accomplished in the Anhui style of acting as he was in the *k'un ch'ü*. He did a great deal to advance the technique of the *hsiao sheng* role and was responsible for developing the present vocal style which combines a falsetto and natural voice. Previously the singing in the *hsiao sheng* roles had been in falsetto only. He was supreme in the role of *Chou Yü* of the *Three Kingdom* plays. Towards the end of the reign of *Kuang Hsü* (1874–1908) he retired to Soochow where he died.

Yü Chen-fei (1902–   )
Yü Chen-fei is the legitimate successor to Hsu Hsiao-hsiang. He is a native of Soochow and the son of Yü Su-lu, a celebrated *k'un*

ch'ü scholar and amateur. From his earliest days Yü Chen-fei was brought up in the traditions of the old drama and although he commenced his stage career as an amateur his background was such that he was trained in professional standards from the beginning. In addition to being a master actor and a scholar well versed in the history of the drama he is also an expert performer on the *ti tzu*, or flute, the principal instrument of accompaniment in the *k'un ch'ü* drama. Yü Chen-fei is the greatest living authority on the *k'un ch'ü* drama today as well as being a distinguished exponent of its acting styles and he is engaged in compiling the plays of the repertoire in their original form. In the *ching hsi* theatre he has been the principal *hsiao sheng* player since he took to the stage professionally and has acted with Mei Lan-fang through several decades. He has a magnificent stage presence and a fine voice, the quality of his stage laughter was remarked upon earlier in this chapter. From 1951 until early in 1955 Yü Chen-fei was in Hong Kong where he first acted with Ma Lien-liang and Chang Chun-ch'iu, later organizing occasional performances of his own when those two actors left for the mainland. His genius was largely wasted in Hong Kong although that city was fortunate in being able to see such an actor for the first time. Finally he was invited to return to Peking by Mei Lan-fang, there being no one to take his place in the theatre in China, and in March 1955 he went back.

Tan ACTORS

Mei Ch'iao-ling (1841–1881)

Mei Ch'iao-ling was born at T'aichow but adopted at the age of eight by a Soochow man. The boy led a rather unhappy life when his foster parent married again and he was sold as an apprentice to a Peking acting company. He led a hard existence at first but finally found a teacher who took an interest in him and eventually graduated as an independent actor. He was skilled in both the *k'un ch'ü* and Anhui styles and became an accomplished female impersonator who was very popular with audiences. His interpretation of a modest and virtuous maiden was only equalled by his acting in the part of a gay coquette and his version of a lady of the Manchu court never failed to receive applause. In the famous painting *Shih San Chüeh T'u,** mentioned at the end of this chapter, Mei is depicted in the costume of such a role. He married in 1859 and had two sons, Yü-t'ien, who became an accomplished theatre musician and Shao-fen, who followed in his father's footsteps, but died just as he was beginning to make his reputation. The son of Shao-fen is the famous Mei Lan-fang. Mei Ch'iao-ling gained great repute as a teacher and he was the founder of the famous acting troupe Ssu Hsi Pan.

Wang Yao-ch'ing (1871–   )

Wang Yao-ch'ing acted regularly with T'an Hsin-p'ei and was noted particularly for his interpretation of the female roles with Manchu style costume, i.e. in plays like *Ssu Lang T'an Mu*, but he was distinguished for all types of *tan* acting in which he made many innovations. Wang had to retire from the stage because his singing voice deteriorated, but he continued as a valuable guide and teacher to the younger actors and Mei Lan-fang received a great deal of encouragement and inspiration from this veteran when he began to devise his newer style *tan* roles. Wang Yao-ch'ing has been important as an advisor and teacher and his name must be linked with the development of the modern school of *tan* acting. He is still alive and director of a new school of experimental classical drama in Peking.

Mei Lan-fang (1894–   )

Mei Lan-fang has been the stage idol of China for so many years that it would be difficult for playgoers to conceive a theatre without him. He was born in Peking and is the grandson of Mei Ch'iao-ling. His father died and he was brought up by his uncle, Yü-t'ien, a well known theatre musician. From the beginning Mei's background was the theatre and he grew up under the strict discipline of the old schools where he early gave evidence of a bright future. Mei himself disclaims any pretensions to natural talent and modestly declares that it is sheer hard work and study which have raised him to his present position. In his memoirs he says that when he thinks of his early days as a pupil actor he can remember nothing except work and more work. It is this spirit no doubt which has made his stage technique unsurpassed in its unity of gesture, expression, and exquisite grace and delicacy of line. His voice has purity and quality and is ideal for the roles he plays, but only strict training and discipline have enabled him to retain his vocal powers so long. In 1913 Mei

Lan-fang was invited to go to Shanghai for the first time by the actor Wang Feng-ch'ing to act as *tan* to the senior man's *sheng*. He was only nineteen at the time and had never left the capital before or acted in large theatres, but only at private performances. He was so nervous that he hardly dare set out, as he has told us in his book, but finally he travelled to the great out-port accompanied by his aunt, his *hu ch'in* player and dresser. After a great deal of thought he had chosen the play *Wu Chia P'o* for his debut in the Shanghai theatrical world. The first performance was a private one but he created such an impression that within a few days he was invited to appear at the Tan Kuei theatre, long vanished from the Shanghai scene. The whole of the city flocked to see the new wonder. In his account of the event, he describes how much grander he found the theatre than those of his native Peking and how vast it seemed when he first peeped through the curtains. Immediately after making his entry however he sensed the friendliness of the audience, his nervousness vanished and his performance was received with wild enthusiasm. Since that day he has never looked back. His partnership with Wang Feng-ch'ing remained unbroken for twenty years, being interrupted by the Japanese war. Mei Lan-fang performed in all the leading cities in China where distinctions were heaped upon him. In 1923 he was accorded high honours by the ex-Emperor Hsüan T'ung and in 1924 he was by general consent voted China's most popular actor. In 1928 he was named one of the five *ch'ao teng* actors in Peking, artists unsurpassed in their own field. In 1924 he visited Japan where he is still remembered with admiration by theatrical people, he toured the U.S.A. in 1930 and the U.S.S.R. in 1935, and in both countries he received high praise. The great powers in those days, it seems, found one aspect of China on which they conspired to agree. During the Japanese war he retired from the stage and the popular story has it that he grew a moustache during this period to emphasize his refusal to act the more effectively. In the troubled times after the war he quickly made a comeback and one of the most difficult things in the world was to be able to get a seat for one of his performances. Shortly before the Nationalist government fled to Taiwan, a colour film was made of one of his plays, *Sheng Szu Hen*, as an experiment, but the technical quality of the photography was poor. He is now said to be working on several new films in Peking, as records of his plays. The position that Mei Lan-fang holds in the history of the *ching hsi* is a notable one and his name will always be remembered as one of the great forces of his country's theatre. He has set standards and created a tradition not only for the actors who have followed but for the many actresses who have risen to prominence of recent years. He proved himself equally adept at playing *ch'ing i*, *wu tan* and *hua tan* roles and although actors like his grandfather and Wang Yao-ch'ing had already begun to defy the conventions whereby *tan* actors specialized in only one of these, it was Mei who finally established the tradition that a good *tan* actor is expert in all three and brought many improvements and additions to the technical styles. He created a number of new plays and in this he was assisted a great deal by the scholar Ch'i Ju-shan. A feature of many of these was the introduction of dances in which the choreography was based on ancient styles. He also devised many innovations and modifications in stage costume and make-up which have become accepted as standard. At more than sixty he is still acting and takes a prominent part in the affairs of the classical theatre and is the director of the new institute for research in the old drama which has been established in Peking. His name is widely used in the cultural political manifestos which are a feature of the new age, the outsider can only accept these with reserve and discretion. He has one son on the stage who, however, does not equal his father in genius. There seems little doubt that Mei Lan-fang, whose achievements span an old world and a new, marks the end of an era of acting in the classical theatre of China.

Kung Yün-fu (1862–1932)

Kung Yün-fu was the supreme interpreter of a role that, more than any of the others, is least understood by actors; the *lao tan*, or aged women roles. There have been few really first class exponents of this role and none who have surpassed the late Kung Yün-fu. He was a jade merchant of Peking who started his stage life as an amateur, being equipped with a remarkably fine natural voice. He first studied the *sheng* roles but his teachers persuaded him to sing the *lao tan* toles in which there were few experts at that time. He mastered the intricate vocal technique and developed a voice which was unrivalled in its tone and quality for these parts. He introduced a greater variety of songs into the repertoire and made many innovations in the technique in general. He eventually created a school of his own for this style which was hailed as the best of its kind by the theatre connoisseurs. In 1928 he was voted a *chao teng* actor, i.e. supreme in his class and one of four other actors to be so honoured in Peking drama circles. He had a distinguished pupil Li To-k'uei who played a great deal with Mei Lan-fang.

Ch'en Te-lin (1862–1930)

Ch'en Te-lin was a female impersonator of the top rank, he too was voted a *chao teng* actor in 1928 when he was aged sixty-six and still appearing on the stagge as an accomplished player of youthful feminine roles. He lost his voice at one point of his career but regained it with careful training and his vocal powers were regarded as unequalled even when he was an old man. He was trained as an actor in the old schools starting his stage career at the age of twelve and gradually gained such popularity that he was summoned to appear in Court entertainments. His appearances in the Imperial Palace enabled him to observe the Empress Dowager at close quarters and report has it that he introduced some of her characteristics and mannerisms into certain of his performances. He was held in high esteem by the younger school of actors who regarded it as an honour to receive instruction from him and many celebrated *tan* actors, including Mei Lan-fang, were his students.

Li Shih-fang (1918–1947)

Li Shih-fang was a young artist of great talent and promise who met his death in an air crash at the age of twenty-eight. He was a very popular actor whose appearance and technique caused him to be nicknamed by theatre people as the 'little Mei Lan-fang', it being conceded by many that he would become the successor to this great actor. He was named as one of the four leading juvenile *tan* actors.

Ch'en Yen-ch'iu (1903–   )

Ch'eng Yen-ch'iu was formerly rated as one of the big four *tan* actors and in his own field at one time achieved a popularity almost as great as Mei Lan-fang. He developed a style of singing

Chang Chün-ch'iu making up

which was much praised by theatregoers. In later years he became somewhat stout for a *tan* actor and retired from the stage at the end of the war. He is now active in the new theatrical research institute in Peking. He commenced his stage life as an amateur.

Chang Chün-ch'iu

Chang-Chün-ch'iu was named as one of the four leading junior *tan* actors, the others being Li Shih-fang, Mao Shih-lai and Sung Te-chu. He commenced his stage career as an amateur and is noted for the high quality of his singing and his decorative appearance in costume. He is at his best in the *ch'ing i* roles and plays with distinction roles such as that of Su San in *Yu T'ang*

Ch'un. During 1950 and 1951, he was in Hong Kong playing with Ma Lien-liang and Yü Chen-fei and for a time organized his own troupe there. Financial circumstances were against him however and he returned to the mainland where he is now acting.

Ching ACTORS

Ho Kuei-shan (1843–1913)

Ho Kuei-shan was the most famous *ching* actor of the last century. He was a native of Shantung province and one of several sons of a district magistrate. After his father's death he decided to take up acting as a profession. He studied under the actor Wang Cheng-shih and later joined the celebrated San Ch'ing company led by Ch'eng Chang-keng who soon recognised his worth as an interpreter of the 'painted face' roles. He appears to have had a voice of tremendous power which, in the customary words of Chinese critics, made the theatre walls tremble. His Chinese biographers also describe him as something of a *bon viveur*, an early photograph certainly shows him as a jovial looking character of powerful build and one can visualize him roaring about the stage in the fury of sound and movement customary to the *ching* role. He had a son who followed in his footsteps although he never attained his father's fame.

Chin Hsiu-shan

Chin was at first an amateur and a deep admirer of the acting of Ho Kuei-shan whose technique he studied. Ho heard him sing and decided to take him as a pupil and Chin became so proficient that he turned professional and earned a reputation second to that of his teacher. His son Chin Shao-shan also became a famous *ching* actor. Reliable information about this actor is scanty and biographers simply state that he died in the early years of the Republic which was founded in 1911.

Ch'ien Chin-fu (1862?–   )

Ch'ien Chin-fu received his training in the San Ch'ing Pan under Ch'eng Chang-keng. He studied *k'un ch'ü* drama first and then later graduated to the *p'i huang* style. He was noted for his skill in the gymnastics of the fighting roles and for the excellent quality of his make up. He acted a great deal with T'an Hsin-p'ei and Yang Hsiao-lou.

Chin Shao-shan (—1943)

Chin Shao-shan was the son of Chin Hsiu-shan and one of the most popular *ching* actors of recent times. He first made his reputation in the role of the Emperor in the famous play *Pa Wang Pieh Chi* playing with Mei Lan-fang. One writer has said that these two actors were so popular in this play with Shanghai audiences that many times the doors of the theatre had to be barricaded against the overwhelming crowds. Chin Shao-shan went to Hong Kong before the war to act with Mei Lan-fang and while there acquired a tiger cub which occasioned the authorities no little concern. He appears to have been a colourful, thriftless character with a passion for pet animals. On the stage he had a good natural voice for his parts and carried on the *ching* tradition with skill and *elan*.

Ch'ou ACTORS

Liu Kuei-san

Liu Kuei-san had a reputation in his own field as high as that of Ch'eng Chang-keng. He was a native of Tientsin and received a good education but according to accounts failed in the government examinations and decided to go on the stage. He joined the San Ch'ing troupe under Ch'eng Chang-keng and here first of all studied the *sheng* roles, but it was as a *ch'ou* that he excelled and finally rose to fame. He brought distinction to his role and acquired a reputation as a great wit as well as a fearless satirist. He created a sensation once by riding his own pet donkey on the stage, in a play which featured such a scene, instead of using the customary symbolic technique of the Chinese actor. He became an actor at the Imperial court but is reputed to have died in prison from a beating, after making satiric references to the minister Li Hung-chang from the stage. Reliable information about this actor is scanty and the dates of his birth and death are unknown, he left no one to carry on his tradition and only his memory survives as one of the great figures of the stage in the last century.

Hsiao Chang-hua (1879—   )

This actor was famed for his skill in all the different *ch'ou* roles although he was especially distinguished for his interpretation of the *wen ch'ou* parts on the stage. He acted a great deal with

Ma Lien-liang and among his many successes was the part of the old jailer Ch'ung Kung-tao. He was a teacher at the famous Fu Lien Ch'eng training school and the instructor of generations of noted actors. He is still active in Peking as an instructor.

Ma Fu-lu (1900–   )
Ma Fu-lu is the most distinguished *ch'ou* actor of recent times and a great favourite with Peking audiences. He was a student of Hsiao Chang-hua.

* *Shih San Chüeh T'u*—Thirteen great *ch'ing* actors by Sun Yung-pu.

CHAPTER V

THE TECHNIQUE
OF THE ACTOR

THE technique of the Chinese actor can be analysed under four broad headings. They are speech and song; movements and gestures; costume and make-up; use of weapons and other stage properties. Collectively they serve a purpose which marks them apart from their equivalents in a more realistic Western theatre, each is related to the other in providing a symbolism which is necessary to the appreciation of stage art. Within these divisions, as listed here, there are variations created according to the four main character roles of the *ching hsi* actor, i.e. *sheng, tan, ching, ch'ou*. A detailed description of the various aspects of technique follows in the order listed above.

Ch'ang pai, speech and song.
In the last chapter a general description has been given of the vocal techniques of the main actor roles, that is to say the aural quality of the singing and enunciation according to the characters portrayed. In considering the actor's speech and song it is necessary to understand the importance of poetic recitative, including the rhyme and tone quality of the Chinese language as applied to the technical construction of *ch'ang pai* which makes great use of prosody. In the past, Chinese writers and scholars have evolved various rules of rhyme for verse construction and these were based not only on sound but on the tones in which the sounds were spoken. Metre or the number of syllables in Chinese depends on the number of words or characters. There is a flat and deflected tone used in Chinese versification. The flat tone is spoken in a level manner with no variation, while the deflected tone may rise, sink or be abruptly terminated. These variations together with the flat version form the four separate tones.

In the *ch'ang pai* of the *ching hsi* stage, rhyme is treated in a much broader way than it is in the subtle complexities of classical literature, the whole aim being simply to provide pleasing effects for the actor. The rhyming formula in use, commonly referred to as *ching chu ch'e k'ou*, consists of thirteen different groups of Chinese characters. They are *chiang yang; chung tung; jen ch'en; yen ch'ien; hui tui; i ch'i; ku su; miao t'iao; yu ch'iu; so po; huai lai, fa hua; mieh hsieh*. The two characters in each group define the types which may be used tonally and metrically to provide rhyming endings to the actor's lines. Within each of these groups are characters which are known as *t'uan tzu*, rounded characters, and others which are called *chien tzu*, sharp characters. The names will indicate their function. On the stage *chien tzu* must be very much sharper in quality than their literary equivalents in order to provide the maximum effect for the audience. One amusing use of rhyme on the stage is called *shu pan*. Sometimes in the middle of a play the music ceases and, accompanied by the beat of the *pan*, the *ch'ou*, or comic actor, will relapse into a recitative whose rhythm has a continuous, almost breathless, quality accentuated by the movement of the actor's eyes and body, both of which are also in time with the rhythm of the words and the beat of the *pan*. This effect is achieved by the actor using words which all follow the rhyme of the first character spoken, that is to say they all belong to exactly the same rhyming class of character. When two actors are singing together they must use the same type of rhymes in their verses.

The *shang ch'ang*, entry and *hsia ch'ang*, exit of the actor is always marked by certain conventional *ch'ang pai* forms which are strictly observed. Every actor playing an important role must use what is called the *yin tzu* on first entering. The *yin tzu* is half sung, half recited, and is not accompanied by music or the *pan*. The *yin tzu* generally contains two or four lines. In the *k'un ch'ü* plays it may have as many as ten. In it the actor may describe his nature and appearance, recite a poem or two sentences called *tui lien*, couplets. The latter are often used by the *ch'ou* or characters of lesser importance. Sometimes an actor coming on recites his *yin tzu* and then seats himself and continues with *tso ch'ang shih* which often outlines the story of the play. It usually consists of four lines. In such a case the preceding *yin tzu* will have described characteristics of the person concerned, his ability to fight and so on. After *tso ch'ang shih* comes *t'ung ming* which describes the character, his family, residence and other matters. It contains several lines not fixed in number. *Chao pan* is the signal for the orchestra that the actor wishes to commence his singing, he raises his voice at the end of the last word to indicate this fact. The following are some of the variations for *shang ch'ang* entries.

Yin tzu shang

As already described this is used in very important roles. The actor stands at the front centre of the stage to recite it and it indicates the fact that he is in his home, or at any rate indoors and not outside.

Tien chiang ch'un shang

This is performed by military characters such as generals. The actor stands in the front centre of the stage and raises his sleeves before his face. It signifies he is on the battlefield or in head-quarters.

Nien shih shang

This is performed by either two or four actors together. They all stand at the front centre of the stage and either recite together or in sequence.

Nien tui lien shang

This is also performed standing in the same position described above and is used by the *ch'ou* or characters of lesser importance in the play. If an important character uses this method it means he has just come from another place.

Ch'ang shang

Here the actor comes straight out singing but in such a case he has previously sung or recited one verse, usually very short, behind the scenes before making his entry. It means that he is coming from another place.

Tao pan shang

One verse is sung by the actor behind the scenes before coming on. The singing is done in a loud voice which is a kind of prelude to indicate the character has come from a far distance or is outside in the streets.

Shu pan shang
This, as already described, is recited to the quick even beats of the *pan* and is often used by the *ch'ou* on entry, as well as in the course of the play or in exit.

K'o so shang
The actor comes on and coughs before he speaks; after this he must recite a *tui lien* or read a poem, nothing else. It means he has come a short distance such as from one room to another.

Nei pai shang
Here the actor recites a verse behind the scenes and then comes out and commences to sing. It serves as a signal to the orchestra. In making an exit, *hsia ch'ang*, all actors may either sing or recite *tui lien*, or if one character has left the stage another may not use *tui lien* at all but simply say, 'I will follow him' and exit. If the *tui lien* is sung the actor usually describes what his next course of action is to be or else sums up past events. Variations are as follows.

Ch'ang hsia
The actor sings three verses then walks towards the exit from which he returns to face the audience and sing one more verse before finally going off. Sometimes he just walks towards the exit laughing, crying or merely saying what is to follow as he goes off.

Nien hsia
After singing the actor walks towards the exit and then faces the audience and recites *tui lien*, after which he sometimes stamps his foot or beats one fist in the palm of the other hand before going off.

Shu pan hsia
This is performed by the *ch'ou* as already described.

Tung tso, body movements and gestures
This is an arbitrary term which covers a wide variety of actions ranging from the delicate gesture of a finger to vigorous poses of the whole body. It also includes a complex series of movements

made with the actor's sleeves, the long pheasant feathers worn on the head-dresses of certain characters and the beards worn in the *sheng* and *ching* roles. For the purpose of identification they are usually referred to by Chinese theatrical people under the categories which follow. *Hsiu*, sleeve movements; *shou*, hand movements; *chih*, finger movements; *chiao*, foot movements; *t'ui*, leg movements; *pu*, walking; *hu shu*, beard movements; *ling tzu*, pheasant feather movements.

Hsiu, SLEEVE MOVEMENTS

Sleeve movements were an important feature of dancing technique in ancient China and were considered essential to add to the grace of the performer. There are many references to the beauty of a dancer's sleeves to be found in old Chinese poems.

'What festival is this, with lamps filling the hall,
And golden hair pins dancing by night alongside of flowery
lutes?
A fragrant breeze flutters the sleeve and a red haze arises,
While jade wrists flit round and round in mazy flight.' *

On the *ching hsi* stage, sleeve movements are a graceful and characteristic feature of the actor's technique and they are exceedingly important in the case of the *tan* actors. Such movements are performed using what the Chinese call *shui hsiu*, water sleeves, so named from their fancied resemblance to rippling water when they are extended. The *shui hsiu* consist of cuffs of thin white silk left open at the seam and attached to the ends of the sleeves proper of the actor's costume. They are between one and a half to two feet long and the lengthier the sleeve the more accomplished the actor, for it requires great skill to manipulate them properly. Sleeve movements are performed in time with the rhythm of the music and nearly all have a symbolical meaning or else serve as the actor's signal to the orchestra. One or two serve a decorative purpose only but they all possess great beauty and no one can fail to be impressed by the grace and delicacy of these gestures when performed by a master actor. There are a great many different movements used in the different character roles and a detailed description follows, the movements of the *tan* actor being listed first. It should be realized that the *shui hsiu* are worn folded double over

* By Hsu Chen-ch'ing. Translated by Herbert Giles. 1906

The actor Yang Pao-sen as 'Ssu Lang'
in the play 'Ssu Lang T'an Mu'

Yang Pao-sen in the role of
Chu Ko Liang

Yu Chen-fei in 'hsiao sheng' costume:
he actress is his wife wearing the stage dress
for a nun. She is holding a 'ying ch'en'

'Sheng' and 'Ching' actors

PLATE I

*Actress wearing the Phoenix head-dress signi-
fying an Empress or court lady of high rank.
It is worn with the 'yün chien' or shoulder cape*

*An actor wearing 'k'ao, k'ao ch'i
'ling tzu' and 'hu wei'*

Stage scene from 'Ssu Lang T'an Mu'

PLATE II

Sleeve movement

the sleeve proper like a large cuff and it is from this position that
the movements are carried out.

1. *Tou hsiu.* When the *tan* actor makes an entry he first stands as
though arranging his costume. The head is slightly lowered and
the right hand, with palm inwards, is swept downwards from the
chest to the right knee and with a turn of the wrist flung backwards and a little to the right. Sometimes the left hand performs
a similar movement either alternately or simultaneously with the
right hand. This movement serves as a signal to the orchestra
leader that the actor is about to commence his speech or song
when the right arm is used. When both arms are used simultaneously it is called *shuang tou hsiu* and often symbolises worry
or anxiety, and when the left arm follows the right it is called
liang tou hsiu and can also symbolize a worried state. *Tou hsiu,*
actually divided into three separate movements, is also sometimes used when there is a pause in the continuity of the actor's
movements.

2. *Tiao hsiu.* This is performed when the actor is in a sitting
position. The sleeves are crossed on the lap to sweep to either
side and the actor half rises from his seat. It is a signal to the
D

orchestra that he is to commence singing.

3. *Jao hsiu*. This is only performed wearing the *kung chuang* costume (see section on *hsing t'ou*). It is regarded as a graceful but difficult movement. The left hand is upraised and the right hand is brought up to chest level with a circular sweep, this is then repeated with alternate arms. It is also a signal to the orchestra that the actor is to commence his performance.

4. *T'ou hsiu*. The two sleeves are flung out together either to the right or left. If to the left, the head looks right and *vice versa*. It symbolizes making a decision or anger and is only performed by the *ch'ing i* actor.

5. *Shuai hsiu*. If addressed by someone to whom he does not wish to listen, the actor turns his body away from the speaker and flings one sleeve out at waist level and then stands with folded arms.

6. *Chao hsiu*. The arm is raised and the sleeve flung forward towards someone who is being called. The action is repeated with alternate arms.

7. *Fu hsiu*. The hands are raised to chest height with the palms upward and the sleeves turned in before being flung outwards.

8. *Yang hsiu*. The left sleeve, hanging down, is held lightly at the end by the right hand with the first finger uplifted and moved forward to the right while the body moves to the left, the head poised as though looking into the distance. It may be repeated in the alternate direction and symbolizes looking far away.

9. *Shuang Yang hsiu*. The hands are raised with the palms down to chest height then turned flicking the sleeves outward. It can also signify looking ahead or sometimes indicates happiness.

10. *Chü hsiu*. This is used when leaving the stage or going round it. The right arm is raised before going off and the left is raised from chest height over the right hand and then the right hand flicked backwards.

11. *Chih hsiu*. The arms are slightly bent and the sleeves, which are at first held in their folded position, are then allowed to drop. If the actor is singing it serves to show that he is about to finish, otherwise it symbolizes the fact that a character is helpless and can do nothing about things.

12. *Fan hsiu*. The left arm is held at waist height in front of the body and the right hand raised above the shoulder when a circular movement of the wrist flings the sleeve upward to hang

down the back. This is used as a signal to the orchestra that the actor is about to sing, the foot being stamped lightly in time with the sleeve movement. It also signifies sorrow at being left behind when parting from a husband or lover and is sometimes used to call somebody to one.

13. *Shuang fan hsiu.* In this the right hand movement described above is performed with both left and right simultaneously, a space of two inches only must separate the hands as they perform the movement while the arms are bent in a curve. The foot is stamped twice on this occasion. It symbolizes deep sorrow and grief.

14. *En hsiu.* The sleeves are held in front of the eyes not touching the face but at about two inches from it with the head a little bent. The elbows are held out slightly from the sides. It symbolizes weeping.

15. *Pai hsiu.* The end of one sleeve is held at waist height with the other hand and the arms are then quickly swept right and left. It signifies someone not responsible for their actions or madness.

16. *Che hsiu.* The right hand is against the chest in an upward direction, the left is bent with the *shui hsiu* held before the face which is concealed. The head is turned away looking downwards to the right. It symbolizes embarrassment.

17. *Yen hsiu.* This is similar to the above movement except that the actor steps back a pace, repeating the action in this order.

18. *I hsiu.* The body is slightly bent and the sleeves held at face height and being made to quiver rapidly. It symbolizes fear.

19. *Chang hsiu.* The left hand is placed on the stomach and the right hand placed at the back of the head. It is used for running or if being beaten.

20. *P'u hsiu.* It is used when two people are happy to meet each other. The sleeves are allowed to hang down on the outside and the elbows of the *tan* actor are held by the *hsiao sheng*. This movement is seen a great deal in *k'un ch'ü* style plays.

21. *Wei hsiu.* This is used by the *tan* and *hsiao sheng* actors together. The *hsiao sheng* has one arm lightly round the waist of the *tan* whose arm rests on his shoulder as they walk along affectionately.

22. *Kai hsiu.* This is done from a sitting position and represents someone who is ill. The hands, covered by the sleeves, are placed

together on the table in front of the actor who half rises to face another person entering.

23. *An hsiu.* Used when an actor is seen writing. One sleeve is placed over the missive to conceal it from the onlooker.

24. *P'eng hsiu.* The two hands are placed together at lip level, as though in prayer, with the sleeves hanging downwards on the outside and in this position the actor moves forward three times to the accompaniment of drum beats. It symbolizes conveying thanks or extending an invitation.

25. *Ta hsiu.* This is performed by two people and symbolizes shaking hands. The actors hold each other's hands at chest height with their sleeves hanging down on the outside.

26. *Che hsiu.* The right sleeve is pulled back a little when drawing a sword, i.e. it is folded back once. The *ching* actor stands with legs wide apart when doing this and holds the sword horizontally in front of him. The *tan* actor does not move his legs and holds the sword point to the front, the *sheng* puts his right foot forward a step with the right arm held into the side and the sword held obliquely across his front. The *hsiao sheng* is the same as the *tan* but the right foot is forward a little and the legs a little bent.

27. *Tang hsiu.* At the beginning of the movement the sleeves are folded over the wrists then the hands are lifted to let the sleeves fall with the body swaying from side to side. It shows the intention of preventing someone passing.

28. *Lan hsiu.* The hanging sleeves are flicked round to turn over the uplifted wrists. This action is done behind another person's back indicating that someone is about to go while still agreeable to discussion.

29. *Po hsiu.* This is performed when an actor is not singing and is a difficult movement to do well. The sleeves are folded over the wrists and held by the hands which of course are not visible. They are then placed together at the left side on the upper waist.

30. *Hsüan hsiu.* This is purely a decorative movement used after a long song passage, when there are no actions to follow. The sleeves are gradually flicked back over the wrists.

31. *Cheng hsiu.* This movement is used by the *wu tan* when wearing the *mang* and *yu tai* (see section on *hsing t'ou*). It is performed when walking, the left arm is curved above the waist with the sleeve neither extended nor fully folded and it is

swung very slowly from side to side in time with the walking pace.

32. *Pei hsiu.* The hands are crossed behind the back in this movement which is used when leaving the stage and walking slowly.

33. *P'ao hsiu.* If very angry the character falls back as though stunned flinging the sleeves forward below waist level.

34. *Yao hsiu.* This movement is literally what is says, biting the sleeve and it is only used by the *hua tan.* It is a sign of affection but not a formal movement. The left sleeve is held to the mouth with the right hand holding the bottom of the sleeve. The head is bowed and no words are spoken.

35. *Lüeh hsiu.* This is used when walking along quickly out of doors. The sleeves are folded over the bent arms which sway from side to side while walking.

36. *Chen hsiu.* This movement indicates a woman who is pleased with herself or admiring her appearance. The left hand with palm upwards is placed over the right hand with palm downwards, the sleeves hang down and are swayed from side to side.

37. *P'iao hsiu.* When a woman falls down or is kicked, the sleeves are flung over in circular movement from above the head to the feet.

38. *T'ung ming hsiu.* This is an entry movement. The actor stands obliquely to the audience, speaks the name of the character he is portraying, and flings the sleeve over from right to left at eyebrow level.

39. *Pei kung hsiu.* The right or left sleeve is raised forward to eyebrow level, the fingers being rounded in a curve within the *shui hsiu* which hangs in place. It symbolizes that the other characters on the stage cannot see or overhear what is going on.

SLEEVE MOVEMENTS FOR ALL CHARACTERS

40. *Tou hsiu.* This is performed in a similar way to the *tan* but with slight variations in the different roles. The *sheng* must nod his head, the eyes look front. In the *ching* parts it is a more powerful movement, the head does not move and the sleeves move to the side with the arms well up. The *hsiao sheng* stands with body bent forward, the toe of the right foot is lifted in front of the left foot and the eyes follow the sleeve. The *ch'ou* stands with knees bent and feet apart. The *wu tan* and the *wu*

sheng are the same as the *ching*.

41. *Shuang tou hsiu.* In this movement the *sheng* actor holds his hands together in front of the stomach then sweeps the arms to the side. The *ching* actor has his hands higher than the *sheng* and keeps his eyes to the front. The *hsiao sheng* and the *ch'ou* movements are the same as the *tan*. In the *liang tou shiu* all characters use the same movement as the *tan*.

42. *Tiao hsiu.* All characters use this movement in the same way as the *tan*.

43. *Tou hsiu.* The sleeve is flung backward over the shoulder with a powerful movement. This is only used by the *ching* and *wu sheng* actors.

44. *Shuang tou hsiu.* This is the same movement but using two arms. It is only performed by the *ching* actors wearing *k'ai chang* costume or the *lao sheng* and *hsiao sheng* wearing the *hsüeh tzu*.

45. *Shuai hsiu.* All characters use this movement in the same ways as the *tan* actor.

46. *Hui hsiu.* It is the same as the *tou hsiu*, the first movement described, but the hands are kept at chest level. It is used by the *sheng, ching, hsiao sheng* and *ch'ou* actors and tells someone to go away.

47. *Chao hsiu.* All characters use the same movement as the *tan* but in a stronger manner.

48. *Ta hsiu.* It symbolizes hitting someone or indicating that one does not wish to listen to another person. It is chiefly used by the *ching* and *wu sheng* actors, the *hsiao sheng* and *sheng* actors using it more rarely. It is performed with two actors facing each other, one leans back and flicks the *shui hsiu* at the chest of the other.

49. *Tang hsiu.* This movement is only performed by bearded *sheng* and *ching* actors. It symbolizes a state of anxiety or anger. The bent arms are held at chest level and the sleeves are flung outwards together with the beard.

50. *Fu hsiu.* This is used by all characters in the same way as the *tan* movement.

51. *Yang hsiu.* The *sheng, hsiao sheng* and *ch'ou* perform this with the left foot forward and the left hand on the front waist. The *ching* actors perform with the left arm bent outwards at the side at chest level with the left foot forward, the right arm flicks the sleeve over to the right.

52. *Shuang yang hsiu.* All characters use this movement in the

same way as the *tan*.

53. *T'ai hsiu*. This is purely a decorative movement with no particular symbolism. It is used by the *hsiao sheng*, the *ching* actor in one play only and by the *fang chin ch'ou*. The left elbow is bent at ear level with the sleeve hanging down over the shoulder behind, while the right arm carries out the movement described in *tou hsiu*, the first movement described in this section.

54. *Chü hsiu*. The methods are similar to the *tan* movement but the *ching* actor must hold his robe with the left hand and the *ch'ou* has his legs slightly bowed.

55. *Chih hsiu*. All characters use this movement in the same way as the *tan*.

56. *Fan hsiu*. This is similar to the movement of the *tan* actor, but with the *sheng* and *ching* actors the right arm must not be close to the head and the *shui hsiu* to the outside of the shoulder. The *lao tan* actor may move his feet in this movement but no other character may do so.

57. *Liang fan hsiu*. The method is similar to *fan hsiu* but the arms are moved one after the other and not together. The *sheng* and *ching* actors place the left hand at the front of the left waist, stamp the right foot and, in time to the music, flick the right sleeve to the right repeating an alternate movement with the other arm. The *ch'ou* must have a bent waist when performing this and the *hsiao sheng* must wear the *mang* or *pei* costume.

58. *En hsiu*. The *sheng* actor performs this in the same manner as the *tan*, only the distance from the face is greater and the sleeve is moved backwards and forwards in front of the face. The *ching* actor has an even greater space between sleeve and face and the movement is stronger altogether. The *ch'ou* performs it like the *sheng* only with waist bent, while the *hsiao sheng* performs in the same way as the *sheng* if wearing *mang* costume and like the *tan* actor is wearing the *hsüeh tzu*.

59. *Pai hsiu*. The only other character who uses this movement other than *tan* actors is a *ching* actor in the role of Li Kuei, when disguised as a woman.

60. *Hsiao pai hsiu*. This movement is as described above only slighter, and is also used by the same character.

61. *Che hsiu*. All characters use this movement in the same way as the *tan* actor.

62. *Shuang che hsiu.* This is the same movement as described above, but with two hands in front of the face. It is only used by the *ch'ou* actor.

63. *Yen hsu.* This movement is only used by the *tan* actor.

64. *Yin hsiu.* This symbolizes sheltering from strong sun or rain or covering the head. It is used by the *sheng* actor and the hand is placed on the head.

65. *I hsiu.* All characters use this in the same way as the *tan*, except that the *ch'ou* has his waist very bent when performing the movement.

66. *Chang hsiu.* This is similar to the *tan* movement, but the *sheng* and the *ching* actors have the left hand on the waist with both hands and legs shaking. The *hsiao sheng* movement is identical with that of the *tan*. The shaking of the *ch'ou* actor is much more violent than of the other characters.

67. *Shuang chang hsiu.* All characters use this movement as described above, but while on their knees with both arms raised.

68. *Tan hsiu.* This represents dusting a seat for an honourable guest or preparing for a wine drinking party. The waist is bent and the unfolded right sleeve is flicked inwards towards the actor followed by the left sleeve flicked away from the body and the right sleeve once more towards the body.

69. *Yao hsiu.* This is used by characters other than the *tan*. The sleeve is waved from right to left in the manner of a fan and signifies that it is extremely hot.

70. *P'u hsiu.* The movement is the same for all characters, but it is chiefly used by the *tan* and *hsiao sheng*.

71. *Wei hsiu.* It is sometimes used by the *sheng* in company with the *ch'ing i*, as described in the section on the *tan* movements.

72. *Kai hsiu.* This movement is as described for the *tan*, but in the case of the *sheng* and *ching* actors, the *shui hsiu* hangs half over the edge of the table, while the whole length of the *shui hsiu* hangs over if performed by the *hsiao sheng* or *ch'ou* actor.

73. *Liao hsiu.* Only the *hsiao sheng* actor uses this movement. When going off the stage the sleeves are flung alternately to either side with a circular motion. It symbolizes self satisfaction.

74. *An hsiu.* All characters use this movement in the same way as the *tan* actor.

75. *P'eng hsiu.* All characters use this movement in the same way as the *tan* actor.

76. *Ta hsiu.* All characters use the same movement as the *tan* actor except that the *ch'ou* actor holds his face very close to the other person.

77. *Che hsiu.* This is similar to the *tan* movement (no. 26) but the *sheng, ching* and *hsiao sheng* actors place their right foot forward. The *wu sheng* has the right knee bent forward and the arms are held up with the elbows bent.

78. *Shuang che hsiu.* This is used by the *sheng* and *hsiao sheng* actors when fastening a shoe.

79. *Tieh hsiu.* This is similar to *che hsiu* only stronger in movement. If one character goes down on his knees in token of respect to another and the recipient of the courtesy considers it unnecessary, the latter pulls his sleeve back just beyond the fingers over the back of the hand, and bends forward to assist his companion to rise. All characters use the same movement but the *tan* actor only bends the legs and not his waist. It is only performed when the two characters concerned have some personal relationship in the play. The closer the relationship the deeper is the bend forward.

80. *Shuang tieh hsiu.* This is the same movement as above (no. 79), only both hands are used in the final movement.

81. *Wo hsiu.* This is used a great deal by the *wu sheng* actor and signifies having made a decision. As the actor is going off the stage he flicks a sleeve forward and catches it with the hand.

82. *Shuang wo hsiu.* This is used by old men or women on the stage and two sleeves are employed, but the movement is more feeble than above (no. 81). It means the character has the will to do something, even if he is a little lacking in the power of accomplishment. The actor sways from side to side while walking.

83. *Heng hsiu.* This movement is used by the *wu sheng* actor. It means that the character concerned intends to fight. The arms are lifted with the elbows bent and pulled outwards with a strong movement.

84. *Liang heng hsiu.* This movement too is only used by the *wu sheng.* The left arm is held straight out sideways at shoulder height with a bold gesture followed by the right arm in the same position. It means that another person may not pass.

85. *Jan hsiu.* It is used by the *wu sheng* going off the stage and sometimes by the *ching* actor. First the sleeves are clutched with

the hands which are then placed behind the back.

86. *Tang hsiu.* This is the same movement as for the *tan* actor (no. 27).

87. *Lan hsiu.* This is the same movement as for the *tan* actor (no. 28).

88. *Po hsiu.* This is the same movement as for the *tan* actor (no. 29).

89. *Hsüan hsiu.* This is the same movement as for the *tan* actor (no. 30).

90. *Cheng hsiu.* This is the same movement as for the *wu tan* (no. 31).

91. *Chan hsiu.* This is used by the *wu sheng* and *ching* actors coming on or going off the stage. The left arm is raised in front with the palm to the body. The right hand takes the left sleeve and places it in the left hand, the right hand then holds the *yu tai*, the special belt described in the section on costume.

92. *Tien hsiu.* This is performed by all characters and has no symbolical significance. The sleeves are flicked back with a few short movements up the cuff of the costume proper.

93. *Ch'e hsiu.* This movement is only seen in one play, *Fen Ho Wan.* The *tan* actor playing the heroine's role, Liu Ying-ch'un, leans forward to speak and clasps the left sleeve which is hanging down with the right hand.

94. *Pei hsiu.* All characters use the same movement as the *tan* actor (no. 32), but in the case of actors playing old people the hands are held higher than the others.

95. *P'ao hsiu.* All characters use the same movement as the *tan* actor (no. 33) except that men's sleeves are at the side instead of in front.

96. *Hsien hsiu.* This is used to express great alarm. The *tan* actor does not use it but all the other actors perform it in the same way. The character is standing and flings the sleeve over the right shoulder and sits down with a bang.

97. *Meng hsiu.* This is used by the *sheng* and *hsiao sheng* actors only. The actor sits with his head on a table and closes his sleeves over the top of the head. It expresses fear.

98. *Shu hsiu.* This is only performed to *pang tzu* music and is therefore infrequently used. The two arms are outstretched and the actor moves sideways with the arms going up and down. It means satisfaction in achieving one's wishes.

99. *Yao hsiu*. This movement is only used by the *tan* actor (no. 34).

100. *Shuai hsiu*. This is only used by the *hsiao sheng* actor who steps backwards, and flings one sleeve after the other as he goes. It is infrequently used and indicates there is an array of military or guards.

101. *Lüeh hsiu*. This movement is the same for all characters as in the *tan* movement (no. 35).

102. *Chen hsiu*. This movement as stated is only used by the *tan* actor (no. 36).

103. *P'iao hsiu*. This movement as stated is only used by the *tan* actor (no. 37).

104. *Tien chiang hsiu*. This is used only as an entry movement when a tune called *Tien chang chun* is used. The actor comes out with the sleeves held in front of his face, and walks to the middle of the stage singing the tune. When he has finished he recites his name and drops the sleeves. All characters use it in the same way, except that the *ching* stands absolutely square to the audience, the other characters standing obliquely. The right hand holds the left sleeve in this movement.

105. *T'ung ming hsiu*. All characters use the same movement as the *tan* (no. 38).

106. *P'an kuan hsiu*. This movement is only performed by *P'an Kuan*, the guardian and administrator of the infernal regions. When he appears on the stage he does a kind of dance which involves several complex movements referred to as *t'iao p'an*.

107. *Pei kung hsiu*. All characters use the same movement as the *tan* actor (no. 39).

Shou, HAND MOVEMENTS

The hand movements of the actor are usually divided into seven principal movements, the seventh, pointing, again being divided into more than twenty different methods. The hand and finger movements of the Chinese actor are a very characteristic feature of his technique and never fail to charm by their grace and precision. The seven hand movements of the different character roles will be described first followed by the *chih*, i.e. pointing of the fingers.

Chang shou. The *tan* actor holds the hands open with the palms upturned. The four fingers are together with the thumb bent on the middle finger. The *sheng* actor holds his thumb straight, the *ching* actor has all his fingers open while the *hsiao sheng* is similar to the *tan* except that his little finger is open a little. The movement signifies embarrassment.

T'an shou. The movement is similar to the above but means to be helpless or there is no way out. In the case of the *ching* and *sheng* all the fingers are together with the thumb straight out.

Pai shou. The right hand is held vertical at shoulder height with the thumb at the centre finger and the palm pushed towards the left. The head is turned to the right. It may be done with two hands, the head still being turned in the opposite direction. The movement is the same for all characters but the action of the *sheng* actor is a little stronger than the *tan*.

Chao shou. The hand is rounded a little with the thumb bent in under the first finger and the palm downwards. The hand is then waved either once or twice. It means to call somebody. The movement is the same for all characters except that the *ching* actor keeps his fingers open.

Ch'üan shou. The first is clenched with the thumb inside the bent fingers but lightly held. The right sleeve is often held with the left hand in this movement which means the character is about to strike someone. It is the same for all characters except that the *ching* actor's fingers are clenched much more forcibly than the others.

Tien shou. The left hand is held out at waist level palm upwards while the right hand, with palm upwards, is swung out in a circular movement from face level and brought down on the-left hand, sometimes with palm upwards and sometimes down. It means very good, agreed, or, 'Aiya! I am wrong or aggrieved'. In the case of the *sheng, hsiao sheng, ching* and *ch'ou* actor, the right hand is brought straight down instead of with a circular movement, the *ching* actor being particularly forceful. With the exception of *ch'üan shou* all the movements described above are performed with the sleeve hanging down.

Chih shih. These are the pointing finger movements. The variations of these movements are numerous and must be done in time with the music and the other movements of the actor's body. The basic finger position of the *tan* actor has the thumb and middle finger touching in a curve while the index anger points upwards, the finger also bent in an upwards curve. The fourth finger is bent slightly above the centre of the middle finger, while the little finger is curved above the centre of the fourth finger. The *ching* actor has the index and middle fingers together for pointing, the thumb is bent on the fourth finger and the little finger is bent. The *sheng* and *ch'ou* sometimes point with the index and middle fingers together and sometimes with the index finger alone. If the latter, the third fourth, and fifth fingers are bent with the thumb on the third finger. The *hsiao sheng* actor's movement is identical with that of the *tan* actor.

Tan yüan chih. Using the basic positions described above according to this role, the actor raises one hand, the sleeve hanging down, and points far into the distance.

Shuang yüan chih. This is a similar movement to that described above only two hands are used together. The hands, which must be kept about a foot apart the whole time, are raised to the pointing position with a circular motion. It is performed in the same way in all roles using the respective basic position of the hand already given.

Fan chih. This movement is often performed when people are talking together on the stage. It has no particular meaning other than gesticulation. The finger points backwards over the shoulder, there being a space of about six to seven inches between the shoulder and the hand. All characters use the same movement except that the *ching* actor's hand is at a greater distance from the shoulder and makes a much more forceful movement.

Tzu chih. Pointing at oneself. In this movement the pointing is done with the left hand while the right hand holds the left sleeve. According to the rules of old technique, the *tan* actor should never point at his face but only his chest, this also applies to the *hsiao sheng* but the rule is different today. The *sheng* and *ching* actors when pointing at themselves do it with the hand, palm upwards, in front of the chest and the thumb open. The *ch'ou* actor may point at his face but his legs must be bent as he does so.

Tu chih. This movement is intense and angry. The pointing is done at another character's face at nose level. The pointing hand is brought from waist level in front of the actor to the right side and then up to nose level and outwards. The *tan* actor must attain a gentleness in the movement even though it signifies anger. The other roles make the same movement with a corresponding increase in vigour.

Ch'ien chih. The right hand is held at face level with the palm upwards and is brought over towards the left shoulder in this position and then swept downwards across the front of the waist out to the right. The left hand rests on the waist either with the hand flat or the knuckles bent inwards. It may be performed with either hand and represents pointing out a destination, or a sign post and so on. In the male characters the action is correspondingly stronger and the left hand is held to the front of the waist or else behind.

Shuang ch'ien chih. In this movement the pointing is done as above only using two hands simultaneously.

Tan hou chih. There are three methods for this. The first is more complicated and all parts of the body must move together. The left hand is bent inwards on the side of the left waist. The right hand points across the chest to the left and the right foot is placed just behind the left with the toe touching the heel. The right heel is slightly raised. The right hand is then drawn across the chest out to the front and then left again with a circular motion. The eyes follow the finger and the waist moves in unison with the hand movement. Only the master *tan* actor is considered capable of doing this well. In the second method the action is the same but the actor points over his shoulder, the hand being held a little higher than in the above movement. In the third method the left hand points across the waist to the right just below the elbow of the right arm. Both sleeves are left hanging. It indicates searching for something or somebody or something interesting has been found. The *sheng* and *ching* actors only use two methods in this movement. The right arm is bent in front of the chest with palm down and pointing below the left shoulder. In this case all the fingers are extended. The second method uses only one finger at shoulder height as above. The *ch'ou* actor uses the same movements but the *hsiao sheng* is identical with the *tan* actor.

Shuang hou chih. The pointing gesture is the same as above but in this case two hands are used at a distance of about one foot apart and moved in time to the rhythm of the music, whether quick or slow. The male characters use their own methods as described but with two hands.

Tan yu chih. In this the actor points directly to the right side, the head is bent and the eyes follow the movement. The left arm may be slightly bent or placed according to the actor's wishes. All characters are the same as the *tan* who, however, makes a much fuller curve with the pointing movement.

Tan tso chih. This movement is the same as the preceding one but to the left instead of the right.

Shuang yu chih and *shuang tso chih*. These are as above but with two hands.

Pei chih. This is used when one character is speaking to another and does not wish a third person to know. The left arm is held at shoulder height and bent at a right angle. The right hand points, palm downwards and with sleeve hanging down, at a point beneath the left arm. The elbow of the pointing arm is also bent at a right angle. The *sheng* and *ching* actors perform this movement with the palm upwards as well as downwards.

Pei hou chih. The left arm is held as in the above movement, but the right points to something or somebody behind the back. The *sheng* and *ching* use two fingers for pointing in this movement.

Pei ch'ien chih. The left arm is held as above but the right hand points to the front. When pointing to the front in this way, the *tan* actor has the right foot obliquely behind the left heel.

Tan shang chih. The right hand points from in front of the chest round to the left shoulder then round and up in the air to the right.

Shuang shang chih. This is a similar movement only done with two hands. It is used sometimes by a woman character feigning madness. In such a case the right foot is moved forward and the left foot placed obliquely to it.

Tan hsia chih. In this one hand points to the ground, but there are three methods of performing it. In the first the right hand is moved from left to right in a half curve and then pointed down with the arm straight. In the second, the right arm is lifted pointing across the left shoulder, pulled back in a curve towards the right and then pointed down to the left. With the third method, the right arm is held above the head at the front, the actor kneeling with right foot just behind the left. The left hand is held on the waist and the right hand points down to the floor from above the head. The *sheng, hsiao sheng* and *ch'ou* only use the first two styles but the *ching* and *wu sheng* sometimes use the third.

Shuang hsia chih. This is as in the first two movements above but using two hands. It is chiefly used by the *tan* actor.

Heng chih. Used for pointing in several directions one after the other. The right hand is used with the palm upwards in the case of the *tan*. The arm is lower than shoulder height and slightly bent. When pointing it is moved from left to right a distance of about two feet. The male characters have the palm down in this movement.

Fan chih. This is only used by the *tan* and *wu sheng* actor and there are three methods. In the first the left arm is akimbo with the knuckles bent inwards on the waist and the body bent to the right. The right hand is brought from the right shoulder in a curve above the front of the head and then pointed to the left. The second method is the same but using different arms. In the third method the right hand above the head points to the ground, palm upwards.

Shuang fan chih. This movement is similar in method but both hands point.

Ch'ü chih. This is only used by the *wu tan* and *wu sheng* and simulates anger. The left foot is crossed behind the right and at a little distance apart. The right arm is in front of the face at eye level. It is pulled from left to right and then pointed sharply and obliquely across the body and down to the left.

Nu chih. This expresses extreme anger and is only used by the *sheng* and *ching* actors. The arm and hand is lifted trembling slightly and is then pointed directly at somebody still using the trembling motion.

Ching huang chih. This is only used by the *sheng* actor and it expresses mixed feelings, a state of both happiness and sadness. The right leg is lifted straight out and the body turned obliquely at the waist. The two pointing hands, trembling a little, are then moved round and round in a circular movement across the lifted leg.

In addition to these movements there are fourteen different methods of pointing at oneself and ten different methods of pointing when holding an object like a fan or a sword.

Chih t'ou. This is pointing at the head. The *tan* actor places right foot behind the left at right angles. The left hand is on the waist with the knuckles turned inwards. The right hand points to the crown of the head with the palm upturned. With the other characters there is no foot movement, the hand is held at a greater distance from the head and the palm faces forward. *Chih mien*. This is pointing to the face, and there are three methods. In the first the right hand is held up with the palm facing forward, i.e., away from the body and the finger pointing at the lips. The second uses the *t'an shou* hand posture to indicate the face, i.e. the right cheek. In the third method the hand is moved across the body to point at the left cheek. The left arm is held lower than the right, the hand covered with the *shui hsiu* and the right hand points to the left cheek from shoulder height. The *tan* actor uses the second and third movements, the *sheng* and the *ching* the first and second. The *wu sheng* and the *ch'ou* often use the third.

Chih pin. This means pointing to the temple, and is only used by the *tan* actor. The same method as the third above is used. Sometimes the temple is touched with the middle finger. *Chih k'ou*. This movement is the same only pointing to the mouth.

Chih po. This means pointing at the upper arm. For the *tan* actor the left arm is bent with the upper arm at right angles to the body and the lower arm horizontal across the chest. The right hand points, with palm turned outwards, i.e., away from the body, at the upper part of the left arm. The pointing finger of the *tan* is bent back. The *ching* and *sheng* actors do it in the same way using their own hand postures.

Chih shou. This means pointing at the hand. Two methods are used, the first being similar to the one above. In the second method the right hand is raised to point over the top of the head into the open palm of the left hand. The *sheng* and *ching* actors use only the first method.

Chih yao. This means pointing to the waist. It can only be done by the *hua tan* when in a costume that has no *shui hsiu*, in which case the right hand must point to the left waist and the left hand to the right. Other characters must never point to the waist but only rest their hands lightly on it, i.e., touch it with the palms. *Chih pei*. This means pointing to the back. The *sheng* and *ching* actors stand with legs apart, knees bent and the right hand held in the small of the back. The left hand is then raised above the left shoulder, palm outwards, finger pointing to the back. The *tan* does not use this method but has the right foot behind the left and the right hand on the waist with knuckles inward. The left arm is then raised to point to the back but lower down than in the other movements.

Chih t'ui. This means pointing to the leg. The *sheng* and *ching* actors lift the left leg, not too high, and the right hand points down at the left thigh in a vertical movement. The *tan* crosses the right leg behind the left, the left foot parallel with the right and the knees bent a little and the body leaning slightly to the left. The right arm is raised at right angles to the body, the hand pointing to the left thigh.

Chih t'su. This means pointing to the foot, and the same movement is used as above for the *sheng* and *ching* but the left leg is held higher. The *tan* actor does not use this movement.

Chih hsiung tu. This means pointing at the chest and stomach, never done in the latter case except by the *ch'ou* actor. Other characters must just use the two hands together and lightly touch the part with the flat palms.

The following are the ten methods of pointing while holding an object.

Ch'ih shan chih. This movement is for pointing with a fan and there are three methods used. First, while holding the fan closed, the actor goes through pointing motions with it. Secondly, the fan may be held against the sleeve behind the palm and between the thumb and little finger, the pointing movements being performed with the index finger. Thirdly, the pointing movements are carried out with an open fan, this is only used by the *tan* actor. The open fan is held in the left hand horizontally and a little below the shoulder. The right hand rests lightly on the fan before going through the relevant pointing movements. Or the fan may be held in the right hand in the same position with the left hand slightly touching the inner edge. This is when both hands are used in a pointing movement.

Ch'ih ma pien chih. This is the movement for holding the *ma ma pien,* the tasselled switch used to symbolize a horse. In holding the *ma pien,* the little finger is first placed through the loop at the top and the hand clasped over the switch with the thumb and first finger straight. There are three methods of pointing with the *ma pien.* It may be held as described above and the pointing movements then carried out with the switch or it may be left hanging down from the wrist by the loop and the pointing done with the fingers. Thirdly, the switch is held at a slight upward incline with the hand bent underneath. The pointing is then done with the left hand. This method is used by the *wu sheng* actors.

Ch'in fu chih. This means pointing while holding the *ying ch'en*, the horse hair fly brush carried by nuns and priests. There are three ways of doing this, the first two being the same as the first two methods for pointing with the *ma pien*. In the third method the *ying ch'en* is held across the chest resting on the crook of one arm and the pointing done with the free index finger.

Ch'ih hu chih. This movement is for pointing while holding the *hu ban*, the tablet carried when holding an audience with the Emperor. There are two methods. In the first the tablet is held at the base and it is used to point with; in the second it is held in the hand so that it rests in the crook of the arm and the index finger is used to point with.

Ch'ih chi wei chih. This describes pointing with the pheasant feathers, the long plumes worn on the head-dresses of certain characters. The two methods are as follows. First, the feathers are held between the second and third fingers and then used to point left and right. To point over the back, the left foot is placed well in front of the right with body leaning well back, the feathers then being used to point towards the rear. In a second method the right hand holds the feather between the second and third fingers and points to the front, at the same time pointing to the left with the left hand feather.

Ch'ih tao chien chih. This is pointing with the sword. The weapon may be held in either hand when used for pointing. Sometimes there is a sword in each hand in which case both are used, the two being kept parallel and one foot apart. At other times the sword may be held turned towards the body, the blade lying along the length of the arm, the free index finger being used to point. The same method may be used with a sword in both hands.

Ch'ih tao ch'ang chih. This is pointing with larger weapons than swords and there are several methods. The weapon may be held at the end and used for pointing, but only to the right. Another way is to hold the weapon at the top by the right hand while the left hand is used to point across it at waist height but only to the front or left. Sometimes the weapon is grasped in the middle and held horizontally behind the back or in front of the waist. In each case the pointing is done with the left hand. Two other methods are to hold the weapon vertically against the body, pointing with the left hand or else the weapon is held at the top in the right hand and used to point, the left hand being moved in time with this gesture to point over the top of the head.

Ch'ih shuang ch'ang chih. This means pointing with two spears and there are four methods. First they may be held in both hands at the base and used for pointing, being kept parallel and a foot apart. A second way is to hold one spear over the head but still parallel with the other to point to the left. Yet another way is to hold the spear in the middle and keeping it vertical behind one arm while the index finger of the hand holding the other spear points, but only to the front.

Ch'ih hsien lien chih. This movement is only used by the *tan* and performed when holding thread, material, etc. The article held is grasped between the first and middle finger, either in one or both hands.

Three other methods of pointing used on special occasions may be mentioned.

Ch'ih chien. A sword in its scabbard is held in the left hand, the weapon being partly drawn. The right hand then points to the sword three times in succession, the movement being done to musical rhythm.

Ch'ih wu chien chih. This means holding a letter, a teacup or similar object. The article is held in the left hand with the palm upwards and at shoulder height. The right hand points to it at this level. If the *tan* actor does this the object is held higher and he points over his head.

Ch'ih ch'eng men. This means pointing to a city gate. The hand points three times in succession to each of the three different characters inscribed over a city gate. The name of the character is repeated aloud by the actor, the whole movement being performed in time to the rhythm of the music.

Chiao, FOOT MOVEMENTS

The actor uses different methods of walking and running according to the role he plays and these foot movements again differ with the type of costume worn. The foot movements of the *tan* actor will be described first followed by those of the other characters.

Cheng pu. This is the normal walking pace. The *tan* actor must walk with the feet close together and take a much shorter step than the actor playing male roles. The quicker the pace the shorter the step. In a short step the feet are parallel and separated by a distance of one inch. The toe of the first foot should only be three inches ahead of the toe of the second. In a long step the leading foot is only two inches beyond the rear foot. The following are the rules for normal walking when wearing specific costumes, details of which will be found in the section on costume.

Wearing the *mang.* The legs are straight and the waist rigid. The hands hold the *yü tai,* the stiff belt round the middle, the head is erect and looks ahead. In this position the movements described above are performed, i.e. *cheng pu.*

Wearing the *p'ei.* The hands are held to the right of the waist though not touching it. The legs are slightly bent and the waist is freer and more flexible than with the *mang.*

Wearing the *hsüeh tzu.* The feet when placed in front of each other turn in a little with a slight swaying of the body.

Wearing *k'ao.* The steps are very small to prevent the flags worn on the back moving irregularly. If the actor moves to the left, the flags must sweep to the right. This is effected by a strong waist movement which is only possible with short steps. One arm holds the *yü tai* and the other the sword or *ma pien.* The head does not move and the arm holding the belt is rounded a little.

Wearing *k'u ao.* This costume has no *shui hsiu* so the hands move from side to side but the head remains still. The steps are as above but there is a certain latitude allowed the *hua tan* actor, who uses this method, in his other movements.

Wearing the *ts'ai ch'ao,* the false feet worn by the female impersonator. The actor using these walks in exactly the same fashion as above, i.e. using the steps described under *cheng pu.*

P'ao pu. This is the method for running, the steps of the *tan* actor must be very short and swift, the body from the waist upwards remaining rigid.

When wearing the *mang* or *kuan i,* the legs are kept straight and even though he is taking quick steps, the actor must appear to run slowly because he is a dignified personage. When wearing the *hsüeh tzu* and running the right hand is often lifted over the head, the actor seldom runs wearing the *p'ei*. When wearing *k'ao* a special skirt is used. This spreads out as the actor moves along giving a decorative effect and heightening the effect of swiftness. The waist is kept rigid and very quick short steps taken in such a case. The running movements of the actor in *k'u ao* costume are the same as when wearing the *hsüeh tzu*. When wearing the *ts'ai ch'iao* and running the waist is moved, unlike the other movements, while the rest of the body is kept erect. The foot movements are as above.

Ch'u pu. This foot movement was originally only used when an actor was expressing worry and agitation, but as it is of pleasing appearance it is now often used solely for decorative purposes. The right foot is placed forward a little and the left foot brought up to it with a short quick movement. This is repeated with every step. The *sheng* actor takes a longer step than the *tan*.

San ch'u pu. This is similar to the above but the steps are very much swifter. Only the *wu tan* uses this movement.

Ch'ih pu. The arms are lifted horizontally on either side and the actor moves sideways, the feet moving together with a tripping motion. It means to go swiftly on important affairs.

Nien pu. This is only used by the *wu tan* actor and symbolizes utter weariness, the feet are together and move with a swivel motion from left to right, the heel and toe being kept on the ground all the time.

Ts'o pu. This is used by the *tan* especially when wearing *ts'ai ch'iao*. It symbolizes a desire to move swiftly but an inability to do so. The feet are together and move forward with very short steps, the body swaying from side to side.

Tao ts'o pu. This is the same movement as above but the actor moves backwards. It is often used to symbolize riding a restless horse.

Yün pu. This symbolizes intoxication or being dizzy. There are two methods. In the first, the left foot is placed apart from the right foot and then drawn up to it sideways three times in succession, the movement is then repeated in the other direction. The second way uses a similar movement but one foot is crossed over the other each time while the body sways drunkenly.

Yao pu. This is only used by the *tan* actor. The left foot is crossed over the right with both hands at the left side, the right foot is then crossed over the left and the hands moved to the right, this

Ts'ai ch'iao

alternating arrangement being repeated as the actor walks along.
Shih tzu pu. This is used to represent the walk of a very graceful
and beautiful woman. The right foot is placed well forward
across the left with a distance of one foot between the heel of the
front foot and the toe of the rear one. The body inclines towards
the left with the right arm held up in front and rounded and the
left arm also rounded held behind the back slightly at waist level.
From this position the actor sways from left to right and right to
left moving the arms and feet into alternating positions while
walking along.
Hua pu. This is used when falling down after quick movement.
One leg is lifted up in front the actor sinking down swiftly on the
other knee.
Teng lou pu. This is used when going upstairs, mounting a city
wall, etc. The skirt is held up with two hands at the front and the
knees lifted to waist level one after the other with very small
steps, the body being bent slightly forward.
Hsia lou pu. This is used when going downstairs. Here the sides of
the skirt are held and the knees are not lifted so high, while the
legs are slightly curved when standing.
Lien san pu. This is used before making a final fall to the

ground and is performed in time to musical rhythm in three distinct movements. The right leg is crossed over the left, and the foot obliquely placed with toes to the right and the arms are placed on top of each other on the left waist as the actor moves to the opposite side, i.e., right.

Hen heng san pu. This is performed when two people are together in a state of helplessness not knowing what to do. The two characters hold hands and crossing their legs move sideways together, e.g. with right leg over left to move left and vice versa.

Ch'üeh hsing pu. This is an acrobatic movement performed by the *wu tan* wearing *ts'ai ch'iao.* The actor supports himself on his bent legs with arms outstretched straight in front of him. He then moves forward kicking each foot up alternately to meet the palm of the hand.

Hsi hsing pu. This is only used by the *tan* actor. The hands are held above the head while kneeling and the head is moved quickly from side to side as the actor moves along on his knees.

Tsuan pu. This is used to symbolize boarding a boat. The right knee is raised and the actor then gives a hop forward on to the right foot at the same time lifting the left. The body sways as though with the motion of a boat on water.

Hsieh tsuan pu. The same as *tsuan pu* for boarding a boat except that the movement is performed sideways.

Hun tzu pu. This is used for a female ghost. The body is kept erect and perfectly rigid, the rigid body sometimes swaying from side to side, very quick short steps being taken in either case.

Peng pu. This is used for jumping. The left knee is first raised and before the left foot touches the ground the right foot is raised, the actor then hopping forward on to the right foot.

T'ao pu. If the *tan* actor uses this movement it signifies walking in a graceful manner. If it is used in male roles it symbolizes strength and vigour. The left foot is crossed over the right but points to the front, followed by the right over left in the same manner.

T'a pu. This is only used by the *tan* actor and is the foot posture assumed when standing still or performing some of the pointing gestures. The right foot is obliquely behind the left heel and the hands together on one side of the waist if not performing pointing gestures.

Hsi pu. This is only used by the *tan* actor when resting. The left knee is slightly bent with the toes of the left foot placed at the middle of the right one and the left heel lifted.

T'ien pu. The right foot is placed in front of the left with one inch distance between the two, the heel is lifted slightly. It is used when looking afar. If the right foot is in front the left arm is raised and vice versa.

Ch'iao ts'u. The right foot is in front of the left and with toes lifted slightly. The hands are crossed behind the back and the left leg a little bent. It is used when listening or waiting in expectation of another's coming.

Tun ts'u. This is used when the actor is portraying a state of regret, his palms are turned upwards and one hand thumps the other. The foot is then stamped lightly.

FOOT MOVEMENTS FOR ACTORS OTHER THAN THE *tan*

Cheng pu. In his normal walking pace the *sheng* actor has both feet square on the ground six or seven inches apart. The right foot is lifted forward fourteen inches and the left foot is then brought up to the right heel and at right angles to it. There is a short pause and then the left foot is lifted forward repeating the movements and so on. When wearing the *mang*, the steps of the *sheng* actor are square, that is to say from side to side. When wearing the *hsüeh tzu*, the movements are not quite so formal and a little freer. When wearing *k'ao* the legs are lifted higher and the steps are very wide. When wearing the *hai ch'ing*, i.e. a costume worn by an old man, the body is much more bent, as are the knees, and the steps are slightly unsteady.

The *ching* actor uses the same walking method as the *sheng* but his legs are lifted wider with more powerful steps. Wearing the *mang*, his chest is thrust out to give a stronger effect. Wearing the *k'ao* the method is the same as the *sheng* but the forearm and elbow are lifted in a semicircle on each side of the body and the steps are made obliquely.

The *hsiao sheng* walks with his feet at the same distance apart as the *sheng* but his movements are more graceful. When he wears the *mang*, he lifts his feet so that the soles of his shoes can be seen, symbolizing a proud young official of high rank. Wearing the *p'ei*, his body is straight unlike that of the *sheng* whose appearance is slightly bowed in this garment. When wearing the *hsüeh tzu* the *hsiao sheng* has a special method, when the foot is

Pao ti k'uai hsüeh

lifted it is done so that the sole is visible from behind. It is the mark of a handsome young gentleman or scholar. When wearing the *k'ao*, the soles of the boots are visible when the legs are raised. Dressed in the *chien i* and wearing a sword the *hsiao sheng* walks so that, for instance, the sole of the right foot when raised is visible at the left side from the back, the actor using a kind of crosswise motion as he walks. In this position the left hand holds the sword and the right hand is placed on the hilt of the weapon.

The *ch'ou* actor uses a little of all these methods in his walk, when playing a servant or an old man he may even improvise a good deal. Wearing the *mang* his basic walk is the same as the *sheng*, but his legs are bent and the body is thrust forward to swing right and left from the waist. It symbolizes a bad character. The *ch'ou* does not often wear the *p'ei*, but if he does he walks with square steps and the body swaying right and left. When wearing the *hsüeh tzu*, his legs are lifted high but he takes small steps moving the shoulders with the swaying of the waist. When wearing the *k'ao* his movements are basically the same as those of the *hsiao sheng* although he is often at liberty to improvise a good deal. If the *ch'a i* is worn, as it often is in the case of the *ch'ou*, the legs are bent, but lifted high although short steps are taken, a similar movement as when wearing the *hsüeh tzu*.

The *lao tan* uses similar walking movements to those of the *tan*, but the movements are much slower and the feet are straight and parallel on the ground when walking; at each step that is taken, the foot trembles slightly before bringing the heel down. When wearing the *mang* the body is bent although not so much as when wearing other costumes. If the *hsüeh tzu* is worn and the *kuai chang*, the long staff, carried, the actor is very bent from the waist and the feet are placed obliquely to take very wide steps.

P'ao pu. Running.

The *sheng* actor does not run when wearing the *mang* except in one play *Fa Men Ssu*, and then it is not really running so much as a quick walk, and the steps must be very short. When wearing the *p'ei* the steps are even shorter. If the actor is wearing a white beard, the two feet must be placed wide apart and he moves from side to side. When wearing the *hsüeh tzu* or *kuan i*, the body is made to appear shorter by a movement from the waist to simulate running. If wearing *k'ao* the flags at the back must not move. If playing an old man the *sheng* actor uses a special method for running, the legs are apart and the body shortened by bending, the arms are swung backwards and forwards, often in anger, and with the beard waving.

The *hsiao sheng* uses the same movements as the *sheng* except when wearing the *chien i* with a sword. In this case the legs are bent and the body, inclined to the left, remains rigid from the waist upwards. When starting to run the steps are at first long, getting progressively shorter and quicker.

When wearing the *mang*, the *ch'ou* actor runs in the same way as the *sheng*. Wearing the *k'ao* he also follows the *sheng*, but he is allowed to move the flags; if dressed in the *ch'a i*, he runs realistically as in real life. Wearing the *hsüeh tzu* he has two methods. If it is worn with a girdle the legs are bent and the head does not move but the sleeved arms are waved back and forth. If no girdle is worn the body is thrust well forward and the steps taken are small but very swift.

The *lao tan* if running when wearing the *mang* takes very small steps with the feet placed obliquely, and wearing the *p'ei* the movement is the same. Wearing the *hsüeh tzu* the movement is similar to the *tan* but if the *kuai chang* is carried, the feet are wide apart and the body thrust forward with one arm holding the stave, the other arm being held stiffly in a half circle with the fist clenched. The head nods in time to each step.

Ch'ü pu. All characters use the same movements as the *tan* actor.

San ch'ü pu. This is only used by the *ching* and *ch'ou* who perform in the same way as the *tan.*

Ch'ih pu. The male characters have their feet apart, the women their feet together when using this step.

Tao ts'o pu. This is sometimes used by the *wu sheng* as performed by the *tan.*

Kan pu. This is only used by the *ching* actor. The two legs are bowed with one foot at right angles sideways and the other pointing front. The actor moves sideways with very small steps, there being a space of two inches between the feet.

Tien pu. It symbolizes riding a stubborn horse when wishing to go quickly. The actor stands very straight and leans back from the waist with high but short steps. It is used in such scenes as a military messenger bringing news to an official or general.

Shih pu. This represents a blind man or groping in the dark. The body is bent back from the waist and the feet lifted in very long steps but slowly and falteringly. It is chiefly used by the *ch'ou* actor.

Yün pu. This is performed as in the movements of the *tan* but the *sheng* takes much wider steps and the *hsiao sheng* and *ch'ou* a little less wide although wider than the *tan.*

Cha kuan pu. This is only used by the actor playing Cha Kuan, the God of the theatre, in the prelude to a theatrical perform-ance. Each foot is kicked sideways in a half circular movement, the actor stopping after each step. Although he takes wide steps he only covers a short distance and the body sways from side to side.

Lao jen pu. The movements are the same as for those described for an old man under *cheng pu* (p. 121).

Ai tzu pu. This is used by the *ch'ou* when portraying a dwarf. The actor moves on toes and heels with bent body. First he squats with knees fully bent poised on his toes with body straight and the elbows held tightly in to the sides. He then moves forward and with each step the sole of his foot must touch his posterior, the clenched fists moving up and down in time to the rest of the movements.

Ch'üeh pu. This represents someone with a lame leg. One foot is poised on the toe with bent knee and the other behind it at right angles. The actor then limps forward on the poised foot bringing up at the same position each time.

Yu yung pu. There are three methods of performing this movement. In one the arm is moved sideways with a swimming motion and at the same time using *cheng pu.* In the second method the actor stands with knees fully bent poised on his toes and the feet twelve inches apart; he then commences to jump sideways on his toes but still with bended knees and working round in a circle. With the first jump the arms are flung crosswise in front of the chest and with the second jump flung outwards and so on. The third method is the same as this only performed standing up.

Hua pu. Falling down. The male characters lift their right leg in front horizontally then, bending the left leg, fall flat.

Teng lou pu. All characters use the same movement as the *tan* except that the males hold their costume at the sides.

Hsia lou pu. This is the same as in the *tan* movement except that male characters hold their dress behind when descending.

Wang pa pu. The legs are lifted high and bent at the knee, both arms are swung outwards over the lifted leg. This is a vulgar style only used by the *ch'ou* actor.

Lung hsing pu. This is used by the *ching* actor and represents swimming. The actor stands poised on the toes of the right foot, the leg slightly bent and the left leg is bent upwards so that the heel touches the thigh. The body is inclined to the left from the waist. The right arm is stretched high to the front and the left to the rear at a lower level. The direction of the feet and arms are then changed as the actor moves forward.

Shang yang pu. The right leg is lifted horizontally forward at right angles to the body; the actor then proceeds to hop on the left leg. It signifies, 'What is to be done', or 'There is no redress', etc.

Lien san pu. This is performed as in the *tan* movement. The *sheng* uses it before turning a somersault and the *wu sheng* and *wu tan* use it in conjunction with the *ch'i pa* movements (p. 226).

Hen heng san pu. All characters are the same as the *tan*, the male characters taking wider steps.

Hsieh hsing pu. This is performed in the same fashion as the second method for *yu yung pu* (p. 125).

T'ui hsing pu. There are two methods used. In the first the left foot is placed behind poised on the toes, the right arm is out-stretched with the left arm across the chest and in this position the actor moves backwards on the toes with very slow movements. It is used by the *wu sheng* and *ching* actors when performing the *ch'i pa* described (p. 226). In the second method the actor is signifying the fact that he is mounted on a horse. The steps he takes in this case are very short, the feet being not more than four inches apart while he moves back on the soles of the feet and not the toes. The body remains rigid and does not move at all.

Tsuan pu. This symbolizes boarding a boat, all characters use the same movement.

San tsuan pu. This is used by the *wu sheng*. It is performed in the same way as in *tsuan pu* but the actor completes it in three movements only.

Peng pu. Other characters use the same movement as the *tan* (p. 120).

Chuan shen peng pu. The *wu sheng* uses this movement which is similar to *peng pu* except that the actor revolves his body while doing it, so that he is actually going round in a circle.

To ni. This is only used by the *wu sheng*. The left knee is first raised and then the actor hops briskly on the left foot lifting the right knee high. He then remains in this position while performing gestures with his arms. It signifies strength.

Tien pu. This is also only used by the *wu sheng*. It is similar to the *tsuan pu* movement but is used as a preliminary to doing *fan hu t'iao*, i.e. performing a cart wheel.

Chien pu. This represents someone walking very swiftly and is only used by the *wu sheng*. The left knee is raised with the thigh horizontal then a very wide step, almost a jump, is taken on to the left foot, raising the right knee and so on.

T'ao pu. This is as described for the *tan* movement (p. 120).

Ting tzu pu. This is only used by the *sheng* actor when he is standing still or resting. The left foot is placed obliquely with the heel against the centre of the right foot. No actor except the *ching* is allowed to stand with both feet pointing to the front.

Heng tzu. This is used by the *wu sheng* and the *ching* actors when standing or resting. The left foot is in front of the right and pointing at right angles to the left. The arms are held bent at the elbows often holding the costume with clenched fists.

Ch'iao tsu. Besides the *tan* actor only the *hsiao sheng* uses this.

T'ien pu. All other characters use the same movement as the *tan* (p. 121).

Ch'o tsu. This is often used by the *wu sheng.* The left foot is placed in front of the right and poised on the toes. The body is bent downwards a little. It signifies preparing to leave.

P'ieh tsu. This is only used by male characters when sitting with the hands on the knees. The legs are wide apart and the feet point right and left. The *ching* actor has his feet turned out at an angle of ninety degrees, the *sheng* at about sixty degrees, the *hsiao sheng* at about forty-five degress and the *ch'ou* at about thirty degrees. The *wu sheng* has his feet at an angle between that of the *sheng* and *ching.* When the *tan* actor sits the two knees are together with one foot slightly in front of the other and the hands crossed at the left.

Tun ts'u. All characters perform this in the same way as the *tan* (p. 121).

San tun ts'u. This is used by the *wu sheng, ching* and *wu tan.* The *tun ts'u* movement is performed three times.

Ts'e tsu. This is used by the *hsiao sheng* and *ch'ou* actors when resting or standing. The left foot is a little apart and to the front of the right and rests on the inner side of the sole which is therefore partly visible from the left.

Fan hsüeh ti. There are two methods used by the *sheng, ching* and *ch'ou* actors. In one the actor sits with legs stretched straight out to right and left resting on the heels. It signifies being at ease. The second is used in the *ch'i pa* movements described (p. 226). The right leg is first lifted across the left so that the sole is visible and then moved out in a wide movement to the right, the sole visible all the time and the toe pointing. The *hsiao sheng* uses five methods. The first two are those described above. In the third the actor wears the *mang* and walks with each leg lifted high and straight forward to the front showing the sole squarely. In the fourth method the actor wears the *hsüeh tzu* and the soles of his boots are then visible from the rear. The knee is bent and one leg slightly crossed over the other when walking to produce this effect. For the fifth way the actor is dressed in *chien i* and wearing a sword, the legs are slightly crossed at the front when walking so that the soles of the feet are visible from the side. *Shuan pu*. Only used by the *ching* actor to express fear or surprise. The actor takes a very small step forward, a distance of three inches, and then a very wide step to each side, making a fan shape with each movement.

T'ui. LEG MOVEMENTS

Naturally foot and leg movements are inseparable in practice but there are twelve special leg movements which may be described independently of the foot movements because of their nature.

Tun t'ui. All characters have a special stance when on the stage but a common factor is to ensure that the legs are not rigid but relaxed and yet controlled. The knees must be slightly bent although the audience should not notice this. This freedom of stance helps other movements in grace and appearance.

Wan t'ui. This is only used by the *wu tan* and the *wu sheng* and is often seen when the actor is represented as mounted on horseback. The actor stands on one leg and the other is lifted bent and at right angles to the body, the lower leg is then slowly raised high to one side and finally down to touch the stage.

K'ua t'ui. This is used when an actor is supposed to be turning a corner on his horse. When turning to the left the actor raises the *ma pien* in a sweep from the left waist into the air at the right with the palm facing front. The left hand touches the left waist and the left leg is lifted with bent knee so that the foot points diagonally to the ground, the actor's body being inclined as he performs the movement. In turning to the right, the right leg is lifted in a bent position so that the heel is above the left kneee. The right leg is then lifted high and outwards to the right and brought to the ground. The two hands hold the *ma pien* at waist height in front of the body which is inclined to the right when performing the movement.

T'i tui. Kicking. This movement is only used by the *ching* and *wu sheng* actors. The actor stands on one leg, the other being raised with the foot pointing to the ground so that it makes a straight line with the leg. It is actually a preparatory movement. The kicking movements are exceedingly difficult to perform and can only be done successfully after long practice commencing in childhood.

T'i t'ui. Different from the movement described above. There are three methods. The first is performed by the *sheng* actor who first stamps his foot to signal to the orchestra then kicks sideways. The second method is used in fighting. The kicking leg is lifted high to the front with the leg in one straight line, the rest of the body must not move. Thirdly the *ch'ou* performs his kicking with the ordinary movement used in real life.

T'an t'ui. In this the thigh does not move when lifted; only the lower leg performs the kicking movement.

Ts'ai t'ui. A slight kick from the ankle is given with the foot. It means sending someone away.

Ch'iao t'ui. The actor is seated with the right leg crossed over the left with the foot held straight out and the sole of the boot in full view. It is used chiefly by the *hsiao sheng* and means a young man who is not very polite.

Shih tzu t'ui. This signifies a great and powerful fighter. The left leg is held partly across the right so that it makes a right angle in the form of a broken cross.

Hua k'ao tu. This is only used by the actors performing *ch'i pa* on making an entry. The *k'ao tu* is the centre portion of the apron of the costume representing armour and often consists of a representation of a tiger's head. The left knee is raised close to the right thigh then the leg raised to the front so that the *k'ao tu* is over the top of the leg which makes a complete circle to point to the left. In the first part of the movement the left leg is not visible until it is moved outwards from under the *k'ao tu*.

San t'ui. Performed when two people grasp the same weapon. The two actors turn to face front with right leg lifted high then brought to the ground with the left foot brought up behind the right heel. They step forward using this movement three times.

T'ai t'ui. This is used when going off the stage after a great deal of fighting. The actor stands facing towards the exit standing on the right leg with body inclined a little to the right. The left leg is lifted with the thigh making a right angle with the body and the left arm is bent across the chest. The right arm holding a weapon is held high with the arm slightly rounded.

Ke Po, ARM MOVEMENTS

Obviously arms and hands must move together but there are a few arm movements which by their nature warrant an independent description.

E

Fan ke po. The two arms are held high above the head but bent, not straight, and the thumbs point to the ground. The movement is chiefly used by the *ching* actor, the other actors using it when wearing the *k'ao*. There is an exception in the case of the *sheng* and *hsiao sheng* who may also use it when wearing the *mang*. If the *tan* uses this movement it is not performed when wearing the *mang*. If the *tan* uses this movement it is not performed with such vigour as the others while the *ch'ou* only uses it in humorous fashion.

Wan ke po. All characters use this movement. The arms are bent with the elbows back making an angle of forty-five degrees. The hands are open with the thumbs pointing at each other. The *tan* actor only uses this posture when wearing the *k'ao*. The *ching*, *sheng* and *hsiao sheng* hold their arms bent at an increasingly greater angle, in the case of the *hsiao sheng* they are almost straight.

Tuan ke po. The arms are slightly rounded with the hands held at stomach level and palms upturned. The distance between the body and the hands in the case of the *ching* actor is three inches, one inch for the *sheng*, slightly less for the *hsiao sheng* and *ch'ou* while the *tan* actor touches the body lightly.

Ning ke po. This is only used by the *tan* actor. When picking an object from the ground the actor turns his hand so that the palm faces to the front but the arm is kept rigid as he picks the article up.

Pao ke po. This signifies being very cold. The *ching* holds his right hand behind the left wrist and the arms are held out from the body, elbows bent. The actor then moves the arms right and left. In the case of the *sheng* and *hsiao sheng* both hands hold the arms near the elbows and the distance between arms and body is very small. The *tan* actor holds the arms with the hands grasping the upper arm below the shoulder and held against the body.

Ch'ui ke po. This means standing with hanging arms but only an actor playing a ghost can allow the arms to hang perfectly straight. All other characters must hold the arms rounded a little and the hands must be level with the top of the thigh. The *tan* actor must not allow his arms to hang at all and the hands must be crossed on the right thigh or the left.

La shan pang. The standing actor turns the top part of his body from the waist to the right. The two arms are held to the left, palms facing outwards and a distance of one inch between. The right arm is then moved to the right side raising the hand to face level first and following it with the eyes as it moves across. The *ching* actor finishes with the hand above the head, the *sheng* at eyebrow level. The *hsiao sheng* and *ch'ou* hold theirs at lip level and the *tan* actor at chest level. It serves as a signal to the orchestra and according to Chinese authority, is based on an old T'ang dynasty dance movement. A movement serving a similar function and having the same origin is called *Yün shou*. In this the arms are held in front of the body with the left one lower, the palm of the hand upturned and the right hand, palm down, held over it. The arms are then moved left and over to the right, the eyes follow the complete movement and are then fixed front. The *ching* actor makes a wider circle with his arm movements than the other actors. The *sheng* and *hsiao sheng* have their shoulders pulled back a little when performing while the *tan* makes a much smaller movement than the others.

Special movements are used by the actors wearing *ling tzu*, the long twin pheasant plumes adorning the head-dresses for certain roles. The *ling tzu*, which are anything between six and seven feet long, were originally used to represent Mongols, barbarians, bandits, etc., on the stage but their decorative quality endeared them to the actors in military plays and they began to use them irrespective of their original meaning. There is one ruling about this, however, in the plays of the Three Kingdoms, *San Kuo Hsi*, actors who are playing roles as representatives of the Han kingdom may not use the *ling tzu* which are only worn by the actors playing the roles of the other two kingdoms. The pheasant feathers are considered to have been used in very ancient times for dancing although they were much smaller. Indeed it is within recent times that those used on the stage have grown bigger as more action was devised to utilize them. The greatest actors now have the longest feathers which require considerable dexterity for graceful manipulation. The feathers are a speciality of the *hsiao sheng* actor's technique. Hsu Hsiao-hsiang, an actor of Ch'ing times who played *hsiao sheng* roles, did a great deal to develop the technique of the feathers and since then it has always been a speciality of the *hsiao sheng* actor. When making a movement with the *ling tzu*, the actor always holds the plume between the second and third fingers. In the case of the *ching* actor feather movements are made high above the head but the *hsiao sheng* movements are at a lower level. The *tan* actor performs with them at shoulder height. There are eleven basic movements given by stage authorities and these are described below.

Jao ling. This movement symbolizes anger. The head is swung round and round so that the feathers sweep round in a wide circle.

Tsai ling. This movement can symbolize either surprise or that the actor is thinking. The head is bent so that the feathers just flick the ground in front and they are then flung quickly back over the head again. The feathers must touch the floor and be raised so that there is no pause in the movement which appears almost simultaneous.

Shua ling. This is purely a decorative movement. The head is first bent to the left so that one feather touches the floor while the other is swept back over the right shoulder. The movement is then repeated in the opposite direction.

Ch'ih ling. This symbolizes looking afar. The first and second fingers lightly hold the feather and sweep down it from the base on the head-dress to the end, curling this in the final movement. It is performed with the right hand while the left is holding a weapon.

Shuang ch'ih ling. This is carried out in the same way except that both feathers are used. The palms face outwards when performing and the feathers are held slightly higher above the head. The actor laughs aloud at the same time. It symbolizes great happiness.

Ts'o ling. It is performed like the movement described above but the feathers are finally raised to chest height and move round and round, first one and then the other, towards the body. The hands tremble a little. It symbolizes a state of agitation or worry.

Wu ling. This is performed like the *shang ch'ih ling* method but the arms are moved in opposite directions above the head. It is used by the *wu tan* actor and performed in conjunction with the foot movement *nien pu* (p. 118) already described.

Shuang fan ling. This is an entry movement. The actor comes on and brings the feathers down to chest height then swings them outwards and upwards above the head on either side, the palms being outwards when this is done. The movement completed, the actor speaks his name.

Mo ling. This is only used by one character, Chou Ts'ang, when he wishes to remain unobserved by others. The actor's back is to the audience and taking the two feathers in either hand he moves them from side to side above his head with his eyes following them. He does this three times and then turning the upper part of his body round from the waist he recites his name to the audience.

Hsien ling. In this movement one feather is held in the mouth. One hand holds a weapon and the other performs the *ch'ih ling* movement already described and finally the feather is placed in the mouth at about six inches from the end.

Shuang hsien ling. Performed as above but using both feathers. The actor must be wearing *shui hsiu*, water sleeves, in this method and must not have anything in his hands.

Besides the feather movements there are also those performed with the beards worn in many of the male roles on the stage, more especially those of the *sheng* and *ching* actors. Beard movements may sound rather curious to Western ears but a great number of the gestures made by the bearded actors have a symbolical or special meaning like everything else that the actor does. There are several different classes of beards worn by the actors which differ in style and colour but these are dealt with fully in the section on costume and make up, here we are only concerned with the various gestures made with the beards.

Lü shu. This is an entry movement used by bearded actors. The actor comes on and slowly strokes the beard from top to bottom. This is done with the right hand, the thumb being beneath the beard.

Pan lü shu. The beard is held at about the middle of its length in the first and second fingers of either the right or left hand. The two fingers are moved a short distance with a stroking motion and the eyes move round and round. It symbolizes thinking.

Shuang lü shu. This is the same movement as described above only using both hands. It is used for smoothing the beard after disarrangement. If the beard is a *san jan* style, i.e., in three portions, it is the centre portion that is used.

An shu. This symbolizes pondering a problem. The beard is patted with the open palm of one hand bowing the head at the same time. The actor lifts his head to show the problem is solved.

Tuan shu. In this movement the two hands with palms upwards lift the beard lightly from the bottom. It is used when looking at another person.

Shuang tuan shu. This is a variation of the above movement. The hands are moved downwards with the palms towards the body then turned out and upwards to lift the beard.

Shuai shu. This signifies an answer in the negative or is used when ordering someone to go away. The beard is swung over the left arm which is held bent and then right over the other arm in the same position. This movement is repeated three times.

Tou shu. This is similar to the method above but the beard is swung within the orbit of the arms and not over them. It means to be unwilling or dissatisfied.

Lun shu. A movement only seen in fighting plays. The beard is flung over the left shoulder and then over the right with a very vigorous motion of the head repeated anything between ten and twenty times. It symbolises an answer in the negative.

T'eng shu. This is used in fighting plays. The two hands with thumbs beneath the beard move downwards to flick the beard out right and left over the upper arm. It means that the actor wishes to arrange his costume or armour.

Liao shu. The first and second fingers are stroked down a short length of the beard moving the fingers in and out all the time. The foot is stamped and the movement is followed by weeping. It symbolizes sorrow and grief.

Liang liao shu. It is used in the *ch'i pa* movements seen on the entry of an actor in military plays. The method is similar to that in *t'eng shu.* The beard is flung to either side and the actor tightens his girdle or his armour and then flings the beard back into position.

San liao shu. The first and second fingers of the right hand flick back a portion of the beard over the right arm and the left foot is stamped. This is repeated with the left hand and the opposite foot, then again with the right hand. It symbolizes great sadness and distress.

Lou shu. This is used when pointing to the distance. The right hand points and the left hand holds the beard and brushes it back to the left. The palm of the hand is towards the body.

Ta shu. This is used in military plays when the actor is going off the stage and moving very quickly. When the actor nears the exit he turns his eyes towards it and taking a portion of the beard in his right hand flicks it over the right arm and moves towards the exit.

T'ui shu. This movement is used when turning the head to look behind. The right hand pushes the middle portion of the beard to the left and the head is turned at the same time.

Kung shu. The actor in military plays sometimes moves his shoulders to arrange the beard instead of his hands.

En shu. Used when wiping the eyes during weeping. The two hands, palm upwards, lift the beard from the bottom up to the face.

Tang shu. The two hands with palms upward hold the beard before the face, the waist is bent and the head turned away. It signifies embarrassment.

T'an shu. The two hands with palm upwards hold the beard which is moved left to right and right to left with a circular movement and then thrown out left as the foot is stamped and the actor cries 'Ai yeh'. It means that he has made a decision or that it is the only possible way to carry out his intentions.

Shuang yang shu. The two hands move down the beard thumb underneath and then flick it out to the front as the actor bursts into laughter. It symbolizes great happiness.

Tang shu. The actor must wear *shui hsiu*, water sleeves, when performing this. He pushes the beard in and out from the bottom and it signifies that he is worried.

Jou shu. This signifies sorrow. The right hand is moved round and round on the beard palm downwards and the fingers flicking in and out alternately as the hand goes round. The other hand may be at the back of the head or placed to the temple.

Mo shu. This expresses satisfaction, e.g. if a hated enemy dies. One or both hands may be used. The hands are stroked from top to bottom of the beard with the thumb in front and not behind. It is done three or five times.

Shuang t'o cha. This expresses anger and is often used by the *ch'ou* actor. The two hands are held with the palms up and fingers outstretched and moved down the length of the beard.

Nien shu. This is also used by the *ch'ou* actor. The ends of the moustache are twiddled with the thumb and first finger, the palm towards the body; for the final twist, however, the palm is turned outwards.

T'o tiao ta. One hand is held forward with the fingers outstretched and supporting the dangling portion of the beard in the palm. It is used by the *ch'ou* actor.

Nieh tiao ta. The *ch'ou* actor uses this when thinking or on suddenly recognizing someone. The thumb, first and second fingers hold the beard at the bottom and are moved round and round in a circular motion.

P'i hsu. This is only used by the actor playing Kuan Kung, the God of War. The two hands hold a part of the beard at the middle of its length and are then moved downwards to divide the beard at the bottom moving the divided portion right and left. At the same time the head turns left, right and centre. It is used when looking at someone.

Shih hsu. The hands are stroked down the beard three times from top to bottom, the thumbs underneath it. It symbolizes cleansing the beard.

Ch'e ch'ou san. The thumbs are placed beneath the beard which is pushed out right and left so that the hands are twenty-four inches apart. The head is bent to the left.

Ch'e cha. The hands hold left and right portions of the beard which are moved out to either side at nose level with the little finger held highest. There should be twelve inches distance between the hands. This movement is only used by a few special characters.

T'ao cha. This is similar to the *lü shu* movement (p. 133) and the method and meaning are the same. However, when the movement is concluded the actor places the fingers on the *erh mao*, the pointed piece of ear which sticks straight up above the ears in the make up of the *ching* actors, and strokes it upwards. The left hand is used for the left side and right hand for the right.

Shuang t'ao cha. The same as above but simultaneously with both hands.

Shang hsia t'ao cha. The right hand holds a portion of the beard upwards to the right above the head and the left hand tugs the other portion towards the left. The actor then surveys the scene around him and having looked swings each portion of the beard round in front of him to let it fall back into place.

Ch'ui shu. This signifies anger, the actor blowing the beard out from his face without touching it. If it is performed by the *ch'ou* actor the movement is a very exaggerated one.

Shan shu. This movement is only used by a bad character. The

actor holds a fan under his disarranged beard and fans it violently.
Yao shu. This is only used by the *wu sheng* and *ching* actors and
symbolizes making a decision. The beard is lifted to the mouth
in the palms of both hands and bitten so that a small portion of
the end protrudes.

Hsi shu. The beard is held in a basin and moved round and round,
the hands stroking it up and down with thumbs behind. It
signifies washing the beard.

Many of the movements described here may sound impossible
to the layman, as of course they are. They can only be carried
out by those whose body and limbs have been subject to long and
arduous training.

THE COSTUMES OF THE ACTOR

The costumes of the actor are known professionally as *hsing t'ou*.
When not in use they are kept in large chests, each costume
being placed in allotted order. An old custom decreed that the
robe called *fu kuei i* was placed on top of the others in the chests.
This costume is worn by actors playing poor and distressed
scholars or virtuous women in similar circumstances. Its name
literally means 'garments of honour and wealth' and the
multicoloured patches which adorn it symbolize an existence of
uncertainty but hopes of a bright future. It was placed first in the
chest because it was considered that the actor who wore it would
otherwise not have good fortune in his profession. There are
men in every theatre whose task it is to look after the costumes,
they are called *kuan i hsiang jen* and are divided into groups, each
of which is responsible for different classes of costume. These are
called *ta i hsiang*, *erh i hsiang* and *san i hsiang*, or principal
costume chest, second costume chest and third costume chest.
Each chest has two men to look after it. They must prepare the
costumes for every play, iron and press them and attend to all
matters connected with the actors' dress. In modern times it has
been the practice for leading actors to have their own costumes,
the wardrobes of men like Mei Lan-fang and Yü Chen-fei for
instance contained garments of the most exquisite colours,
materials and workmanship, literally worth thousands of pounds.
Those for supporting players are rented by the theatres, however,
there being firms whose function is to hire out all kinds of
theatrical costumes and accessories as well as make them to

Actor wearing Lo mao and tz'u ku yeh

order. It is said that the practice of actors owning their personal costumes is now frowned upon in China, but whether this is correct or not the writer is unable to verify. Chinese stage costumes are made from silks and satins of many textures either richly embroidered, ornamented with appliqué designs or simply of plain colourings. Cotton is used for some of the simpler costumes, particularly those of the clowns.

Each dramatic role has its own particular costume style which is faithfully adhered to by every actor playing that role. His costume portrays a type rather than an individual, and generals, officials and scholars, to name a few, will all wear dress identical in form and detail according to their types although in fact they each represent different individuals. It was said in the first chapter that society in old China was distinguished by a strict etiquette in costume styles according to rank and class, and this is seen carried to an extreme on the classical stage as a further aid to the system of conventional roles described earlier in the book. On the other hand there are some roles which portray characters, particularly mythological ones, unique in their appearance, but even in their case component parts of the costume are interchangeable and may be seen used in other roles. Different combinations of units of costume are often used to produce a variation in style and symbolism.

Stage dress has evolved from actual costume worn in the T'ang, Sung, Yuan, Ming and Ch'ing dynasties but it would not be correct to say that plays are dressed with historical accuracy, for styles of different periods are freely intermingled in the same drama for the sake of stage effect. It is stage effect which is considered solely in their design as well; many modifications or exaggerations in styles have been introduced into the costumes which make them much different in appearance from their original models, if far more decorative from a stage point of view. A good example of this may be seen in the Manchu lady's costume which is often worn by the *tan* actor and which is distinguished among other things by its headdress, called *liang pa t'ou*, the whole hairdressing style being referred to as *ch'i chuang t'ou*. There are many older people who still remember this style in Peking before the 1911 Revolution and there are many photographs extant which give a clear idea of its appearance. From these alone it is possible to see how exaggerated the stage version has become and admittedly much more theatrically impressive. This is but one small example of a process which is seen repeated in a number of instances in costume design. In the play *Ssu Lang Tang Mu*, described later, the heroine, the Princess of the Iron Mirror, appears in the opening scene wearing the dress described above. Her husband, Ssu Lang, wears costume which is based on that of a high ranking courtier of the Ming dynasty, although no courtier would ever have recognized the symbolic accessories and modifications which have been used in this case. The action of the play itself is set in the Sung dynasty, a typical example of the indifference shown to historical accuracy when stage effect is the first consideration.

Colour plays a very important part in the symbolism of stage costume and is supplemented by the many motifs which are derived from traditional patterns and ornament. Different colours indicate different rank and status as well as the general personal character of the wearer. These colour rules are unvarying in their application. There are five colours known as the *shang*, or pure colours and five known as the *hsia*, or secondary colours. The first named are red, green, yellow, white and black, and the last named purple, blue, pink, turquoise blue and a dark crimson called in Chinese *chiang*. Good characters of high rank wear red, men of high virtue wear green, the Emperor wears yellow and very old or very young people wear white, which is also the colour of mourning. Black denotes men of fierce or aggressive character but it can also indicate simple and informal everyday attire. In the case of women it shows virtue and modesty under conditions of distress or adversity. Pink and turquoise blue is worn to represent youth and sometimes old age, blue indicates high rank irrespective of personal character, dark crimson is worn by usurpers to a throne, barbarian generals or military advisers, while purple is often the prerogative of the *ching* or painted face actor.

The ornate patterns which are often superimposed on costumes are based on the symbolism found in Chinese art and literature and a few of the important motifs commonly used are described here.

The bat in China is emblematic of long life and happiness and its shape is constantly used for decorative purposes on stage costume and some of the hair ornaments worn in the women's roles. The form has been conventionalized until in some cases it appears almost butterfly-like in appearance. The Chinese characters for bat and happiness are pronounced the same and are therefore connected. The characters for longevity, *shou*, and joy, *hsi*, are written in a variety of conventional forms which are widely used in decorations of every conceivable type including those on stage costume.

The phoenix, or *feng huang*, was a bird of good omen in ancient China which was said to appear in times of prosperity and good government. It was used a great deal as a decorative motif in ceremonial costume by the Empresses of China and is still preserved as an Imperial emblem on stage dress as well as for hair ornaments. After the phoenix came the crane, which was regarded as a messenger of the gods as well as a symbol of longevity. It is used constantly in stage dress design and in past times was embroidered on the Court robes of civil officials. The dragon is perhaps the most celebrated creature in Chinese mythology and was said to ascend to the heavens and bring the rains for the crops. A five clawed dragon was an emblem devoted to the special use of the Chinese emperor and is in consequence seen a great deal as a decoration on stage costume denoting Imperial rank. The tiger in China symbolized masculinity and fighting power as the lord of the animal kingdom. A tiger's head often figures prominently as a decoration on the costume of military characters on the stage.

Among flowers the plum blossom is one of the most famous and commonly regarded as a symbol of long life because it appears on the leafless trees far in advance of other blooms. It is also indicative of wisdom as well as feminine charm and is much used as decoration on costume. The peony is an emblem of Spring and feminine beauty and is often seen as a decoration on women's dress.

In addition to pictorial motifs such as all these, there are more abstract patterns like the border designs based on the swastika. The latter is of Buddhist origin, it denotes resignation of spirit and is styled 'the ten thousand character'. From this evolved the key or meander pattern known to the Chinese as the 'thunder pattern', another variation of which is the T pattern. They are all used in theatrical costume decorations. The best known Chinese abstraction is the *pa kua i* or eight diagrams. This is an arrangement of cabalistic signs which consist of straight lines arranged in a circle enclosing the *yin* and *yang* symbol. The *pa kua* were said to be derived from the markings on the back of a tortoise shell after placing in a sacrificial fire. The earliest interpretation of them appears in an abstruse and ancient classic known as The Book of Changes, a work containing the elements of metaphysical knowledge, divination and geomancy. The *yin* and *yang* symbols represent the origin of life, the two segments of the circular motif represent the interaction of the celestial and earthly principles. A good example of the use of this design for costume is seen on the dress of the celebrated strategist Chu-Ko Liang, who appears so often in the *San Kuo* plays. His blue or purple robe is embroidered with line combinations of the *pa kua i* in heavy gold and the *yin yang* symbol appears on his robe as well as on the front of his hat, signifying his great metaphysical powers. As a last example of the many abstractions used in design that called the *ju i* may be mentioned. The *ju i* was actually a kind of sceptre used as a symbol of supremacy by the ancients and the head of the hilt was carved in the shape of a fungus called *ling chih*, the plant of immortality. The conventional form of the *ju i* head is often embodied in a border ornament used in stage costume. The symbolism of Chinese design motifs is a considerable study in itself and it is only possible here to indicate a few of the important features as related to the actor's dress.

Although at first Chinese theatrical costumes may appear complicated in their variations and confusing in number, in actual fact they are based on a limited group of standardized forms each of which has several variations in colours and decorative motifs. Women characters often wear costumes which are identical in nomenclature with those of the men, variations in cut and decoration providing a feminine version of the male style. Among the purely feminine costumes, the plain white skirt worn by the *ch'ing i* actor is sometimes used by male characters as a form of apron arranged round the waist, an example of that interchangeability already mentioned.

The different kinds of hats, hoods and head-dresses which are worn by the actor are described under the name *k'uei t'ou*. They range from the very simple to the exceedingly ornate and complex. Many of them bear a strong resemblance to the actual headwear of former times, as reference to paintings, prints and old illustrations will readily show. On the other hand there seems to be considerable doubt as to the historical origin of many of them and it is probable that quite a number are stage creations which show little resemblance to historical prototypes.

Stage footwear is less complex than costume, broadly it may be divided into three classes. There is the high boot with soles ranging from one to three inches thick. This is worn by male characters for travelling, fighting and on ceremonial occasions; women do not wear this style. Next comes the flat-soled slipper type of shoe in several variations, worn by both male and female characters indoors and for informal occasions, although women wear it out of doors as well. Thirdly there is a special type of flat-soled boot which is used by male, and sometimes female, characters whose roles are largely acrobatic or aggressive in character and require a great deal of vigorous movement.

Kao fang chin, scholar's hat

In addition to these three main styles, the *ts'ai ch'iao* or false feet of the female impersonator must be mentioned. These are made of wood and shod with brass being secured to the leg with a wide cotton bandage, they enable the actor to simulate the bound foot gait of ancient China although acrobatics are performed when wearing them that no lady of old would have remotely considered. The *ts'ai ch'iao* is shaped so that the actor's foot rests against a wooden support and is poised in an almost vertical position. Only the tip of the false foot is visible beneath the wide trousers worn over this unique contraption. The illustration will give some idea of its appearance. Within recent years some actresses have taken to wearing a less difficult invention, also shown in the illustration; it is a minute shoe with a built-up sole inside which enables the wearer to stand poised in rather the same way as on the old *ts'ai ch'iao*, although the true effect is not achieved quite so successfully, if more comfortably. The art of using the *ts'ai ch'iao* is a hard one to learn and is only mastered by those actors who have been instructed since childhood days. The photograph on pl. III shows a student at the Peking dramatic training school being instructed in walking on *ts'ai ch'iao*. The picture was taken in 1935 and gives a good idea of the process described. The pupil later became Sung Te-chu, a famous *wu tan* actor. His teacher is Chu Ju-hsiang and it will be noticed that he carries a small baton in one hand. It was customary for a teacher to direct his pupil's movements with this and which was also used to give a sharp tap to those who proved careless in following.

Hsing t'ou

The following is a list of the principal costumes found in the theatrical wardrobe.

Fu kuei i. As this is the first garment seen when the costume chest is opened it will be described before the others. It is a plain silk robe patterned with large diamonds of green, red, blue and yellow cloth sewn on to it, and is worn chiefly by the *hsiao sheng* actor although occasionally the *ch'ing i* also wears it. As described earlier, it indicates that the wearer is very poor and going through times of adversity but that later difficulties will be overcome. The *fu kuei i* has *shui hsiu*, water sleeves, and is cut on similar lines to the *hsueh tzu*, the informal robe described a little later on. The version worn by women characters is only half length and worn over a plain white skirt as against the full length garment of the *hsiao sheng* actor. It is called the *nü fu kuei i*.

Mang

This name covers an important group of robes worn by both male and female characters. It is based on the style originally worn by high officials in the Ming dynasty on formal occasions and therefore on the stage serves a similar purpose, being worn as formal attire by actors playing members of the Imperial family, high officials, military officers and the like. The version worn by women characters is three-quarter length worn over a skirt, instead of full length as in the case of male roles. The variations in the *mang* apart from this lie in colours and patterns which symbolize ranks of society. The *mang* is a voluminous

Ch'ou actor wearing mang, sha mao and yü tai

robe, which covers the feet in the case of the male robes. It has a low cut circular neck opening beneath which is worn a *hu ling*, a kind of thick white silk stock which is worn cross-over style. It has very wide sleeves to which are also attached *shui hsiu*, water sleeves, and it is slit at either side and fastens at the right. The silk material of the garment is richly embroidered in gold and silver and hangs in heavy folds. Round the waist is worn the *yü tai*, or jade girdle. This is a large stiff hoop-like girdle which far exceeds the circumference of the actor's waist and is attached through loops on the sides of the *mang*. It is decorated with brilliants and small mirrors. The pattern on the *mang* is always a dragon one with a wave design marking a very wide border on the hem of the robe. The dragon pattern may be one of three kinds, *t'uan lung*, *cheng lung* and *hsing lung*. In the first the dragon is contained within a roundel, in the second the head of the dragon is on the chest when the *mang* is worn and the body curling away in a writhing loop, while in the last a walking dragon is depicted. The wave pattern at the bottom may be one of two types, *p'ing shui* or *li shui*. The first means ordinary waves in which case the pattern consists of diagonal lines of various shades of blue and silver, while the second represents the conventional curling 'storm' waves of Chinese art in similar colouring. There are five styles of *mang* in the *hsiang* colours and five in the *hsia* colours. They are listed as follows.

Hsiang colours.

Hung mang, or red style.

This is worn by very important officials who are generally of good character. There is one exception, Ts'ao Ts'ao may wear the red *mang*.

Lü mang, or green style.

This is also worn by a good and virtuous character of high rank who is also a high military personage, generally played by a *ching* actor. Kuan Kung is a good example of the type of role in which this garment is used.

Huang mang, yellow style.

This is only worn by the Emperor. There is also a colour called *hsing huang* which is not a pure yellow, having a brownish tone. It is worn by an old official or general.

Pai mang, white style.

This is worn by characters who are either very old or very young men but in any case are of good character and responsible for their actions.

Hei mang, black style.

This is worn by *ching* actors when playing high officials or generals and when their painted face make-up has black as a predominating colour.

Hsia colours.

Fen hung mang, pink style.

This is worn by *hsiao sheng* actors when playing the part of a young general.

Hu se mang, turquoise blue style.

Like the white style it is only worn by the very young or old, usually in the role of a general.

Chiang se mang, dark crimson style.

This is worn by usurpers to the throne, and by Mongolian and barbarian Emperors. It is sometimes worn by a military adviser.

Lan mang, blue style.

This symbolizes an important official no matter what his personal character.

Tzu mang, purple style.

This is only worn by the *ching* actors who use it for the same kind of roles described under *hung mang*.

T'ai chien mang, eunuch's style.

This is only worn by actors portraying palace eunuchs. It is in colours of green with a snake instead of a dragon pattern.

The *mang* styles worn especially by women characters follow.

Nü mang, women's style *mang*.

This is shorter than the men's version, being worn over a skirt. As a variation it may have a phoenix instead of a dragon pattern and a *yün chien*, or tasselled shoulder cape, is always worn with it.

Nü hung mang, red style *mang*.

This is worn by very high officials' wives and daughters or an Emperor's concubine.

Nü huang mang, yellow style *mang*.

This is worn by the Empress or the mother of the Emperor only.

Nü ch'iu hsiang se mang, olive green style *mang*.

This is only worn by the *lao tan* actor.

Another group of robes similar in cut and design to the *mang* are the *kuan i*, literally official costume. The difference in these garments lies in the fact that they are patterned instead of plain, having only a single embroidered square panel on the chest, while two broad plain coloured flaps stand out along the length of the rear side of the slit on either side of the garment. As in the case of the *mang* the *yu tai* is worn with this robe of which there are several colour styles.

Hung kuan i, red style.

This is worn by high officials between the first and fourth ranks. A scholar taking a first class pass in the examinations also wears it.

Tzu kuan i, purple style.

This is worn by the same characters as above only they are elderly people.

Lan kuan i, blue style.

This is worn by officials between the fifth and seventh rank, e.g. a local governor.

Hei kuan i, black style.

This is worn by ranks lower than the above.

Yüeh pai kuan i, literally 'moon white style'.

This is worn by scholars.

Chiang se kuan i, dark crimson style.

This is worn by an official adviser.

The women's style *kuan i* is in two colours only, red and olive green, the last being used only by old women and the first now not often used at all.

The *kuan i* is always worn with the hard double crowned hat with protruding 'fins', called the *sha mao*, for male roles.

The next important style of dress is the *p'ei*, an outdoor garment worn by people of higher rank. It is worn over the top of the *hsüeh tzu* described later. It is sometimes worn as an outdoor garment on less formal occasions than those requiring the *mang* to be worn. The garment for men is worn full length but that for the women characters is three-quarter length, being worn over a skirt. In both cases it has very long *shui hsiu*, or water sleeves. It is made of stiff satin and opens down the front and fastens with silk tapes. It has a low collar revealing the *hu ling*, or white stock, and in the case of the male version has a split up each side. There are several different colour styles ornamented with various patterns, often designed in roundels. The yellow style *p'ei* has a dragon pattern as it is used by princes.

Hung p'ei, red style.

This is worn as formal dress by young people, e.g. on the occasion of marriage or promotion to higher rank. It is also worn as ordinary dress sometimes by very high officials.

Lan p'ei, blue style.

This is usually worn by elderly men of affluence.

Huang p'ei, yellow style.

This is worn by princes.

Tzu p'ei, purple style.

This is the ordinary wear of old or retired officials of high rank.

T'ien ch'ing p'ei, or sky blue style.

This is sometimes plain and sometimes patterned in white. It is worn by all types of officials and scholars and as mourning after the burial of relatives.

Fen hung p'ei, pink style.

This is worn as the ordinary dress of a youthful official of high rank.

Yueh pai p'ei, moon white style.

This is worn as mourning for young people.

There are women's versions of all these colour styles but there are also two other styles used only in female roles: they are *kuei men p'ei* and *kuan yin p'ei*. The first named is made of soft material instead of the stiff satin of the ordinary *p'ei* and ornamented with flower patterns. It is worn in scarlet, pink, pale and duck egg green and is the dress of young unmarried women. The second style is only worn by the goddess Kuan Yin and is in white with a blue or black bamboo pattern.

The next robe on the list is the *hsüeh tzu* which is seen in many styles and might be called the general purpose clothing of the Chinese actor. It is used as informal dress on all kinds of occasions as well as being worn as an undergarment with other styles. It has an open neck, fastens to the right, has *shui hsiu* and is worn with a soft girdle round the waist. There are two main styles: *juan hsüeh tzu*, made of soft material, and *ying hsüeh tzu*, made of stiff satin. It may be plain or patterned. It should perhaps be noted here that the common pronunciation for the Chinese character describing this garment is *tieh tzu* but among Peking theatre people themselves it is always called *hsüeh tzu*.

The various types are as follows.

Hung juan hsüeh tzu, soft red style.

This is worn as an undergarment with the *mang* by both men and women.

Lü juan hsüeh tzu, soft green style.

This is worn as an undergarment with the *mang* by the *ch'ou* actor.

Huang juan hsüeh tzu, soft yellow style.

The Emperor wears this an an undergarment with the *mang*.

Hu se juan hsüeh tzu, soft light purple style.

This is worn by students and scholars.

Fen hung juan hsüeh tzu, soft pink style.

This is worn by the *hsiao sheng* actor.

Yüeh pai juan hsüeh tzu, soft moon white style.

This is also worn by the *hsiao sheng* actor.

Lan juan hsüeh tzu, soft blue style.

Again this is worn by the *hsiao sheng* actor.

All the above are plain and used as undergarments.

Ch'ing lien se juan hsüeh tzu, soft lotus coloured style.

This is only worn by the *wu sheng* actor.

Tzu hua ts'u ch'ou hsüeh tzu, natural silk style.

This is worn by old men.

Tzu hua pu lao t'ou.

This is used by old men and a shorter version is sometimes used by the *ch'ou* actor.

Hei juan hsüeh tzu, soft black style.

This is used by actors playing poor or distressed people.

Nü hung hsüeh tzu, women's red style.

This is worn by young unmarried women at home.

Fen hung nü hsüeh tzu, women's pink style.

This is worn as the ordinary costume of the wives and daughters of men of affluence.

Ch'ing lien se nü hsüeh tzu, women's lotus coloured style.

This is only worn by poor people.

Tsa se nü hsüeh tzu, women's style in other colours.

These are worn by maids in waiting to concubines and by slave girls.

Tzu hua ts'u ch'ou nu hsueh tzu, women's natural silk style.

A natural silk style worn by old peasant women.

Hung ying hua hsüeh tzu, red stiff satin style.

This is worn by stage heroes and men of high character.

Lü ying hua hsüeh tzu, green stiff satin style.

This is worn by bad characters, particularly those portrayed by the *ching* actors.

Pai ying hua hsüeh tzu, white stiff satin style.

This is worn by the young hero.

Huang ying hua hsüeh tzu, yellow stiff satin style.

This is the ordinary dress of the Emperor or his relatives.

Hei ying hua hsüeh tzu, black stiff satin style.

This is worn by heroes portrayed by the *ching* actors.

Tsa se ying hua hsüeh tzu, stiff satin style in other colours.

These are worn by bad characters. It should be noted that the six stiff satin styles named are all patterned.

Su ying hsüeh tzu, plain stiff satin style.

There are four colour styles for this: red, worn by the Emperor but not often used; blue, worn by officials and scholars; black, worn by merchants; and *ku t'ung se,* a dark brown colour worn by old heroes. The *pa kua i* robe is a style of *hsüeh tzu.* This is decorated with the *pa kua i* symbols mentioned earlier in the chapter and is only worn by military strategists or men possessing metaphysical knowledge and magical powers. Chu-ko Liang is the classic example. There are three colour styles, blue, purple and white. The blue version may be worn without a beard, but not the purple, which is worn by a high ranking Taoist. The white version is worn as mourning.

Hsiao i is a *hsüeh tzu* style in pure white cloth or satin, which is worn by women on the stage as mourning though it may be also used on occasion for a ghost.

Ch'ing p'ao.

This is a black *hsüeh tzu* style garment made of cloth and worn by the assistants to local government officials.

Hai ch'ing.

This is a black satin *hsüeh tzu* worn by an old servant of good character in a wealthy family The *ma pu hai ching,* made of coarse black cloth, is worn by an ordinary servant. *Ch'a i,* this is a short *hsüeh tzu* style garment made of blue cloth which is worn by a boy servant, a waiter and so on. It has very short *shui hsiu,* water sleeves.

Shih shih hsüeh tzu, modern style *hsüeh tzu.*

This is an important garment worn by women characters which has been universally adopted on the stage during the last fifty years although it is never used by the *lao tan* actor. It is made of soft satin and is of knee length worn over a skirt. It opens down the front, has a high collar, long *shui hsiu* and is worn with or without a sash. There is a twelve inch slit on either side. It is used a great deal by the *ch'ing i* actor, when it is in black with the collar, cuffs, hem and slits decorated with a one and a half inch border of turquoise or royal blue silk with white silk piping one eighth of an inch wide running down the centre of the border. This style is the prerogative of the *ch'ing i* actor but the *shih shih* type of *hsüeh tzu* in other colours has largely replaced the forms described previously for women characters except

where worn as an undergarment, or by the *lao tan*.
Ho ch'ang.

This is a *hsüeh tzu* type robe similar to the *pa kua i* except that it is decorated with a crane pattern instead. It is only worn by two mythological Taoist characters.
Fa i.

This is a wide flowing cape with no sleeves worn by a Taoist magician when carrying out a special ritual. It has a border all the way round it decorated with the *pa kua*, or a crane pattern.
Chia sha.

This is a red robe with a white brick-like pattern and is worn slung across the left shoulder. It is used by an important Buddhist dignitary.
P'ien shan.

This is a grey robe very similar to the genuine costume of a Buddhist monk and is really a *hsüeh tzu* style.
Tao p'ao.

A blue *hsüeh tzu* style robe representing the informal wear of a Taoist.
Tou p'eng.

This is a wide cape with no sleeves which hangs to the feet and has a low collar. It is often red in colour, patterned, and worn to represent travelling or bitter weather. It can also signify that the wearer is ill or out of doors late at night.

The *pei hsin* is a sleeveless garment which opens down the front and is worn to knee length. A shorter version worn at waist length called the *hua pei hsin* is worn by a palace maid or a slave girl. It may be red or green with various patterns which are never in roundel form. It is commonly used by the *hua tan* actor.
Tao pei hsin.

This is green with no pattern and worn by a Taoist when played by the *ching* actor.
Hei pei hsin.

This is black and slightly longer than knee length being worn by an old slave woman. The *ch'ou* actor sometimes uses it in his old woman impersonations.
Seng pei hsin.

This is patterned with a bold blue and white rhomboid pattern and worn by a high ranking Buddhist dignitary generally impersonated by a *ching* actor. It is also worn as part of the costume of a Buddhist nun in which case the *pei hsin* is worn over the decoratively coloured *shih shih hsüeh tzu* usually worn by the *tan* actor. There is nothing sober or lacking in decoration in the stage nun.

Yün chien.

This is a decorative shoulder cape which is worn with the *mang* or the *kung i* described later. It is made in different colours often with a richly embroidered gold pattern and has a tasselled edge. The tassels are yellow in the case of an Empress; other characters use red or alternating colours. A simple version of this, whose serrated edge is made in the shape of the *chu i* pattern, is called the *ju i chien* and worn by palace maids and attendants.

The *k'u ao* is the name given on the stage to the short tunic and wide trousers which were the ordinary woman's attire during the latter part of the Ch'ing dynasty when actors first introduced it as stage costume. Today it is regulation stage costume for the *hua tan* actor though never worn by the *ch'ing i*. It was formerly known as *shih chuang* modern style costume. It is used to represent informal dress indoors for maids, slave girls and humble people. The *k'u ao* may be in plain colours or, as is often the case, in bright and colourful floral patterns. When made of ordinary blue cloth it is called *lan k'u ao* and is used for very poor women. The tunic of the *k'u ao* has no *shui hsiu* and the real sleeves are cut well above the wrists. It is short with slits on either side, has a high collar and fastens to the right. It is always worn with a broad and ornamented sash. The trousers are wide and of the same design. Sometimes a skirt is worn instead.

Wei tsui.

This is an apron worn over the normal costume by the *hua tan* and *ch'ing i* actors. It hangs from the chest to knee height and is fastened over the shoulders and round the side with tapes tied at the back of the actor. The top of the apron is cut with a semicircular edge being plain in the case of the *ch'ing i* and ornamented for the *hua tan*. It is worn when the character is performing some household or domestic task.

The skirts worn in the women's roles, *ch'ün tzu*, may be plain or highly ornamented. They are all long and cover the feet.

Pai pien ch'ün tzu.

This is made of plain white silk which is pleated at either side with a panel at the front and back. The panels are outlined with the same plain blue border that decorates the *hsüeh tzu* of the *ch'ing i* actor. The skirt is made in the form of a long rectangular piece of material which is wound round the waist and fastened with tapes. A pure white version of this with no blue border is used as an accessory in both male and female roles. In these cases it is used to symbolize that the wearer is poorly dressed, ill and distressed or going on a long journey. An example of its use in male roles is quoted in the description of the play *Chi Ku Ma Ts'ao*. The *ch'ing i* actor sometimes fastens this second skirt high round the chest, the loose ends being attached to the little finger of each hand with a small ring. It is called *chan ch'ün*, or *yao ch'ün* and is associated with some very graceful and decorative posing and gestures. When the skirt is worn by male characters as described it is called *pu ch'ün*.

Tsa se ch'ün.

This skirt is made in different colours and patterns and is often worn by the *hua tan* with the *k'u ao* costume instead of trousers. It has panels at the front and back but no pleating at the sides.

Hung kung ch'ün, red palace skirt.

This skirt is even longer than the normal ones described above, the feet do not show at all; in the others the point of the shoe is visible. It is red and ornately embroidered with flower patterns in the panels and has as many as one hundred pleats. It is worn with the *mang* or *kuan i* costumes. There is a green version, the *lü kuan ch'ün* worn by the *lao tan* actor.

K'ao

This is the name of an important group of costumes which represent the armour of the warriors and generals. They are made of stiff and heavily embroidered satin and the fishscale pattern is prominently used throughout. The costume is in separate parts, the front and back being apron-like panels hanging to the feet, the two side panels are shorter and a broad girdle-like portion fits round the waist, embroidered with a tiger's head. The sleeves are tight and cuffed and a butterfly wing-shaped piece forms a type of small cape over each shoulder with a broad semi-circular piece fitting round the neck as a collar. There are two main styles of *k'ao*, *ying* and *juan k'ao*. The *ying k'ao* is distinguished by a unique feature, four large triangular pennants called *k'ao ch'i*, which are strapped to the back of the actor behind his shoulders. The *juan k'ao* does not have these pennants which are richly embroidered in colours to match those of the main costume. The *k'ao* are designed in the *shang* and *hsia* colours, the first being worn by commanders in chief and high ranking generals and the last by barbarian and foreign generals.

Hung k'ao, red style.

This is worn by a commander-in-chief or a very strong fighting character.

Lü k'ao, green style.

This is worn by high ranking warriors and by *ching* actors who have a red make-up.

Huang k'ao, yellow style.

This is worn by the brothers of the Emperor or an old general.

Pai k'ao, white style.

This is worn by a young warrior of high rank.

Hei k'ao, black style.

This style is worn by a bad character. It is also used in some *ching* roles where the make-up is black.

Fen hung k'ao, pink style.

This is worn by a young general who is also well versed in scholarship.

Hu se k'ao, coral blue style.

This is worn by a handsome young general of great renown.

Chiang se k'ao, dark crimson style.

This is often worn by the *ching* actors and by usurpers to the throne.

Lan k'ao, blue style.

This is worn by a low ranking general with an ugly countenance.

Tzu k'ao, purple style.

This is worn by a low ranking officer.

Chien k'ao, arrow style *k'ao*.

This is only used for a particular play. It is red in colour and has three pockets in the chest in which arrows are inserted being invisible from outside. Cords are attached to the arrows which enable them to be pulled out to simulate being killed by these weapons. The military costume representing armour and worn without the flags is called *k'ai*; it has no tiger head and the apron piece in the centre is fish-tail shaped and is worn by military characters of low rank. There are red, yellow, green, white, black and blue styles, yellow and blue only being worn by the guards of the Emperor. The armour style worn in the women's roles has numerous coloured and embroidered silk streamers hanging down to skirt length and the panels are somewhat shorter than in the male costume. The *k'ao ch'i*, or armour pennants which are strapped to the actor's back fit in a single socket from which they fan out. They are embroidered with dragon, phoenix and flower designs and there is a long silk streamer attached to each one. They symbolize a token of authority bestowed on the wearer by the Emperor, that is to say they are worn by military officials in positions of command.

Hua ying hsiung i.

This is a costume worn by brave and fearless fighters who are outlaws and not members of the Imperial forces. It consists of tunic and wide trousers. The tunic has tight sleeves and a double frill along the hem, and with silk cords laced across the chest. It may fasten down the centre or to the side, and is patterned in light and brilliant colours of various designs although never the dragon or tiger. There is a plain black version of this costume which indicates a similar character but of lower rank and circumstances. When old men wear this dress it is in *ku t'ung se*, literally brass coloured silk.

Shang shou i.

This is a similar style costume to the above but it is not frilled or patterned and generally brown or black. It is often worn by four actors who appear together to represent the Emperor's army.

Hsia shou i.

This is the same type of costume as the one above but generally blue in colour and is worn by the four men who represent the opposing army to the Imperial forces.

Lung t'ao i.

This is the costume worn by the four men called *lung t'ao* who follow a general in military plays and represent his forces. The robe is a long one which hangs to the feet and in theory is in the same colours as those of the general whose forces they portray. There is a wave pattern border at the foot of the costume which also has short *shui hsiu*, water sleeves. The robe opens down the front and is decorated with a dragon pattern.

Hsiao p'i kua.

This is a short sleeveless tunic which fastens down the front and has a circular collarless neck hole. It is cut in rather the same style as the *pei hsin* described earlier. It is decorated with a roundel on the chest containing the character *ping*, meaning soldier, or *tso* which is an older term. It is generally red in colour and worn by those playing the parts of ordinary soldiers.

Hu p'i p'i kua.

The same garment as the one described above only with a pattern of tiger stripes. It symbolizes a ghost soldier.

K'uai i.

This consists of a black tunic and trousers. The jacket buttons up the front, has a high collar and rows of buttons along the sleeves as decoration. It is worn by non-military but fighting characters, often engaged in nefarious deeds by night. The *wu sheng* and the *wu ch'ou* wear it.

Chien i.

There are three styles of this garment, the *lung chien i* or dragon style, the *hua chien i*, or patterned style, the *su chien i* or plain style. The robe is a long one which fastens to the right in Chinese style and has no collar but a low neck opening in which the *hu ling* or white stock is visible. It has tight sleeves with *ma t'i hsiu*, horse hoof cuffs. These can be turned down to cover the hands and are so called from the fancied resemblance to a horse's hoof on such an occasion. The garment is always worn with a wide, stiff knotted sash known as the *luan tai*, which is also worn with the *ying hsiung i* already described. It is worn to indicate travelling as well as being the dress of fighters who do not wear armour. The dragon style is patterned with dragons and the wave design on the hem of the garment. Emperors and very high officials wear it in yellow and others in red or blue. The flower style is patterned with floral designs and is often worn by fighters. The flower designs are contained within roundels in this case. The plain style *chien i* has no pattern and is generally in black or blue and it is worn by general's aides, messengers and retainers and signifies people of lower degree than in the other two styles. The plain *chien i* sometimes has a border design round the hem and the opening of the robe, the key pattern being used in various colours.

Tuan ta actor in chien i and luan tai with ch'ou actor in hsüeh tzu

Ma kua.

This is formal dress worn when travelling and riding. It is made in two colours only, yellow and black, and patterned with roundels containing a dragon or flower design and a wave pattern round the hem. It is a short jacket of waist length with wide sleeves, and is worn over the *chien i* described above. Only the Emperor wears the yellow version. A style of *ma kua* worn only in plays depicting the Ch'ing dynasty is called *ch'in ping i.* It is black with a white roundel on the back and front in which are inscribed the characters *ch'in ping.* It is worn by one who is a general's retainer and carries his weapons, etc.

Yung tzu ma chia.

This is similar in style to the *shao p'i kua* but is black and decorated with the character *yung,* meaning brave. It is worn by soldiers.

Kuei tzu shou i.

This consists of a *ma kua* worn over the plain white skirt in the

pu ch'ün fashion described earlier. It signifies an executioner.
Ch'i chuang.

This is the Manchu style costume. See p. 216 for description.

The following are some accessories to the principal costumes.
Shui i.

A robe made of white cloth with *shui hsiu* and worn beneath all other stage costumes which have *shui hsiu*.
Luan tai.

A stiff silk girdle four inches wide with tasselled ends and worn with the *chien i* or *ying hsiung i*. It may be in yellow, white, purple, blue, or orange. If patterned it is called *hua k'ou tai* and is worn by the *wu sheng*.
P'ang ao.

This is a padded, sleeveless underjacket which is worn by the *ching* and *wu sheng* actors to give width and bulk to their shoulders and bodies.
Szu t'ao.

These are the silk cords sometimes worn across the chest by the *wu sheng* actor; they are also used to fasten armour, although in such a case they are invisible.
Tz'u ku yeh.

A small inverted prong-shaped ornament seen on the front of the head-dresses of fighting characters. It is based on the form of a water plant (*saggitaria sagittifolia*) and symbolizes courage. The *ch'ing i* actor often has this made in black gauze and worn at the right side of the coiffure.
Ts'ai k'u.

The trousers worn by male characters with the high boots. They are black or red, the latter colour always being worn by the *lao sheng*. The boots and shoes worn by actors have the following names.
Kuan hsüeh.

These are the high black satin boots worn in the male roles for all military and official occasions. They have thick white soles which slope up in a flat wedge shape at the front. The *ch'ou* actor wears a version of this style with a much lower sole. A patterned variety worn by fighting characters is called *hua chan hsüeh*.
Pao ti ku'ai hsüeh.

These are ankle length boots of soft black satin with flat soles

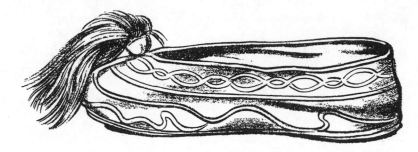

Ts'ai hsüeh

and bound to the actor's legs by tapes. They are worn by actors who play parts requiring swift acrobatic movements and serve a practical purpose in enabling him to gain a firm stance on the floor. There are coloured versions as well as black: see illustration, p. 122.

Ts'ai hsüeh.

These are the flat soled slippers of various colours worn by the *tan* actors. They are ornamented with a silk tassel on the front and embroidered in various designs: see illustration above. When the *tan* actor wears *ch'i chuang* or Manchu style costume one of two styles of shoes may be worn, the first style being called *ch'i hsüeh*. The foot is fitted into a slipper type shoe to the sole of which is fixed a white wooden stilt about three inches high. The base is rectangular but the sides are deeply concave. It is placed exactly in the centre of the sole and is a stage replica of the old Manchu style which requires great skill in wearing. The second type is called *hua p'en ti* and has a sole which curves up at the front and back. The name means 'flower basin' sole and refers to their curious shape. The ordinary black cotton flat soled Chinese slipper style shoe is also worn on the *ching hsi* stage by the *ch'ou* actor and those playing poor people. A slipper-style with a thick white sole, sometimes embroidered with a pattern and sometimes plain is often worn by the *lao sheng* and *hsiao sheng* actors in non-military attire.

Ku'ei t'ou, THE HEAD-DRESSES OF THE ACTOR

Many of the head-dresses worn by princes, generals, Empresses, chief concubines and the like are extremely elaborate and decorated with all kinds of accessories. The irregularity of their

The actress Ch'in Yü wearing 'ch'i chuang'　　　Yü Chen-fei, 'hsiao sheng' actor

A student of the Peking Dramatic Training School being taught to walk on 'ts'ai ch'iao' (1935)

PLATE III

A Shantung temple stage

The stage of Kuang Ho Lou Theatre, Peking (circa 1898)

PLATE IV

shapes and complex designs makes it impossible to describe them adequately without individual illustrations. Their numbers make that impossible in a book of this size and only some of the principal basic styles are listed. Generally speaking, the more important the character the more elaborate the head-dress, although there again, it depends upon the circumstances in which the wearer is portrayed. Ornaments of many different kinds are used, brilliants, pearls, beads, tassels and artificial flowers to name a few. A favourite item is the *jung ch'iu*, a silk pom pom made in many different colours and sizes and used singly or in quantity as decoration. Barbarian Emperors and generals have their head-wear adorned with long sweeping pheasant plumes and *hu wei*, white fox tails (see p. 211).

On ceremonial occasions the stage Emperors wear a style called *t'ang mao*. This is a high creation in gold with a dragon pattern at the front right and left sides with a large pearl in the centre. It is ornamented with *jung ch'iu* of different colours and has two long yellow silk tassels hanging down over the shoulders. Empresses and women of high rank, when wearing the *mang*, have a head-dress called *ta feng kuan*, or phoenix head-dress, which is a large aureole of pearls and sparkling ornaments with a phoenix decoration in the centre. A flat semi-circular jade ornament called the *pao tsuan* is suspended from it at the back above the nape of the neck. There are less elaborate styles of this for wear by ladies of lower rank. A very characteristic hat worn in the male roles by civil officials is the *sha mao*. This is made of stiff black felt with a double semi-circular crown. From the back at either side protrude two fins, *ch'ih*, which are so constructed that they quiver slightly with the actors' gestures. It is a style based on the hats worn by the officials and scholars of other days as a reference to old paintings will readily show, although the stage style has been greatly modified for dramatic purposes. The *ch'ih*, or fins, may be of different shape. Those in the style called *fang ch'ih sha mao* are shaped rather like the blade of a small oar with rounded ends and are worn by high officials and men of good character. When the fin is oval shaped, *yuan ch'ih sha mao*, it signifies a low grade official and it is often used by the *ch'ou* actor who must wear this style of hat. A broad leaf-shaped fin is worn by men of bad character, e.g., Ts'ao Ts'ao, while he is still a low rank official. A version of this hat style with red fins, gold

F

flower decorations and a large red *jung ch'iu* at the front is only worn by P'an Kuan, the Guardian of the Underworld. A similar type of hat with a square instead of a rounded double crown and two very long and narrow fins which turn up at the end is called *hsiang tiao*. It is worn by prime ministers and is used a great deal by the character Ts'ao Ts'ao. The illustration on p. 143 shows the *kao fang chin*, the hat of an ordinary scholar. It is usually black but can be worn in other colours as well. There are many styles in the *chin* class, one is the *hsiang chin* which is square and slightly wider at the top than at the base, with two short flat pieces protruding above the back of the hat. It is used as the ordinary wear of a prime minister. The *hsiao sheng* actor often wears a hat called the *wen sheng chin*, which is the mark of a young scholar in good circumstances. The crown of the hat is surmounted by two curled butterfly wing shaped pieces from which are suspended long silk tassels. It is seen in a variety of colours, richly embroidered and set with a jade ornament in the front. Another class of head-dress is the *lo mao* which has several styles. It is worn by fighting characters, particularly the *tuan ta* actors. It may be stiff, *ying*, or *juan*, soft. It is like a hexagonal tam o'shanter (see illustration) and may be in plain black satin or coloured with a flowered design. The plain black version *hei lo mao* is often worn by a family retainer or a personal servant. When the *tuan ta* actors wear the soft kind it is pulled down at a rakish angle over one ear. This style of hat is commonly worn with the *ying hsiung i* and the *shang shou i* costume as well as the *chien i*. The *ch'ou* actor sometimes wears a white woollen cap with a turned-up edge and broad tasselled fringe on the crown, called *chan mao*. It is also worn by actors impersonating old men of the lower classes. Another style worn by the *ch'ou* is the *niu chien tsuan* which is more or less a replica of a fashion common among elderly women until after the revolution of 1911. It consists of a bandeau which narrows towards the back of the head where a small queue, bound and decorated with a flower, protrudes with a comical upward twist. In conclusion something must be said about the actual hair styles of actors, for these are not wigs but are built up using articles which are common in both male and female roles.

The *wang tzu* is a semi-circular skull cap made of horsehair and bound with silk. It is open at the back where there are two

Lo mao

tapes for fixing it to the head. A hole in the crown allows the *shuai fa*, a long plume of hair on a short vertical mount, to be secured. This is worn when actors are in distress or playing the part of a prisoner. The *shuai fa* is often swung round and round with a vigorous movement of the head at emotional climaxes in a play. The *wang tzu* is fixed even more securely on the head by the *shui sha*, a fine gauze net four feet long and sixteen inches wide which is bound round the first-named article in the form of a bandeau. The *wang tzu*, *shuai fa* and *shui sha* on occasion constitute the sole head-dress of the *sheng* actors particularly in a dramatic climax. In the case of the *lao tan* or an old man, a white or grey *wang tzu* is worn to represent the hair. For old men roles a little coil of grey or white hair called *fa chiu* is often worn on the crown of the head. The coil is bound to a metal ring which is fixed under the *wang tzu*. The latter is an important

accessory which not only acts as hair but serves as a foundation
for other coiffures as well. Before the *wang tzu* is fitted to an
actor's head a narrow black tape, several feet long, is bound
tightly round the head, being crossed over on the brow so that
the top eyelids are lifted back towards the temple. It is an un-
comfortable and even painful process for the uninitiated and is
responsible for the deep slant of the eyes in the *tan* and *hsiao
sheng* roles. The general hair style used in feminine roles, the
ta fa, literally great hair, has the same foundation and its basic
components and method are described in detail therefore. Besides
the *wang tzu* and *shui sha* other accessories called respectively,
ta ting, *hsien i tzu*, *t'ou fa shui p'ien i fu* and *ta tsan* are required.
The *ta ting* is a thick switch of real hair which is used to form the
decorative chignon at the back of the head in *tan* roles. By
combing and dividing it in certain ways the variations of appearance required in different parts are created. A long strand of the
ta ting left hanging down at one side of the head gives a feminine
equivalent to the *hsuai fa* of the *sheng* actor. A small pad of
artificial hair is placed underneath the *ta ting* to increase its
height when in place. The *hsien i tzu* consists of numbers of
strands of thick silk thread bound to a length of cord which is tied
round the head and beneath the *ta ting* so that the strands hang
down the actor's back almost to the heels. The *t'ou fa shui p'ien i*
are spear-shaped pieces of natural hair bound at one end and
looped over to make flat coils of diminishing size which fit round
the forehead and the side of the face. There are seven which are
fitted around the line of the forehead to below the eyebrow and
two larger pieces which fit around either cheek to the jaw line
ending in curved points. These two pieces are important because
they can be used to broaden or narrow the appearance of the face
by skilful arrangement. Two more pieces are looped over each
ear. The coils of hair are held in position by a special fixative made
from thin shavings of wood which are taken from a tree whose
botanical name is *machilus pauhoi kaneh*. Before the individual
pieces are placed in position they are combed and dipped into a
thin solution of the fixative which is smeared on lightly with the
finger. The fixative is prepared by squeezing the shavings together
with water in a small bowl, the pieces of hair being laid out on a
small board after treatment ready for use. The *ta tsan* is a metal
hair ornament pointed at either end which serves a practical

purpose. It acts as a support behind the chignon beyond which it protrudes slightly at either side. The loose ends of hair and various binding tapes are held secure by the *ta tsan*. It was actually used by Chinese women in hair dressing in former days and indeed can still be seen worn by peasant and fisher-women, although of a smaller size than the stage counterpart. The complete method of making up this coiffure follows.

First the face is made up completely and the eyes drawn back with the tape already mentioned. Then the first and smallest coil of hair is gummed in position over the centre of the forehead. A second pair are then gummed on either side of this in a slightly lower position, followed by a third pair which practically touch the eyebrows. The tails lie across the hair of the actor, which is generally protected by a light cotton skull cap, and the long tape which binds back the eyes is given a second twist round round to hold the coils firmly in position. The third pair of coils is then gummed on just below the eyebrow line and the tape taken over these also. Next the two long pieces fitting over the cheeks are gummed in place. The ends of these are bent at an angle across the top of the head from left to right and vice versa. These are then fixed with the tape and the ear pieces placed in position, the tape being knotted to hang down at the nape of the neck. The *hsien i tzu* is next tied round the head fairly high up and the *wang tzu* fitted over the crown of the head and tied in place at the back. The *ta tsan* is inserted through the back of the *wang tzu* whose tapes are tied round it. The switch of false hair is placed over the back of the head and tied to the *ta tsan*. The *ta ting* is tied to the *ta tsan* with the bound end facing towards the front of the head and the loose switch hanging down the back. It is combed back over the pad of false hair, smoothed out, divided into two at the bottom of the pad and each parting taken round the top of the pad again from the opposite side at the bottom, i.e. the two pieces of the *ta ting* are crossed. The loose ends are firmly fixed round the false pad and made even more secure by winding strands of the *hsien i tzu* round and round it. Sometimes in the *ch'ing i* roles a long strand of the *ta ting* is left free to hang down the left-hand side. After this the *shui sha* is wound broadly round the head from forehead to back and knotted underneath the *ta ting* to hang loosely down the back beneath the *hsien i tzu*. When this is completed, the various hair

ornaments and decorations are pushed into place, the *shui sha*
serving as a base for clips and pins. In the case of Su San for
instance, the character described in the play *Yü T'ang Ch'un* in
Chapter VI, the following steps are taken after the *ta fa* has
been made up. A broad silk turquoise blue scarf is wound round
the head over the *shui sha* and looped into a big knot with
the wide ends hanging down at the right side of the face. Then
large hanging ear-rings are clipped on the ears and a single plain
silver stud on a short pin fixed in each of the coils of hair round
the forehead. Similar studs mounted on a tape are wound round
the *ta ting* and two long silver pins with ornate heads are stuck
in the top of the chignon. Two spatula shaped silver ornaments
are then fixed in the base of the chignon at either side. Following
this, a silver brooch in a conventional bat design is clipped in
behind the blue scarf at the right of the base and plain silver
studs mounted in rows of seven on long pins, of which there are
six, are fitted across the front of the head from left to right. The
coiffure is then complete. It takes two men to complete such an
operation. They are called *pao t'ou ti* and every actor of note
playing *tan* roles has two of these men in attendance. Even in the
case of actresses, men still perform this task and display great
skill and dexterity in their unusual craft.

Two other hair styles used by the *tan* actors besides the *ta fa*
are the *ku chuang t'ou* and the *ch'i chuang t'ou*. Although they
make use of the same accessories they are prepared in different
ways. The *ku chuang t'ou* are coiffures based on historical
models, many of them were introduced by the actor Mei Lan-
fang. The *ch'i chuang t'ou*, the Manchu style, is worn with the
ornate head-dress known as *liang pa t'ou erh:* see illustration on
pl. III. A good example of this hair style is seen in the play *Ssu
Lang T'an Mu*.

Pan hsiang, THE MAKE-UP OF THE ACTOR

The make-up of the *ching hsi* actor is, generally speaking, non-
realistic. In the case of the *tan* roles the face is white, the eyes are
surrounded by a deep red graded away into a pink which merges
with the white of the cheeks and the sides of the nose, the bridge
of which is left pure white. Except for the *lao tan* and the comic
women roles, this style is used for all femine roles although there
may be variations in the depths of gradation according to indi-

vidual tastes. The eyebrows and corners of the eyes are finely pencilled to slant upwards and the mouth is small, being whitened out and painted to suit the conventional requirements. The following procedure is adopted for this make-up. First the face is smeared with a clear honey mixed with water to make a foundation. Next, a white cream made of rice powder mixed with water is smeared matt over the whole face with the palms of the hands. Then a pale magenta-toned rouge is smeared into the cheeks and on the eyelids with the palm of the hand followed by a crimson tone which is rubbed dry on the eyelids and cheeks to give a deeper colour. The forehead and the bridge of the nose are left white. The deepest red is on the eyelids and beneath the eyes, the tint of the cheeks is graded off at the side of the nose leaving the upper lip and chin white. The eyebrows are drawn in with a small brush and elongated to the line of the natural hair. The eyelashes and rims of the eyelids are painted with eye black and the mouth painted in with lipstick.

The make-up of the *hsiao sheng* actor is similar to this although the contrasts in the tints on the face are not so marked. The *lao tan* actor wears no facial make up and the bearded *sheng* actor very little. The *ch'ou* decorates his face with a white patch round the eyes and nose superimposing certain markings in black for different roles. By far the most complicated make-up on the stage is that used by the *ching* actor whose *lien p'u*, or painted faces, are such a striking feature in the *ching hsi* theatre. In these make-ups the whole of the face and forehead is painted with bold and colourful patterns, many of them extremely complicated and all of them symbolic. It appears to be a matter of uncertainty when this technique was first used in the Chinese theatre, but it was a well established practice by the time of the Ming dynasty (A.D. 1368–1644). Records of designs used in this period still exist although they differ a great deal from those seen today, being simpler and of lighter colours. The *kumadori* or painted make-ups of the Japanese *kabuki* theatre almost certainly owe their origin to those of the Chinese stage. The principle of these painted faces is the representation of personal character by colour and symbolic pattern, although bizarre design for pure stage effect is also taken into consideration and sometimes given more emphasis than pure character symbol. The designs are based on the shapes of the butterfly, moth and bat, the eyes and nose being the basis for front and back wings,. the eyebrows the feelers, and the space between the eyes and nose the rest of the body. Naturally the basic outline in these cases is carried a long way beyond any naturalistic representation of the forms. The paint used for the make-ups is made in powder form and mixed to a stiff liquid, oil is used with certain colours to give a glossy shine to the surface. The actor, having first applied a foundation dressing of powder, paints on the colours before his mirror using Chinese brushes. The designs take anything up to an hour to complete and are executed with extreme skill and care. The eyebrows are painted in first followed by the area about the eyes, nose and mouth and lastly the cheeks and minor details. There are various styles which may broadly be divided into six kinds. First there is the 'old' face which shows age and decrepitude. The eyes droop towards the corners and pale colours are used in the areas around the nose. Integrity and purity of character is shown in what is called a 'whole' face. In this nothing is painted between the eyebrows and the eyes or by the corner of the eyes; that is to say only whole areas of colour are used. All make-ups cover the whole of the face with paint, whatever the style. The 'broken' face is the opposite of the whole face and shows a complicated character. Designs which are irregular in their complexity are called 'flower' faces and when the forehead and cheeks are painted in large conspicuous areas of colour it is called the 'three tile' face. When an animal's face is represented it is called a 'demon' style face, and a 'clean' face refers to one in which extremely simple colour and pattern are used.

The principal colours used in the designs are red, white, blue, black, yellow, green, purple and gold. White indicates cunning, treachery and licentiousness, but in such characters the whole face is painted dead white with comparatively simple markings in black and grey. White can also be used in broken up patterns on faces which represent brave and upright men. Red indicates loyalty, bravery and generosity, blue means fierceness and bold courage. Black means integrity and a straightforward character. Yellow is the sign of a clever thinker who conceals his feelings, and purple indicates filial piety and loyalty. Green is commonly used for spirits, often evil ones, and gold is the adornment of gods and supernatural beings. There were as many as five hundred different designs known to the pre-war theatre of

項羽   包拯   曹操

Three painted face designs

Peking but many of these are no longer used: they included of course all types of minor characters as well as the main roles. It has been the practice for famous actors to modify designs for their own use and invent new ones. The young *ching* actor has to learn every stroke of the designs he must use and be able to paint them on skilfully and accurately without aid, a task not easily mastered.

The number of designs and the limitations of colour printing in this book make it impossible to illustrate a great number of these make-ups in detail but three famous ones are shown which are in black and white only, at the same time they are representative of the type of symbolism used throughout in the painted faces of the *ching* actor.

Hsiang Yü

Hsiang Yü was the king of Ch'u and lived towards the end of the Ch'in dynasty (232–201 B.C.). He was a brave warrior but of a quick and impulsive nature and with a violent temper. His temperament was his undoing and all his schemes came to nothing. Yü Chi, his beautiful mistress, killed herself rather than live to serve his opponent as Hsiang Yü suggested when defeat stared him in the face. He himself committed suicide shortly after the death of his favourite and his faithful horse drowned itself in a rushing mountain torrent. These incidents are immortalized in a play *Pa Wang Pieh Chi, The Emperor's Farewell to his Favourite,* and the illustration shows the make-up used by Hsiang Yü in the drama. It is in black and white and the pattern above the eyebrows represents a double pronged spear used in ancient China, symbolizing pugnacity. The black patches round the eyes and the white tip of the nose represent integrity and courage but the design as a whole portrays a man of staunch character defeated by his destiny.

Pao Ch'eng or Kung

Pao Ch'eng was a famous judge who lived in the eleventh century. This make-up is also only in black and white. Pao Ch'eng was reputed to hold office simultaneously on earth and in the nether regions and he had power to enter the lower world. The crescent on his forehead and the white pattern above the eyes symbolize the disappearance of ghosts and evils under a bright moon. The predominant black in the design symbolizes his integrity and devotion to justice.

Ts'ao Ts'ao

This is the make-up of the crafty Prime Minister who appears in so many of the *San Kuo* plays. His face is painted a leaden white; in this case no oil is mixed with the paint so that there is no shine, with thin black lines known as 'flies' feet' which represent wrinkles of cunning. They are painted in grey when he is represented as an older man. This is a good example of the painted face of a bad character.

BEARDS, *hu hsü*

Beards are an important part of the make-up of the *sheng*, *ching* and *ch'ou* roles. They are made of hair bound to a wire frame which fits over the ears and rests just above the mouth on the upper lip. Conventional designs are used for certain roles and may be in either black, red, grey or white.

Man jan.

This is a long full beard which completely obscures the mouth and spreads in one broad swath of hair over the actor's chest. This style is worn in black, grey, or white and is largely worn by the *ching* actors. It symbolizes a high and powerful personage.

Kuan Kung jan.

This is a long and wide beard which hangs in five separate portions. It is black and only worn by the actors portraying Kuan Kung.

San jan.

This is the normal style worn by the bearded *sheng* actors. I is long and in three portions, the broad middle piece over the mouth having a narrower strip of hair of the same length on either side. It is not worn by the *ching* actors but is used only with the natural face without any make-up as seen in the *sheng* parts. The colours used are black, grey or white.

Cha jan.

This is a long full beard similar to the *san jan* except that it has an aperture which exposes the mouth unlike the former style. It is worn a great deal by *ching* actors playing characters who are noted for their courage rather than their intellect. The character Chang Fei in the *Three Kingdoms* plays is a good example.

Cha tsui jan.

This is a similar style to the above but is shorter and worn in minor roles played by the *ching* actors.

The *ch'ou* actors wear a variety of styles of their own, many of them extremely comical. Some principal types are listed here.

Ch'ou san jan.

This beard is in three long narrow strips on the same principle as the *san jan* but much less full in appearance. It is worn when the *ch'ou* actor portrays a petty official or in a role in which the character has a pretension to some intellect.

Ssu hsi jan.

This consists of a short pointed beard over the mouth and two wisps protruding at either side of the face. It is worn by characters such as watchmen, jailers and the like.

Wu tsui jan.

This style combines a drooping moustache over the mouth, a bushy wisp at either side of the face and an Imperial below the chin which is suspended on wire to dangle with the movements of the actor's head. It is in black, white or grey and it is used by the *ch'ou* in civil roles.

Erh t'iao.

This consists of a bristling moustache with two upturned ends. It is worn by the *wu ch'ou* and sometimes the *tuan ta* actors.

Pa Tzu.

This is a large moustache whose two ends protrude forward. It is in white, black or red.

I tzu jan.

This is a broad fringe of hair which runs round the face and may be in red or black. Another version called *erh tzu jan* has a

small dangling tuft below the chin as well.
I ch'o jan.

A single sharp-pointed wisp which sticks straight out from the top lip. It is in black.
Wu tsui jan.

A thick fringe of hair round the face ending in a broad piece hanging at either side of the mouth with a dangling goatee below, similar, although larger, than the styles described previously. It is white and therefore worn by old men.
Ch'iu jan.

This is a short curly half beard which extends round the face and is sometimes worn in certain *ching* roles as well as by swash-buckling characters in the *Shui Hu* plays. The two sharp-pointed tufts of hair which protrude above the ears of the *ching* actors are called *ku jen erh mao*.

WEAPONS AND OTHER STAGE PROPERTIES

A variety of weapons are used by actors, some of them being worn or carried simply as accessories to costume but often they are employed in acrobatic feats particularly in the fighting plays. Two weapons used a great deal by the *ching* and *wu sheng* actors are the *tao* and *ch'iang*. The *tao* is a kind of pike which has a large curled blade with a portion cut away and a red silk tassel pendant hanging from the lower edge. It is mounted on a decorated haft about six feet long. The *ch'iang* has a narrow spear-shaped blade on the end of a haft of the same length and decorated with a white silk tuft where the blade joins the haft. Both are used by the actors in the swift parry and thrust movements which develop into what are literally dances of martial prowess particularly in the *San Kuo* plays. The *p'u tao* is a short sword or scimitar which is wielded by the *tuan ta* actors and used by fighting characters who are not military men. There are a whole series of graceful movements and postures associated with this weapon. The *chien* or two edged sword is carried in an ornamented scabbard with silk tassels on the hilt and is worn at the waist. The *pao chien*, as it is called in the theatre, is some-times used in pairs for dancing.

In addition to the weapons there are a number of small properties which are used in various symbolic ways. The *ma pien*, already mentioned, is a noted example. It is a riding

Tuan ta actor with p'u tao

switch with a loop at one end and four silk tassels hanging from it at equally spaced intervals. The tassels are in different colours, which often represent the colour of the horse, and there are conventional movements and gestures performed when the actor carries it to represent riding, dismounting, backing and tethering a horse. These movements constitute some of the most graphic and decorative symbolism on the stage and are in great contrast to the much more realistic horse of the Japanese *kabuki* for instance. The *ying ch'en* is a long plume of white horse hair on a handle with a thong and is carried by nuns, priests and high ecclesiastical dignitaries as well as Taoist magicians. It is actually based on an article formerly used by Buddhist priest as a symbol of their religious functions and a protection against flies which their creed did not allow them to kill. Embroidered silk flags serve a variety of purposes on the stage. Black ones called *feng ch'i*, or wind banners, represent gales of wind and actors in groups of four run across the stage waving them to indicate a storm. *Ch'e ch'i* are flags with a wheel pattern embroidered on them. An actor holds a pair of these horizontally at waist level and another actor stands, runs or walks between them to represent being in a chariot or wagon. A white banner with a broad crimson border and the Chinese character *lin* embroidered in the centre is a banner carried by soldiers to represent an order given to an army. Similarly a banner embroidered with the character *shuai* in crimson and gold is held by an attendant above a commander-in-chief leading his army. Armies are represented by attendants, in groups of four, carrying flags each of which represents one or two thousand men. *Shui ch'i* flags patterned with a wave design represent water; they are usually carried by actors in groups of four and are shaken constantly to represent sea and river. A city wall is represented by a dark blue cloth patterned to represent the mortared bricks of a city wall and supported on two bamboo poles which are held aloft by two attendants. There is an opening down the centre of the cloth to allow it to be furled on either side to represent the opening of the gate and to allow actors to pass through. To represent a city tower, tables are placed on top of one another with a chair on top of that behind this cloth. The actor then climbs up on to the chair to appear above the top level of the wall cloth as though standing on a tower. A bed is represented by an embroidered satin curtain on bamboo poles fixed upright. The curtain may be divided in the centre and folded back, such a construction also serves as a canopy for high officials in session. To represent nightfall lanterns suspended on bamboo poles are carried by minor actors. The lantern carried before members of the Court is elaborately created with hanging crimson tassels, but the ordinary type consists of a piece of crimson silk draped in a cylinder and hanging from a green wooden top. To represent being on board a boat an actor carries a light wooden paddle or follows another actor who represents a boatman and who carries out a series of movements as though actually paddling. A decapitated head is represented on the stage by a small, round bundle wrapped within a crimson cloth. An official seal is symbolized by a square wooden block wrapped in yellow silk standing on the table representing the desk of an official or magistrate.

Two plain wooden chairs, with an equally plain table, form the principal stage properties. The chair may serve as the seat of a high dignitary or it may simply be a bench in a simple cottage. It is used to represent many other things as well. If an actor playing a jailer stands behind a chair and tilts it sideways, it indicates that the prison gates have been opened to allow someone through. If the jailer simply bends to peep through the struts of the chair, it shows he is looking through the peephole in a prison gate. To show weaving at a loom an actor sits on a chair facing a second chair whose back is to the audience and over which has been hung a broad strip of silk. The actor then passes a shuttle under and out from the cloth to symbolize weaving. A chair placed at one side of the stage sometimes represents a well or a precipice. An actor who mounts it and leaps down on the other side has jumped from a great height, and then disappears quickly offstage. If he leaps over it, it symbolizes drowning in the well. An actor standing on a chair placed on top of a table at the rear of the stage indicates that he is on a high mountain or promontory: if he is playing a god or spirit it shows that he is in the heavens. A table with a chair at the side, both placed at the side of the stage, represents a hill or high wall. The actor throws a length of rope across the table where it is held by the property man and then he mounts the table and chair in turn clinging to the rope to symbolize scaling a wall or steep slope. Some further uses of the chair are described in the *shang ch'ang* movements which conclude this chapter. When a table is placed in the centre of the stage with a single chair behind it, the seat is called *nei ch'ang ts'o*, inner seat, and when placed in front of the table, *wai ch'ang ts'o*, outer seat. If an actor speaking or singing at the front of the stage turns to sit on the chair he must adopt one of two procedures. For the 'outer seat' he turns left after finishing his words and then walks in an S-shaped line to the chair where he turns right face and seats himself. For the inner seat he turns right after finishing his words, and follows a line shaped like an inverted S extending round the left of the table to the rear where he turns left face and sits.

A few more characteristic symbolic representations of the actor may be given before going on to list *shang ch'ang* and *hsia ch'ang* movements. Opening and closing a door is a typical piece of mime often seen on the *ching hsi* stage. The type of door indicated is always the double style found in old Chinese houses bolted in the centre with a horizontal sliding lock. When opening the door from outside the actor uses the thumb and index finger of the left hand with the palm outward as if holding the bolt of the lock and the right hand removing it. The hands are then placed together with the palms outward and pushed forward and apart, being gradually inclined as if forcing the doors apart. Opening a door from inside involves a slightly different procedure. The left hand is held with palm outwards and the thumb and first two fingers of the right hand as though they are grasping the horizontal bolt, which is moved to the right. The hands are then placed together in front and drawn inwards as though pulling open the doors. Next, the actor steps towards the left, raising his hands with palms outwards as though pushing back the heavy doors, first left and then right. There was always a very high threshold in Chinese entrances and the actor indicates this by lifting his right foot high as though stepping over, the left foot being lifted backward before completing the motion. When a door is to be closed from outside, the actor first 'crosses the threshold', *k'ua men chien*, turns back, places his right foot over the imaginary threshold once again, and draws the left door forward with the right hand while stepping back, repeating the movement with the left hand for the right half of the door. The locking movement as first described is then performed in reverse. To close a door from inside the movement is performed as when opening from inside, except that the doors are pulled into place instead of being pushed back, and are locked instead of unlocked.

When riding a horse the actor performs the following movements using the *ma pien* or riding switch. When reining up his horse the actor moves the switch backwards and downwards in a curve, completing the curve by holding the switch rigid in front of him. When leading his horse he holds the switch vertically by the handle with the tip downwards. When a horse is led by a groom to the rider, the switch is held horizontally with the handle towards the rider. The right hand is extended at the side at shoulder height. The actor playing the groom stands in front of the rider with his back towards him while performing this movement. When dismounting his horse, the actor moves his right arm with the switch upwards and towards the right in a sweeping circle, and then brings it into a horizontal position in front of him with the left hand touching the tip, at the same time the actor looks at the audience. Then, with a circular wrist movement, he turns the switch downwards to the right, slips his little finger out of the loop and changes the switch to the left hand and lifts his right foot. The left hand holding the whip is moved as though gathering the reins, and a step is made with the left foot as though getting out of the stirrup. The switch is then placed in the right hand again, to be taken away by a groom. If the switch is thrown on one side of the stage it means the horse has been turned out to graze. When mounting a horse, the actor raises his right hand with fingers outstretched but together, and closes his left hand as though to hold the reins. The third finger of the left hand is placed in the loop of the switch and the hand clasps the haft. The switch is drawn backwards and the left foot lifted as though to the stirrup, the switch is lowered as though on to the horse's back and the right foot thrown across the saddle. The left hand then performs the motion of tightening the reins and the rider faces the audience with the switch uplifted.

When boarding a boat an actor jumps forward (see p. 120 in the section on foot movements) and sways his body gently back and forth as though balancing himself against the motion of the boat, and picks up the wooden paddle which is placed on the stage. If more than one person boards the vessel, the first one holds the paddle horizontally towards the others in turn as a support. If an actor appears through the exit carrying a paddle it signifies that he is already on board and when he holds out the paddle is receiving passengers. When anchoring a boat, the actor runs in circles making motions with the paddle as though steering the boat; he then places the paddle on the stage and jumps forward as though stepping ashore. He then turns about, stoops down, and mimes the action of drawing a boat nearer the shore and mooring it with a rope.

The *tan* actor often portrays a maid preparing thread for sewing the soles of shoes. The soles of the traditional Chinese shoes are made of layers of cloth quilted together with a strong thread which is first twisted and rolled. The *tan* actor first pretends to draw out a long thread and places it over an imaginary hook with one end between his teeth and the other between the palms of his hands which are held with the finger pointing vertically, and the thread is then rolled briskly between the palms. The ends are then changed and the opposite half rolled in the same way. The twisted thread is now ready from release on the hook and is let loose in preparation for threading through a large needle. It is a graceful piece of mime which, when performed by the skilful *hua tan* actor, never fails to charm the eye.

When a besieged city is depicted on the stage, groups of actors run in wide circles across the stage from either side, those players entering through the exit disappearing through the entry and vice versa. The curtain representing a city wall is hung at the rear of the stage during this action. If it is a small group of people only who are surrounded, they come on in the same way but stay in the centre of the stage with their backs to the audience.

Shang ch'ang AND *hsia ch'ang* MOVEMENTS

The *shang ch'ang*, entry, and *hsia ch'ang*, exit, techniques, have already been listed under music and speech or declamation and the following are conventional movements and groupings used by the actors on these occasions.

Shang ch'ang, entry.

Chan men shang.

Four *lung t'ao* appear first or four eunuchs or four slave girls. They enter in twos after which the principal actor appears and recites the *yin tzu*. The *lung t'ao* are minor actors who represent armies and they normally stand at each side of the stage in groups of three or six. They have no speaking parts and merely carry banners and go through a series of different movements according to the nature of the scene. The first and third men are the important ones as they must take the lead and therefore know every twist or turn which has to be made.

Ch'i pa shang.

This is used in fighting plays although it represents a scene indoors. Four generals appear and perform the *ch'i pa* movements used by fighting characters (see p. 226). The principal character then enters and recites the *yin tzu*.

Hsieh men shang.

Four *lung t'ao* form into pairs on either side of the entry and the principal character enters and stands just beyond the four men and sings. The *lung t'ao* then go to the opposite side of the stage and the principal character stands in the centre and sings. It signifies that he is on a journey.

I tzu shang.

Four *lung t'ao* enter and stand in a line at the right of the stage followed by the principal character who places himself in the front of the line at the centre. It signifies a powerful and important personage.

T'ang ma shang.

The actor makes his entry with a running horse symbolized by appropriate actions with his *ma pien*. It means he is coming from another place.

Tsou pien shang.

This is only used by the *wu sheng* or *wu ch'ou*. The actor is on tiptoe with arms outstretched as though walking stealthily either by the side of a road or wall or at night time. It means he is appearing from another place.

Hsieh i tzu shang.

Four *lung t'ao* enter and stand in an oblique line stretching from the entry across the right front corner of the stage, the principal character in the front centre of them. He finishes a song or speech before they move across the stage. It symbolizes the quick marching of a number of men.

Shuang hsieh i tzu shang.

Two oblique lines of *lung t'ao* across the right side of the stage with the leader in front indicates an even greater number of men than in the above.

I tzu chan men shang.

Four officials or generals come to the front of the stage and stand in a line. The first and second to enter stand in the centre of the line with number three on the right side and number four on the left, so that in the order of their entry, they now stand three, one, two, four from right to left. Each one then recites a line and announces his name in order and they then withdraw in pairs.

T'ai chiao shang.

This is similar to the movement described above except that

the actors do not change places when forming up. It is used by
sedan chair carriers.

Ssu chiao chan men shang.

Four actors enter and form a square, number one and two in
front, three and four behind. It represents a meeting in home or
office.

Erh lung ch'u shui shang.

Generals of opposing sides with their soldiers make entries from
the exit and entry sides simultaneously. The soldiers stand to one
side and the generals stride forward to meet each other.

Men tun tzu shang.

One or two actors enter and take a seat or seats at the front of
the stage. This entry is used on military occasions and symbolizes
an urgent situation or that an emergency has arisen.

Ssu pa men i shang.

This is performed in the same way as *i tzu chan men shang*
except that the four characters sit instead of standing.

Wu pa men i shang.

Five actors stand in a straight line each on a chair. It indicates
the arrival of spirits from distant places by riding on
the clouds.

Hsieh men i shang.

When an actor making an entry stands on a chair and sings
or declaims before proceeding across the stage, in the case of a
spirit it indicates riding on a cloud or else ascending high ground.

Cheng men i shang.

The actor enters and then stands on a chair which is at the
front of the stage in the centre. It symbolizes riding on a cloud
and so is only used by supernatural characters.

Ch'u tung shang.

In this movement the actor makes his entry backwards.

San hsieh men i shang.

The actor makes his entry, stands on a chair and sings, and
then goes off. He then reappears from the exit side, stands on
another chair and again sings before going off. Finally he reappears from the entry side once more, repeats the performance
and then gets down. It symbolizes that he is surrounded by
enemies.

T'iao shang.

An actor playing a spirit or god stands on a chair or table when he first enters to symbolize coming down from the clouds or high ground.

Hui chen shang.

A general enters and takes his stand on the stage followed by another who comes from the exit side. It symbolizes meeting to fight.

Ling shang.

The actor enters with an attendant who carries either the water or wind banner. It symbolizes being washed ashore or blown by the wind.

Ch'e ssu men shang.

There are many variations of this entry which represents the actor as coming from another place and conversing while walking along. It is used by the *tan* actor.

Tsou yüan ch'ang shang.

A variation of the above is used by Su San in the play, *Yü T'ang Ch'un*, when she is travelling with her jailer.

Pai tui chang.

A general comes on followed by *lung t'ao* representing his army. Another character appears from the exit or opposite side to be met by the general.

Hsia ch'ang, exit.

Pei huan hsia.

This is used when calling to another who is plunged in absent-minded thought. One actor, having made his exit, calls from back stage for the second actor to go off. Alternatively one actor pats the shoulder of another standing in thought and they go off together.

Wo hsia.

This is used at the close of a meeting between the Emperor and high officials. The Emperor stands between two files of actors and then turns and goes off, the files divide and go off at entry and exit sides simultaneously.

Hsieh men hsia.

This is used when four servants stand in an oblique line at the right of the stage facing the exit. Their master stands in front of them and they wait until he has left before they too depart.

Tao t'o hsueh hsia.

This is performed as above but there are several files indicating officers, aides, soldiers, etc., the first file being the most important, followed by the next most important in the second file and so on. The files go off one at a time.

She t'ui p'i hsia.

Four files of *lung t'ao* stand obliquely facing the exit. The front file marches round to the back by the right leaving the second file in the front. The procedure is followed by each file in turn until the original fourth file has become the front file. They then march off stage, the left hand man in each file leading off. It represents troops in military formation.

I tzu hsia.

A principal character standing in front of a line of four men at the right of the stage goes off. When he has left, the two outer men step forward to form a four and they march off.

Wan shou erh hsing hsia.

Two characters go off hand in hand together. It signifies that friends of equal rank have met each other after one of them has returned from a long journey.

Pai tui hsiang ying hsia.

A host and guest stand with four attendants each in a line behind them, the host is at the exit side and the guest at the entry. The first attendant from both the guest's and host's files, i.e. the man nearest the front of the stage, turn to face each other and go off by the exit, passing between host and guest who are still facing each other. The second pair of attendants follow and so on. When the two files have departed, host and guest go off together. If the guest is of low rank he precedes the host and vice versa.

Hsi hsing hsia.

This is only used by the *ch'ing i* actor. The actor is on his knees and moves rapidly along on them towards the exit; often he faces the audience while performing this so that he is moving sideways. It symbolizes a state of great distress or agitation.

P'ao hsia.

This means running off the stage, the various roles using their own special techniques. It is often used by the *hua tan* and *hsiao sheng* actors to symbolize playfulness, embarrassment or fear as the case may be.

Peng tzu hsia.

This is used by the *wu sheng* or *wu tan* and symbolizes coming to a decision. The actor is standing at the exit side of the stage and jumps once in the air before going off.

Hsieh i tzu hsia.

This is often used in military plays when crossing a bridge or narrow path. A file of actors jump on and off a chair or table in turn and make their exit.

T'ang ma hsia.

This is used when an actor is mounted on his horse. He goes round the stage in a circle holding out his *ma pien* and then goes off.

Chui hsia.

This describes two people running with one in pursuit of the other. The second actor goes off when the first has made his exit.

La hsia.

One actor pulls another off the stage either by one arm or else by tucking the arm of the second person under his own and forcing him to move.

Ting hsia.

When one person does not wish another to pass, this is used as an exit movement. The first actor with arms akimbo walks towards the other who takes a step back and then another until he finally backs off the stage.

Hsiu hsia.

This is used by the *tan* actor to signify embarrassment. The appropriate sleeve movement, i.e., *che hsiu* is performed and the actor goes off quickly.

La ma hsia.

This is used when leading off a horse. The *ma pien* is held upright in the actor's left hand with the right hand in front of the body, and in this way the actor makes his exit.

Pei hsiao hsia.

This symbolizes there is a fire. The actor tries to go this way and that way before he finally leaves the stage.

T'ao hsia.

When a character has killed another and runs away, it is described by this name. The actor keeps looking behind him as he runs off.

T'o hsia.

Four actors go off carrying another above their heads lying absolutely rigid on their palms. It signifies someone who has died or collapsed with fear.

Tzu wen hsia.

The actor runs quickly off stage with his head lowered, having killed himself with a sword or other weapon in the play.

P'eng tzu hsia.

A character kills himself by running his head into something. The player falls down after symbolizing this action, then runs quickly off.

Pei sha hsia.

An actor rises and runs quickly off after he has been killed by someone else in the play.

T'iao shui hsia.

The actor portrays suicide by jumping in water, then runs off quickly.

Ts'eng hsia.

This describes the actor going off slowly, limping and holding one arm after being wounded.

Fan hsia.

This is used by the acrobats and means going off performing a cart wheel.

I tzu t'ui hsia.

This is performed when a group of actors wish to show that they are returning to the place from which they came. They turn to face the back stage before going off.

Ling hsia.

This is the same as *t'ao hsia* but the character concerned is accompanied by a flag bearer to show that he is someone of high military rank.

Finally, to close this chapter, a few words must be added concerning the technique of specialists so far unmentioned, the *wu hang*, or acrobats. They are a class of players apart, who do not speak and are different from the *wu sheng* actors. They come on to the stage in groups and may represent bandits, soldiers of fortune, or similar characters, but their main function lies in providing the audience with an entertaining display of gymnastic feats as an interval in the action of the play. Their technique consists chiefly of incredible hand springs, cartwheels and dives over various objects or they twirl metal bars about with lightning speed and perform dizzy gyrations on one leg. Their bodies literally appear to be made of rubber and they leap about with the agility of monkeys and land on their feet as delicately as cats, until the audience is breathless with their antics.

THE PLAYS
OF THE CHING HSI

THE plays of the *ching hsi* are arbitrarily divided into *wen hsi* and *wu hsi*, as we have already seen, the former being concerned with domestic and social affairs and the latter with military events, the exploits of brigands and the like, both styles being intermingled if necessary to suit the dramatic occasion. The plots of a great number of plays are drawn from two sources of paramount importance, the novels *San Kuo Chih Yen I*, or *Romance of the Three Kingdoms* and *Shui Hu Chuan, The Water's Edge.* * Both these celebrated works have been the subject of a good deal of research, argument and speculation among Chinese scholars and literary historians and it is not intended here to record the various detailed theories which have been set out. The Yüan (1280–1368) and Ming (1368–1644) dynasties are attributed as the periods in which these works were created, and the names of several writers are associated with them by Chinese authorities. Whatever the real facts of authorship may be, it seems fairly obvious now that the writers were largely responsible for compiling in literary style tales and collections of tales, which already existed in oral and written form and had been handed down for generations long before certain individuals refined and perfected them as popular novels.

The Romance of the Three Kingdoms commences with an account of a tottering throne, the machinations of scheming ministers and generals and exploits of military heroes. It deals with that period in Chinese history when the Eastern Han dynasty (A.D. 25–220) was succeeded by the period called *San Kuo* or Three Kingdoms (A.D. 220–265). At the end of the reign of the Emperor Hsiao Ling Ti, China was thrown into a state of confusion by a rebellion and internal wars, from the chaos of which arose three leaders, Liu Pei of Shu, Ts'ao Ts'ao of Wei and Sun

---

* Generally referred to in English as *The Water Margin*, which always seems a clumsy title to this writer.

Ch'ien of Wu. The exploits of these three men and their various followers form the basis of the novel and have inspired the plays called *San Kuo hsi* which have taken their themes from it. In the matter of historical accuracy it should be remembered that the novel often deviates from true facts and the plays doubly so, for in them the playwright is chiefly concerned with dramatic effect at the expense of everything else. Among the many plays which make up the *San Kuo* repertoire one of the most famous is *Ch'ün Ying Hui* or *The Meeting of Many Heroes*, a lengthy drama which actually consists of six distinct episodes, some of them now performed singly, each episode under its own name. Before describing these in any detail a short outline of events and people portrayed in the novel itself will be useful as a background when considering the *San Kuo* plays.

In the story Ts'ao Ts'ao is the villain of the piece, a traitorous Minister and usurper of great perspicacity and cunning. He murdered the Emperor's wife and her brother and married his own daughter into the royal family as Empress. Liu Pei, opposed to these nefarious schemes, was defeated in battle by T'sao T'sao who captured his two wives and Kuan Kung, a sworn blood brother. Ts'ao Ts'ao employed the tactics of winning men of ability to his cause by treating them kindly when in his power or else offering bribery. He attempted to gain the allegiance of Kuan Kung in this fashion, but he would have none of it and managed to make his way back to Liu Pei, escorting the wives, breaking through five barriers and smiting down six of Ts'ao Ts'ao's great generals in the exploit. Later Liu Pei sought audience in a humble hut of the learned recluse Chu-Ko Liang, whom he finally asked to be his generalissimo and help in directing the affairs of the Shu kingdom. Chu-Ko Liang was a strategist of great repute who, by his cunning, defeated the forces of Ts'ao Ts'ao at Hsin Yeh. Because of the numerical strength of his opponent's forces Liu Pei had fled to the kingdom of Wu for protection under Sun Chuan, the second son of Sun Ch'ien. During the period of conflict Liu Pei's infant son was rescued from Ts'ao Ts'ao's clutches by the brave general Chao Tzu-lung. Sun Chuan had two advisers Chou Yü and Lu Su while Huang Kai and Kan Ning were his chief generals. Chou Yü was a clever but narrow-minded young man who became jealous of his rival Chu-Ko Liang and his uncanny power: he tried to discredit his rival, but in vain, and eventually Chou Yü died from rage and despair. During this time the old general Huang Kai had been despatched as a pretended traitor to Ts'ao Ts'ao's camp, part of the scheme being to fire the fleet of the Wei leader. Both the land and sea forces of Ts'ao Ts'ao were defeated and he himself fled to the Hua Yung pass where he pleaded so well with Kuan Kung who guarded it, that the latter allowed the defeated leader to escape with his life. Later Liu Pei had a dispute with the leader of Wu over territory which he refused to give up and which was guarded by Kuan Kung. The latter was killed by an agent of Wu, and Chang Fei, the second sworn blood brother of Liu Pei, tried to avenge his death but was himself murdered. Liu Pei sent his forces against Wu in revenge but using fire, his opponents inflicted a crushing defeat on him. On the death of Liu Pei his strategist Chu-Ko Liang supported the son of his late leader and they joined forces with Wu in a combined attempt to destroy the power of Wei under Ts'ao Ts'ao. The latter died and was succeeded by his son Ts'ao P'ei who placed himself on the throne. The general Ssu Ma-i guarded the territory of Wei and in him Chu-Ko Liang met his match for, unable to inflict a defeat, he withdrew his armies and died a heartbroken man. The son of Ssu Ma-i later assumed supereme power in Wei and united what had once been three separate kingdoms as an entity.

As can be seen from this very sketchy outline, the novel portrays a background of plot and counter plot with the complex psychological delineation of ministers, general and warriors who seem interminable in their numbers. The theatre has drawn upon all this to provide plays which emphasize the technique of stage fighting and colourful action, departing from identical interpretation where dramatic effect warrants it and ignoring chronological arrangement.

The Meeting of Many Heroes, *Ch'ün Ying Hui*, in its various episodes provides a representative array of some of the most important and interesting personalities of the *San Kuo* romance. The first episode is generally called *She Chan Ch'un Ju*, *A Battle of Words with a Gathering of the Literati*. Chu-Ko Liang was invited to a conference at headquarters in the state of Wu. His master Liu Pei was considering an alliance in view of his retreat before Ts'ao Ts'ao who had mobilized a gigantic army and was making a rapid advance against his opponents. As a test, the gathering at the Wu headquarters tried to belittle Liu Pei and his cause while picking holes in Chu-Ko Liang's schemes. The latter talked so convincingly and showed such erudition that he quickly silenced his critics and proved the soundness of his strategy in spite of the brilliant verbal opposition.

The second episode *Chiang Kan Tao Shu*, *Chiang Kan Steals the Letter*, features a clever ruse of Chou Yü, the brilliant but jealous young adviser of the Wu stage. Chiang Kan, Ts'ao Ts'ao's secretary and a childhood friend of Chou Yü, came from across the river one day ostensibly to visit his old acquaintance. Chou Yü on hearing this was secretly pleased for he realised there was an ulterior motive behind it all. He hastily wrote out a letter over the forged signatures of the two admirals of Ts'ao Ts'ao's fleet and placed it among the official papers on his desk before going out to welcome Chiang Kan. The latter had actually been sent to persuade Chou Yü to surrender, but he was given no chance to talk for his host pretended that he was glad to see an old friend at a meeting of so many heroes and ordered his followers to kill any man who started talking politics on such an auspicious occasion. After showing his guest round the camp Chou Yü gave a banquet at which a great quantity of wine was consumed, although in actual fact both host and guest secretly emptied their cups on the floor. After the feast Chou Yü simulated intoxication by doing a spirited dance with his sword and singing a military song before they retired for the night. Once everything was quiet and Chou Yü seemingly sunk in drunken slumber, Chiang Kan got up and searched his host's quarters by candlelight. Finding the forged letter on Chou Yü's desk he opened it and amazed at what he read, slipped it inside his sleeve, hastily stole out of the camp and escaped across the river back to Ts'ao Ts'ao's headquarters. He delivered the letter to his master who was filled with anger on reading that, according to the document, his two chief admirals were secretly plotting against him and were supposed to deliver Ts'ao Ts'ao's head to Chou Yü within seven days. Ts'ao Ts'ao ordered his admirals to be beheaded immediately and so Chou Yü by his ruse disposed of two important tacticians on the enemy side. The part of Chou Yü is a favourite one for the *hsiao sheng* actor for whom it offers full scope in his technique. It is a role in which the actor Yü Chen-fei excels, giving full play to the subtle shades of facial expression and gesture which mark the occasion. Chiang Kan is an important role for the *ch'ou* actor.

The third episode also concerns Chou Yü, but portrays him in a less favourable light being outwitted by the strategist Chu-Ko Liang, sent to work with him against Ts'ao Ts'ao who had discovered the trick played upon him and his admirals. Chou Yü feared the power of Chu-Ko Liang and being bitterly jealous, he decided the occasion was ripe to discredit him. He asked Chu-Ko Liang to have one hundred thousand arrows made within ten days ready to attack the new invasion fleet being prepared by Ts'ao Ts'ao. Chu-Ko Liang thereupon said he would procure the arrows in three days. Chou Yü, secretly rejoicing, made his rival sign an order verifying his promise and agreeing to suffer the extreme penalty if he failed to comply, for, said Chou Yü, there could be no joking about serious military affairs. He was sure that Chu-Ko Liang would not be able to complete such a superhuman task and had therefore signed his own death warrant. For two days Chu-Ko Liang did absolutely nothing and on the third day Lu Su, a good natured member of Chou Yü's retinue, went to see how he was getting on. Chu-Ko Liang simply asked for twenty war boats, a large quantity of straw and a few hundred men. That evening he invited Lu Su to accompany him in a boat on the river. Each vessel was thickly built up with straw and Chu-Ko Liang ordered them to be rowed towards the enemy bank through a thick mist which had now come down over the water's expanse. The boats were moored within arrow shot of Ts'ao Ts'ao's headquarters, a long row in mid-stream, and Chu-Ko Liang ordered his men to beat gongs and drums and cry out as though they were an attacking force. Ts'ao Ts'ao's men hearing the din and being unable to see through the mist fired their arrows in the direction of the noise. When the straw-filled boats were thickly planted with arrows on one side Chu-Ko Liang ordered them to be turned round in order to receive the arrows on the other side until eventually both sides were a bristling mass. All this time Chu-Ko Liang and Lu Su were drinking wine in the cabin of one of the boats but while the strategist quaffed his wine calmly, Lu Su was terror stricken and trembling and poured his drink anywhere but in his mouth. This scene never fails to raise a laugh from the audience. The boats returned to their base at dawn and were found to have collected not only the hundred thousand arrows but another thirty thousand to spare. Even the jealous Chou Yü was forced to congratulate Chu-Ko Liang on his success but he only smiled and remarked that he was grateful to Ts'ao Ts'ao for the generous loan. When asked how he knew there would be a mist over the great Yangtze river, Chu-Ko Liang merely answered, 'If a strategist knows nothing of astronomy how can he be competent?' This episode in the main drama is named *Ts'ao Ch'uan Chieh Chien*.

The fourth episode, *Ta Huang Kai*, *Beating Huang Kai*, features yet one more trick of Chou Yü. Ts'ao Ts'ao sent two of his followers as spies to the Wu headquarters where they were received as guests by Chou Yü who realized their intentions, although on Ts'ao Ts'ao's instructions, they pretended to surrender themselves with a feigned grudge against their leader. Chou Yü, having first arranged matters with his faithful lieutenant, the ageing general Huang Kai, ordered the old man to be flogged for a trivial error in front of Ts'ao Ts'ao's men. After this Huang Kai simulated disloyalty to his chief and secretly conferred with the two spies, telling them of his intention to decamp with a squadron of boats laden with provisions and supplies and join Ts'ao Ts'ao's forces. This was reported in secret to Ts'ao Ts'ao, who was deceived by the apparent dissension in the enemy camp. In fact Chou Yü's idea was for Huang Kai to take boats filled with incendiary materials which would be fired at the right moment and so destroy Ts'ao Ts'ao's fleet by the resulting blaze. In the meantime Chou Yü had despatched a famous wise man and hermit, Pang Tung, to Ts'ao Ts'ao's camp to advise him to lash his boats together in groups in order to make it easier for Ts'ao Ts'ao's crews, all Northerners and unaccustomed to life afloat, to perform their daily tasks. Ts'ao Ts'ao, falling into the various traps, agreed to the schemes.

The ensuing series of events is covered by the two episodes *Chieh Tung Feng*, *Calling the Wind from the South-east* and *Huo Shao Chan Ch'uan*, *Burning the Battle Fleet*. Chu-Ko Liang, although not informed by Chou Yü of the intended plot, nevertheless had noted what was going on and understood everything. Chou Yü invited his rival to his headquarters one day and in the presence of Lu Su, asked him for his opinions on the method of attacking Ts'ao Ts'ao and received the reply there was only one possible way. Forbidding Chu-Ko Liang to state it Chou Yü then hastily wrote a character on the palm of his own hand hinting at the proposed scheme, and asked Chu-Ko Liang to do the same. When the two men held up their palms each had written the character for fire. This is a famous scene in the play calling for subtle gesture and posing. Chou Yü was astonished that Chu-Ko Liang had reached the same conclusion as himself, but decided that he was even more dangerous as a rival than he had feared. Some day later while out of doors reconnoitring, he suddenly realized that a strong winter wind was blowing from the north-west which in view of the relative position of the two camps would utterly defeat his scheme to destroy Ts'ao Ts'ao's fleet and overcome with exasperation, he had a stroke and had to be carried back. Physicians failed to diagnose his ailment but Chu-Ko Liang declared that he understood what the trouble was and could cure the sick man. He wrote some lines of verse saying that the lack of a strong wind from the south-east was responsible for Chou Yü's breakdown. Chou Yü admitted the truth of this diagnosis and Chu-Ko Liang then told him not to worry, he would procure the south-east wind for he knew how to command the elements. He ordered a high three-storied terrace to be built in the hills over-looking the river and wearing his Taoist robes he ascended the terrace and by prayers and spells brought the desired winds. Chou Yü, now convinced that Chu-Ko Liang far surpassed him in ability, sent two men to kill the strategist and sorcerer, but when the assassins arrived their quarry had already fled, for he had anticipated the attempt on his life, and a small boat had been sent to convey him back to the Shu headquarters. Huang Kai achieved his object that night in the great battle of the Red Cliff, when, owing to the gale from the south-east and the ruse by which the boats were lashed together, the whole of Ts'ao Ts'ao's fleet was destroyed and his army routed on land and river.

The last episode in the cycle of events is named in the drama *Hua Jung Tao*, the *Flight to the Jung Tao pass*. Chu-Ko Liang held a council when he arrived back at his own quarters and commissioned various people to guard all routes and mountain passes by which Ts'ao Ts'ao was likely to escape. He left Kuang Kung until the last in order to arouse both eagerness and resentment in that brave warrior and finally sent him to guard the

Jung Tao pass. Chu-Ko Liang had learned through astronomical signs that Ts'ao Ts'ao was not yet destined to die and so he purposely provided the opportunity for Kuan Kung to spare the fugitive's life as his had been spared by Ts'ao Ts'ao in the past. Ts'ao Ts'ao arrived at the pass a weary and broken man with a handful of men scorched by the flames. Seeing Kuan Kung barring his way the wily old minister shed tears and in a trembling voice piteously pleaded with Kuan Kung to remember his friendly act in the past. Filled with compassion at seeing the mighty fallen and respecting justice, Kuan Kung allowed Ts'ao Ts'ao to escape. Chu-Ko Liang, with his tongue in his cheek, ordered Kuan Kung to be punished, but Liu Pei pleaded earnestly on behalf of his foster brother.

There are many other *San Kuo* dramas besides the cycle described above in which some or all of the personalities named figure with many more besides. These plays provide great scope for the *ching* actor in his various styles, a lesser number of them lay emphasis on the kind of singing roles which are the speciality of the *sheng* actors. Women appear infrequently in the *San Kuo* plays. It is worth while looking at some of the important characters who figure on the stage in this romantic interpretation of a turbulent period in the ancient history of China. Ts'ao Ts'ao is the epitome of treachery, cunning and resourcefulness and yet there are more likeable qualities noticeable at times. His face is painted the matt white which symbolizes an evil character, with thin black lines round the eyes, nose and cheeks. They represent wrinkles of cunning which are increased the greater his age depicted. He wears a full black beard and his costumes tend to be of a single colour. He sings and speaks with the powerful vocal technique customary to the *ching* actor, his shoulders are tremendously broad, he wears special padding beneath his costume for the purpose, and his whole demeanour must express cruelty and cunning but courage as well. A good interpreter of Ts'ao Ts'ao must be tall and have both the physical and technical qualifications which enable him to play this role. He usually wears the hat known as *hsiang tiao*, a square, black doubled crowned head-dress with long 'fins' protruding from either side at the rear. This is a symbol of a prime minister. If depicted in his younger days the hat has a rounded double crown with two large leaf-shaped 'fins' protruding and this signifies he has not yet attained the highest rank. Chu-Ko Liang is China's supreme strategist and wise man of all time. The actor appearing in this role wears a long robe, the *pa kua i*, which is either of a rich purple or deep blue and patterned in gold with *pa kua*, the eight diagrams or mystic symbols of Taoism. In his hand he carries a feather fan. He wears a black beard, his face bears scarcely any make up and he wears the wedge-shaped hat of a Taoist official which bears the *t'ai chi t'u*, another mystic symbol, on the front. Chu-Ko Liang, also sometimes known as Kung Ming, has a calm, unruffled and scholarly bearing that must be conveyed by the actor playing the part which is a *sheng* role. He must therefore have a good singing voice and one play in which Chu-Ko Liang is the central figure, *K'ung Ch'eng Chi, The Strategy of an Unguarded City*, has a leading place in the repertoire of every *sheng* actor worthy of the name.

Liu Pei is shown on the stage as a brave and loyal leader of the house of Han, liked by his people and with a strong attachment to his two foster brothers Kuan Kung and Chang Fei for whom he shows affectionate concern. At times he gives evidence of more selfish motives and the ability of a politician to manoeuvre himself one step nearer the throne. The actor playing the role wears a black beard and no facial make-up. In some plays he wears Imperial robes of scarlet embroidered with gold dragons and his hat is of gold and covered with crimson silk pom-poms. On the battlefield he wears a riding habit, carries a whip and has a cloth hood over his head. The play *Ch'ang Pan P'o* which depicts the flight of Liu Pei after being defeated by Ts'ao Ts'ao shows Liu Pei in the costume first described. The two wives of Liu Pei appear in this drama, on the battlefield and under the protection of Chao Tzu-lung, one of the Liu Pei's five tiger generals. The actor who portrays this general wears no beard but his face is made up to suggest the clear complexion of a courageous youth. He wears stage armour which is of white satin embroidered in black and carries a white hafted spear decorated with a white silken tassel. He must be well versed in gymnastics and stage fighting, singing being less important; it is therefore a role for the *wu sheng* actor and one in which the actor Yang Hsiao-lou gave distinguished performances and was much beloved by Chinese audiences in the past.

One of the most intriguing characters on the *ching hsi* stage

G

must be Chang Fei, one of Liu Pei's two sworn blood brothers. He is depicted as a rash and impulsive character, rough and ready but good hearted and intensely loyal, with a tendency to fly into towering rages. The actor playing the role wears a long black beard with two impish tufts of hair sticking up above the ears, his face is painted in a complex pattern of black and white with scarlet lips and pink on the cheeks if shown in his youth. To represent the passing of the years the black pattern on the upper part of his face is painted in grey. The curved lines of the design are said to be based on the form of a butterfly and the design is regarded as one of the most difficult ones to paint. Chang Fei leaps and roars around the stage like a whirlwind, stopping occasionally to strike a bold pose in which he pulls the strands of his long beard towards the heavens and twirls the tufts of hair above his ears with two fingers while rolling his eyes in a fury. It is a notable part for the *ching* actor and a great favourite with theatregoers.

Kuan Kung, the other sworn blood-brother of Liu Pei, is a very different character for so deeply is he revered, that he has literally become a deity, being recognised as the God of War as well as a theatrical divinity to whom, in the very recent past, it was still customary for actors to pay respect, and there were many traditions and superstitions associated with the Kuan Kung role. The role of Kuan Kung is a special one which certain actors have been noted for alone; the part requires singing ability and an equal talent for the vigorous technique of military action. The singing style is a little different from that of the ordinary *sheng* actor, being more robust and requiring lower tones. Besides this the actor should have a commanding presence and display great majesty in his bearing and movements. He is also expected to justify his role off stage both in his personal character and habits: a Chinese critic describing a famous Kuan Kung actor, Lin Shu-shen, who died in Shanghai in 1925 at the age of seventy-six, said that he would not allow himself to be photographed in the stage dress of the role because of his reverence for the hero he portrayed. The costume and make-up is a striking one. The face is painted a brilliant scarlet only relieved by a few thin black lines traced round the nose and eyes. The beard is long, full and black, though towards the end of his days it is shown as greying. The actor wears stage armour of green silk embroidered with gold thread and bordered by an orange fringe and carries a large curved blade with a long haft, the *kuan tao* or green dragon blade as it is called. He is often followed by an attendant who carries a green silk banner embroidered with the character *kuan*. There are a whole series of *Kuan Kung* plays including five which are related to each other and based on only one portion of the *San Kuo* romance. There are many other aspects of the *San Kuo Hsi* which it is not possible to consider here, but this outline touches on some of the main features of a group of dramas which, in many ways, can be said to constitute the very backbone of the *ching hsi*, providing, as they do, some of its most colourful roles.

The second source of many important plays mentioned at the beginning of the chapter, the *Shui Hu Chuan*, is a novel of a very different kind. Its background is the China of the eleventh century during the Sung dynasty (A.D. 960–1279): it deals with a period when a great reform programme, devised by the statesman Wang An-shih and supported by the Emperor Shen tsung (1067–85), had come to grief through the sabotage of the ultra-conservative members of the ruling caste, forcing the ordinary people to suffer the more extreme abuses of Confucian traditionalists once again. Their indifference to the common welfare caused many kinds of people to withdraw from ordinary walks of life and try to remedy the social evils in much the same way as the English Robin Hood and his men. The number of these chivalrous outlaws was one hundred and eight and they gathered round the edge of the lake at Liang Shan Po where they performed daredevil deeds, robbing and killing the oppressors and helping the oppressed as well as slaying fierce tigers. Their prevailing philosophy was the celebrated maxim 'All are brothers within the Four Seas'. The novel is a long one full of realistic detail with psychological interpretations, and of deeds of valour skilfully related. During the centuries it has attracted the attention of many writers, scholars and commentators and there have been several editions as well as additions to the story. It is not surprising that this enormous work, of which it would be true to say that practically every Chinese has either read or listened to its exciting stories in his time, was responsible for the creation of a repertoire of plays which are distinguished for their portrayal of swashbuckling heroes, fierce swordsmen and the trials and tribulations of the ordinary people. Like the *San Kuo Hsi*, the *Shui Hu* plays are also full of colourful painted face characters, although of a somewhat different type. A perennial favourite of the *Shui Hu* play cycle is *Ta Yü Sha Chia*, *A Fisherman's Revenge* or literally *A Fisherman Slays a Family*. It was also sometimes called *Ch'ing Ting Chu*, *The Lucky Pearl*. This play is popular with everybody, with the new China as much as the old, its theme being highly approved, and it received great praise in Russia when it was staged by Mei Lan-fang on his visit to that country in 1935. The story is as follows. Hsiao En, who had formerly been one of the chivalrous bandits, in his old age became a fisherman and lived in a small hut by the river. He was very poor and his wife was dead but he had a beautiful daughter Kuei Ying, who was betrothed to Hua Feng-ch'un, the son of his old friend. As a memento the Hua family had presented the fisherman with a rare pearl, *ch'ing ting chu*, a lucky jewel to be worn on the crown of the head. When the play opens the fisherman and his pretty daughter are shown on the river in their boat. This is indicated with the customary symbolism, the actors holding a wooden paddle and making the motion of rowing while they are singing. The play provides good roles for the *sheng* and *ch'ing i* actors who take the principal parts and there is a good deal of singing by the two characters in the course of the play.

Mei lan-fang is noted for his delightful interpretation of the part of Kuei Ying with the *sheng* actor, Wang Shao-lou as the fisherman. While Hsiao En and his daughter are mooring their boat two old friends, Ni Jung and Li Chun, also members of the band of valiant outlaws, appear on the river bank to greet their old comrade and are invited into the boat to share an evening meal of newly caught fish and some wine with the fisherman and his daughter. As they are merrily eating and drinking, a messenger from the local landlord appears to demand payment of a fishing tax levied solely on his own authority. Hsiao En replies that he has no money just now, and he and his two companions become annoyed at the messenger's overbearing attitude. One of them, Li Chun, shouts at the messenger that he had better tell his master to waive the tax as it is quite illegal and make arrangements with the local magistrate to ensure this is done, otherwise, he, Li Chun, will make it hot for him. The terrified messenger flees back to his master and tells him what has happened. The fisherman's two friends after consoling with him go off saying they will procure money to enable their friend to pay the tax in case of trouble. The landlord flies in a rage when he hears what has transpired and sends four professional boxers and strong men to deal with the unruly fisherman. A fracas follows in which the fisherman, in spite of his age, gives the four men a sound thrashing and they take to their heels. Realizing that trouble will follow, Hsiao En goes off to the local magistrate's yamen to lodge his complaint, but is simply flogged with forty strokes and told to go and apologize to the landlord next day. Hsiao En returns wearily home in the evening to be met by his daughter who is distressed by her father's absence. That night the two of them proceed to the landlord's mansion under pretence of giving him their precious pearl, allegedly fished out of the river, as an offering. Once alone with their persecutor they take out sharp swords and Hsiao En slays the evil landlord: the two of them then dispatch their victim's bodyguard who arrive in force to seize them and make off into the night, Kuei Ying to join her betrothed and her father to take to a bandit's life once again. This is the gist of the old version: there may well be new twists given to the present one but that the writer is unable to say. The play is a swift moving one, partly a burlesque, and has always delighted audiences for the quality of the singing in the *sheng* and *tan* roles, as well as for the repartee and knockabout comedy that ensues in the scenes with the landlord's minions, which acts as a foil to the social satire inherent in the play.

Other literary sources from which *ching hsi* plays have derived inspiration are novels like the great work *Hung Lou Meng, The Dream of the Red Chamber;* the famous tale *Hsi Yu Chi,* or *Trip to the Western Regions,* a dramatization of the introduction of Buddhism into China, and popular romantic works of the Ch'ing dynasty such as *Shih Kung An, Yang Chia Chang* and *Pao Kung An,* all dealing with periods in China's past history, must also be noted. There are also a number of plots borrowed from the *k'un ch'ü* drama and adapted to the particular style of the *ching hsi*. There are also the plays called *pen hsi*, dramas which have been written and devised within recent times for well known actors. These were based on old material and constructed for traditional methods of acting but were completely new in the *ching hsi* repertoire. Mei Lan-fang introduced a number of *pen hsi*, mostly devised for him by the critic and scholar Ch'i Ju-shan. Ch'eng Yen-ch'iu and Ma Lien-liang are other actors who have given their personal plays to the stage. One of Mei Lan-fang's *pen hsi*, *Tai Yü Tsang Hua*, *Tai Yü Burying the Flowers*, was adapted from *Hung Lou Meng*. Tai Yü was a beautiful young girl who, as she was an orphan, lived with her grandmother. She was poetic, highly emotional and in delicate health. She was also deeply in love with Pao Yü, her spoiled cousin, but it was considered improper to reveal their affections. One morning in spring she awoke full of melancholy because she had been denied admittance to Pao Yü's quarters the evening before and was filled with jealousy and doubt. It was actually a servant who had ignored the knocking on the young man's gate, thinking it was a joking maid. Tai Yü felt herself neglected and lonely like the falling petals of the late spring flowers and in this moody state she went out and gathered the blossoms and placed them in a bag suspended on the end of her small hoe. Then she proceeded to a corner of the garden where a mound was built as a burying place for the blossoms and here she reflected mournfully as to who would bury her in the event of her untimely death. Her lover meets her there and after explanations and accusations there is a reunion. The interest in this slight and romantically morbid piece on the stage lay in the graceful and delicate interpretation of a maiden's emotions and gestures by the master *tan* actor. It was first produced in 1915, and was one of the plays in which Mei Lan-fang introduced costume faithfully reproduced from ancient fashions, in contrast to the more conventionalized women's styles seen on the *ching hsi* stage.

In a chapter of this scope it would be impossible to give descriptions or a comprehensive list of plays from a repertoire that literally contains several hundred titles. The synopses which follow are of those plays which for one reason or another have been mentioned throughout the text, so that the reader will wish to know a little more about them. After these, one other play has been selected for analysis in some detail for the purpose of enabling the reader to relate various matters discussed in the chapters on music and technique with an actual drama as it is seen on the stage.

Chi Ku Ma Ts'ao (see p. 47).

This unique drama belongs to the *San Kuo Hsi* and is mentioned in the chapter on music as being one in which the actor personally must give a skilful performance on the *t'ang ku* or large drum. It depicts the conflict between two arrogant personalities, the scheming minister Ts'ao Ts'ao and a learned and eloquent scholar called Mi Heng. Ts'ao Ts'ao was trying to secure the allegiance of a celebrated general, Liu Piao, to his cause. In order to achieve his aim, he asked one of his followers to suggest a suitable man to send as an envoy to the general and was advised to use the scholar Mi Heng. The latter was a proud and obstinate man who secretly disliked Ts'ao Ts'ao but he obeyed the summons he received and presented himself at Ts'ao Ts'ao's court. When he arrived he was at first awestruck to see the panoply of the scheming minister and the display of weapons; he saluted Ts'ao Ts'ao who, however, reproached him for not kneeling when appearing before a superior. Mi Heng quickly took offence at this and proceeded to laugh contemptuously before the assembled gathering. When Ts'ao Ts'ao queried this strange behaviour, Mi Heng proceeded to revile the Minister to his face and to belittle his followers as being only of use to butcher pigs and dogs, beat drums and gongs and attend to minor public affairs. They were a worthless rabble, Mi Heng cried, but he himself was a man so illustrous in scholarship that he stood beside Confucius in virtue. Ts'ao Ts'ao curbed his anger and restrained his lieutenants who wanted to slay the arrogant scholar on the spot. Deciding to bring shame on Mi Heng, he stated that he was to give a banquet for his ministers on the morrow and as he was short of a drummer he offered the post to the scholar. The latter decided to insult the Minister further in public and accepted the offer. When he appeared at the banquet the next day he wore his shabbiest clothes and laughed on being remonstrated with by the officials. He then proceeded to the drum outside the banquet hall where he gave a spirited and skilful performance, after which he stripped naked and finally stalked before Ts'ao Ts'ao and the assembled guests who were horrified at the appearance of the perverse scholar. When asked the reason for his behaviour by Ts'ao Ts'ao, Mi Heng retorted that by showing his body he proved that he was a gentleman by birth, pure and immaculate. There was then a passage of words in which Mi

Heng continued to revile everybody present until they were on the point of having him killed. Ts'ao Ts'ao remained calm and finally managed to silence Mi Heng by saying that if he accepted the mission to General Liu Piao and accomplished it successfully he would be rewarded with a high official position. Mi Heng finally accepted the offer and departed with Ts'ao Ts'ao reflecting after he had gone, that such arrogance would probably soon cut short the life of the scholar.

This play is noted for its singing parts for both *ching* and *sheng* actors but one of the highlights is the scene where Mi Heng beats the drum. The actor playing the role must be able to give a spirited and accomplished rendering which the audience eagerly waits for. Mi Heng wears simple black trousers tucked into the black high-soled boots used by the *sheng* actor, and a black tunic tucked into the trousers. It has an open neck revealing a white stock and he wears no head-dress, the *wang tzu* (see the chapter on costume) only being seen. Round the waist a white skirt, of the type worn by the *ch'ing i*, is girdled so that it is caught up at the back of the actor's legs rather in the manner of a tail coat. This dress is the stage convention which represents his shabby condition. There is great dramatic power in the posing of the actor when he raises the drumsticks and the deep notes resound throughout the theatre while the sombre simplicity of his costume adds to the general effect.

Chin So Chi (See p. 22).
This play, *The Story of The Golden Locket*, was originally a *k'un ch'ü* drama which has undergone many changes since it was originally staged. It is also often referred to as *Liu Yueh Hsüeh*, *Snow in June*, or *Chan Tou O*, *The Execution of Tou O*.

Tou O, the pretty daughter of a good family, was betrothed to Ts'ai Ch'ang-tsung, the son of a court official. The bridegroom's family presented a golden locket as a token of the event. Shortly after the wedding young Ts'ai set out for Peking to compete in the Imperial examinations. He was accompanied by a servant Chang Lü-erh or Donkey Chang. Donkey Chang was an evil-minded fellow who cherished desires on his young mistress and while crossing the Huai river in a boat, he pushed his master overboard and returned with a story of death by misadventure. The mother of the ill-fated Ts'ai, striken with grief at the news, fell ill and, in her weak condition ,asked for some broth. Donkey Chang, with a view to achieving his evil desires, poisoned the broth in the hope of removing the last obstacle in his plot. The old lady smelt something suspicious about the broth however and refused it, whereupon the mother of Donkey Chang, being a thrifty soul, drank the broth herself and died almost immediately. Taking advantage of the accident the wily Chang accused his old mistress of poisoning his mother but made it known that if he was given Tou O in marriage he would say nothing further on the subject. The old lady refused and was dragged off to prison on the strength of Chang's accusations and tortured to make a confession. Tou O followed her mother-in-law to the courts and unable to bear the sight of the hardships inflicted on the prisoner, confessed that she herself had poisoned Donkey Chang's mother. The magistrates thereupon set the mother-in-law free and sentenced Tou O to death instead. The young wife was cast into jail where she suffered a great deal at the hands of a cruel woman jailer. She was visited by her sorrowing mother-in-law and the two women prayed together to heaven that justice would eventually be done. But the edict arrived from Peking ordering Tou O to be executed in the market place and she was led forth by the jailers to her death. It was a June day when she was dragged to the execution ground but, as the tragic company made its way along the streets, a biting winter gale blew up and heavy snow began to fall. A government official on tour in the district realized that the strange weather was a sign from the gods that Tou O was innocent. On making enquiries at the magistrate's office, a fresh trial was ordered. Tou O's neighbours, who had never been able to believe her guilty, presented a petition as the result of which Tou O was acquitted and the real criminal, Donkey Chang, convicted. Shortly afterwards, the husband of Tou O unexpectedly appeared: he had escaped drowning by a miracle and proceeded to the capital where he had secured high honours in the examinations. There was a happy reunion and all ended well after the many hardships and sorrows which had ensued since the betrothal commemorated by the golden locket. This play with its somewhat naïve plot is marked by the opportunities provided for the poignant singing in both the *tan* and *lao tan* roles represented by Tou O and her mother-in-law. There is a famous scene where Tou O is led to the execution block. She is dressed in scarlet tunic and trousers with white skirt over the top, a costume worn by condemned women on the stage. Her hands are bound behind her back to which is strapped a wooden tablet inscribed with characters signifying she is a condemned criminal and a corrupt woman. Jeering jailers escort her and there are some striking group poses accompanied by the pathetic songs of Tou O in *fan erh huang* tempo. A climax comes with the snowstorm, symbolized by small pieces of paper scattered over the stage. This scene is very often presented by itself under the title *Snow in June*, the melancholy singing and the posing of the character concerned having a special appeal to audiences.

Yü T'ang Ch'un, the Story of Su San the Courtesan

Su San is a stage character who has a great hold over the hearts of Chinese theatregoers and her story is said to have had a foundation in fact. The play is not often given in full today, but extracts are given from it under their own titles and are among some of the best loved pieces in the theatre. Two of the scenes most often staged are *Nü Ch'i Chieh*, *A Maiden Journeying under Arrest* and *San T'ang Hui Shen*, *Three Officials Hold Court*. The full story of the plot of *Yü T'ang Ch'un* is as follows. In Ming times there was a young scholar of Nanking called Wang Chin-lung who fell deeply in love with Su San, a beautiful sing-song girl at one of the houses of assignment. Su San returned his love and the two were blissfully happy, the young man building a pavilion *Yü T'ang Ch'un*, the *Happy Hall of Jade*, in the gardens of the house where they whiled away the lotus-eating hours. The mistress of the establishment took advantage of the young man's infatuation and bled him dry. When she saw that he had squandered all his means she turned him out on a bitter winter day. The young prodigal eventually took refuge in a temple where he eventually met Chin Ke, a flower vendor whom he had patronized in his prosperous days. The flower vendor offered to arrange a meeting with Su San, who he said still pined for her lover and the courtesan arrived at the temple one day on the pretext of making an offering to the gods. She wept bitter tears on seeing the plight of Wang Chin-lung and embracing him, presented him with three hundred ounces of silver which she had managed to smuggle out. With

Su San

this money she begged him to go to Peking and compete in the Imperial examinations, saying that she would wait for his triumphal return. They parted with tears but unfortunately on his way to the capital the young scholar was robbed and had to become a beggar. He returned to his old haunts and one day Su San recognized his voice pleading to the passers by outside: she hurried out and smuggled him up to her room where, on hearing his story, she gave him another sum of money and sent him on his way. This time Wang Chin-lung reached Peking safely, passed his examinations with honour and was appointed a circuit judge and inspector. In the meantime Su San, pining for her lover, refused to entertain guests any longer in the house of assignment, whose mistress decided to sell the girl off as soon as possible. A private deal was concluded with Shen Yen-lin, a rich merchant from Shanghai who had long coveted Su San. She was enticed to his home by a story that her lover Wang Chin-lung had been given an appointment and sent for her. Too late she found that she had been trapped and to make matters worse, the virago wife of the merchant, P'i Shih, hated the girl and finally attempted to kill her with a bowl of poisoned noodles. Su San had refused to eat since she entered the merchant's house and would not touch the noodles which Shen Yen-lin swallowed himself and dropped dead within a few minutes. His wife came rushing in on hearing Su San's shrieks and immediately accused the girl of murder. Su San was dragged off to the court where the merchant's wife liberally bribed the magistrate and unable to bear the pain of the flogging to which she was submitted, Su San confessed to her alleged crime. She was thrown into the cells to await confirmation of the death sentence from a higher court. While in the cells a fellow prisoner of Su San wrote out a true statement of her case which she managed to conceal on her person. Soon after an order came for her to proceed to the higher court at Tai Yüan for a new trial. It so happened that her lover Chin-lung had arrived at this town on circuit to examine all the cases referred to him by the various district magistrates. Su San set forth on her journey to Tai Yüan with her hands manacled in the *cangue* placed round her neck and accompanied by an old warder, Ch'ung Kung-tao, who took pity on his charge. He allowed her to take off the *cangue* and gave her his stick to help her on her weary way. In return for the old man's kindness Su San offered to be his adopted daughter, much to his delight. She asked him what was the best thing to do to ensure that the statement she carried would be seen by the judges, and the older warder told her to put it between the locking device of the *cangue*, where the paper would be seen as soon as she was released at the trial. While they were travelling along, Su San sang a song of hatred against everybody who had treated her so badly, crying that there was not a single honest man in the place from which they had come. The old warder interrupted her several times and finally became mortally offended by her condemnation which also reflected on him. Su San pacified him by skilfully concluding that there was one exception, her adopted father Ch'ung Kung-tao. They finally reached their destination and Su San was brought to trial the next day. Her petition dropped from the *cangue* when it was unlocked and was presented to the presiding judge, none other than Wang Chin-lung himself. He was supported by the provincial judge and the provincial treasurer, the former having an inkling as to the past relationship between the prisoner and his senior. He questioned Su San unmercifully about her personal life, much to the embarrassment of Wang Chin-lung who finally adjourned the court in his mortification at the insinuations made by the provincial judge. That evening he disguised himself and visited Su San in the cells and the provincial judge, anticipating this move, also visited the cells at the same time on a pretended tour of inspection. There was a denouement in which the provincial judge threatened to impeach his senior but was eventually dissuaded by the more tolerant treasurer who said that such lovers deserved a better fate. The case closed with the real criminals brought to justice and Su San and her lover being married in the presence of the whole court under the direction of Wang Chin-lung's colleagues. The trial scene in this play calls for some arduous singing on the part of the actor playing Su San who, on her bended knees before the judges, must sing her past life for an hour or more, a feat which only the most skilful *tan* actors accomplish successfully, as it requires great stamina as well as a first class voice. The journey scene with Su San and the old warder is a perennial favourite with Chinese audiences. Su San comes on wearing scarlet tunic and trousers with a white skirt folded back behind her legs, a white sash with a blue bordered design hangs down in front and a turquoise blue silk scarf is knotted round her head to hang in two wide folds at the right of her face, a costume accessory which symbolizes travelling out of doors. Her hair is studded with plain silver ornaments and hangs down in two long plaits. The *cangue* is in the form of a silver metal fish, clamped round her neck with both hands manacled with silver chains and thrust up through the holes in the tail end of the fish which protrudes in front of her face. She wears dainty tasselled slippers and altogether is as decorative a prisoner as one could wish to see. The old warder walks with bent legs and a stoop and has a long white beard. He wears a simple blue gown with a yellow and blue sash knotted round his waist to hang down in front and on his head a black, red-tasselled hat of the type worn by minor officials in Ch'ing days. He carries a stave and has a small bundle round his shoulder. His face is made up with the comical white patch of the *ch'ou* actor. There is a celebrated opening in which the warder, wagging a reproving finger at Su San, exclaims:

Ni shuo ni kung tao,
Wo shuo wo kung tao,
Kung tao pu kung tao,
Tzu yu t'ien chih tao,

'You say you want to take one way, I say I want to take the other way. Whichever way is right only heaven knows'. The comic speech and bearing, yet fatherly kindness, of Ch'ung Kung-tao, makes a notable contrast with the charming but tragic figure of Su San in this interlude, which provides great scope for the pathetic style singing of the *ch'ing i* role as well as some of the coquetry associated with the *hua tan*.

Huo Cho Chang San-lang, Catching Chang
San-lang Alive (see p. 77).
This is a ghost play which originally came from the *k'un ch'ü* drama. The story concerns Chang San-lang, a scholar who, sitting over his books late one night, was visited by the ghost of his former mistress, a courtesan. The maiden was formerly the paramour of Chang San-lang's teacher who had tired of the girl and finally killed her when he discovered that she had read a letter which revealed his identity as a member of a secret society. She died with her love for Chang San-lang still ardent within, and so her spirit returned from the other world to fetch him to join her. After a terrifying chase the ghost finally strangled the scholar whose rigid corpse was found by servants the next morning. The part of Chang San-lang is one for a *ch'ou* actor, but the comedy in this case borders on the nightmarish and the play is noted for the facial expressions and contortions which the master actor uses in his representation of the fear and agony of a ghost-haunted man. The only musical accompaniment is a flute whose clear high notes heighten the dramatic effect. The spirit of the dead maiden is a striking figure with long black tresses and a deathly white make-up relieved by a scarlet gash painted down the centre of her forehead. Clusters of long strips of white paper hang from beneath either ear, a stage convention for a ghost. Her costume consists of a white skirt and white tunic whose *shui hsiu*, or water sleeves, hang practically to the ground, the arms of the actor being held rigidly against the sides, another convention adopted for ghosts. When making an appearance the actor makes three rapid gyrations, a reminder that spirits are supposed to ride on

Chang San-lang

whirlwinds, and moves swiftly round the stage with the arms still held to the sides but the body leaning forward or sideways at a steep angle. The effect of the supernatural is most effectively realized and the play is intensely dramatic in its symbolic action. A characteristically humorous touch relieves the tension at the conclusion of the play when the body of the dead Chang San-lang is picked up, the actor playing the part holds himself rigid as an iron rod and in this fashion is held aloft above the heads of the men who carry him off the stage.

Ssu Lang T'an Mu

The play which follows has been selected for descriptive analysis for several reasons. In the first place it used to be one of the most popular dramas on the Peking stage. Its airs would always set heads swaying and voices humming, while some of the most famous actors of the last century have graced its roles to delight the hearts of Chinese theatregoers. Today it is not performed because, according to the authorities, it is no longer wanted by theatregoers. This means presumably that authority has decreed this to be so, the reason being according to official pronouncement that 'the play projects a concept of personal virtue that is quite compatible with attachment to alien rulers against one's own people. Both performers and audiences now see that this is a harmful distortion of the proper relation between public duty and personal sentiment, so they no longer like the play.' Whether they now do or not, *Ssu Lang T'an Mu* makes full use of the different roles and traditional techniques of the *ching hsi* theatre of which it may be said to be a typical play.

The plot of *Ssu Lang T'an Mu* is taken from a well known romantic novel of the Ch'ing period called *Yang Chia Chang*. The book tells the story of the Yang family during the Sung dynasty (A.D. 960–1279) but many of the legends incorporated are said to have first become popular during Yuan times (A.D. 1280–1368). The play was one which the actor T'an Hsin-p'ei made particularly famous and the technical descriptions given here are based on his version. Later actors have introduced their own variations without deviating from the general form of the plot, a common occurrence in *ching hsi* plays. This is especially noticeable in the texts of plays when actors often substitute words of similar meaning to suit their own preference. The outline of the story of the play follows and afterwards a detailed technical description of the opening of the play with relation to the musical forms and the techniques of the actor.

During the reign of the Emperor T'ai Tsung (A.D. 976–97), General Yang Chi-yeh and his eight sons embarked on a campaign against the Mongols which finally ended in a bloody battle where many perished and the fourth son Yen Hui was taken prisoner by the enemy. When the Empress Dowager of the Mongols saw her captive she was greatly pleased with the young man and finally gave him her attractive daughter, the Princess of the Iron Mirror, in marriage. Yen Hui did not reveal his identity when he was taken prisoner and gave his name as Ssu Lang under which pseudonym he lived with his Mongolian wife for fifteen years. A child was born to them near the end of this period and it is at this point that the play opens. One day Ssu Lang heard that his mother and sixth brother had launched a new campaign against the Mongols and that at that moment they were actually within travelling distance. As he sat in the palace he reflected sadly on his long exile and bewailed the fate which brought his old mother so near and yet prevented him meeting her. The tears came to his eyes and while he was sunk in grief, his wife, accompanied by a maid carrying their infant, entered the room where he was sitting. His troubled bearing was immediately noticeable to her and she pressed him to tell her the reason of his sorrow. At first trying to pass it off, Ssu Lang finally agreed to let her guess what was on his mind, and after several attempts she finally succeeded. Ssu Lang then revealed to her all the details of his story and although the Princess was astonished by what she heard, she was none the less very sympathetic and promised that she would devise a way for him to visit his mother provided he promised to return before daybreak, and this Ssu Lang swore to do. To pass through the Mongol lines it was necessary for Ssu Lang to possess the mandate arrow issued for safe conduct by the Empress Dowager herself, but it was quite impossible to ask for this, circumstances being what they were, and so the princess thought of a ruse. She went to the Empress's apartments carrying her baby and, once inside, pinched it violently so that the child howled at the top of its voice. The Empress Dowager, anxious for its welfare, asked what ailed the child. She was told that the baby was howling because it could not have the precious arrow of mandate to play with, and being a very indulgent grandmother, she handed the token over with the instruction that it must be returned to her before the next morning. The Princess hastily handed the arrow over to her husband in secret and sped him on his way with injunctions to remember his promise. Ssu Lang was quickly through the Mongol lines and rode swiftly through the night, but approaching the Chinese lines he was captured by a young officer, in reality his own nephew, aud taken before the commanding general who turned out to be none other than his own brother. He was recognized and there was a happy reunion in the inner camp where he met his white-haired mother once again as well as his former wife, now living as a widow, and other members of the family. Happiness was short lived when they heard his story and the conditions which attached to his visit. It was long after midnight when Ssu Lang amidst tearful pleas and entreaties finally broke away from his family and said a sad farewell before he rode away towards the Mongol lines. The Empress Dowager had discovered the ruse during his absence and Ssu Lang was arrested immediately he arrived back and dragged before his angry mother-in-law. He was sentenced to death but the Princess interceded on his behalf. The Empress was at first adamant but eventually her human feelings got the better of her and she pardoned her son-in-law, ordering him to a command in the far North where there would be no possibility of him rejoining his own family again.

By no stretch of imagination could this plot be regarded as sophisticated and it is a little difficult to take it as seriously as Chinese authorities apparently now do. The real interest in this play to theatregoers lies in the many opportunities for the different character roles, *sheng*, *ch'ing i*, *lao tan*, *ch'ou* and *hsiao sheng* are all featured with their various singing styles. In short it provides the audience with a generous measure of their favourite stage techniques and therefore dramatic entertainment.

When the play *Ssu Lang T'an Mu* opens the stage is bare except for a single chair on which is a cushion, set in the centre. The orchestra strikes up the prelude *ta lo ch'ung t'ou* followed by *hsiao lo ta shang* (see the chapter on music) and Ssu Lang makes his entry from the right of the stage, i.e. left of the audience. The part of Ssu Lang is a noted one for the *sheng* actor and the costume worn on entry is striking. The reader should refer to the chapter on technique for the technical names used in describing the costume here. The actor's robe is a scarlet *mang* with a dragon pattern, water sleeves and the *yu tai*, or jade girdle, round his waist. He wears the black silk boots with thick white soles called *kuan hsueh*. On his head is the black and round double-crowned hat called *sha mao* with its two 'fins' protruding at either side, but it is decorated with other accessories which make it different in appearance from its usual form. The crown

of the hat is decorated with *jung ch'iu*, silken pom poms, and surmounted by two sweeping *ling tzu* or pheasant feathers while *hu
wei*, white fox tails, hang from the rear of the hat down the back
of the actor. The headwear is referred to as *fu ma t'ao ch'ih*. Ssu
Lang's beard is black and of the style called *san jan*. The head-
dress and its accessories symbolize that although Ssu Lang is
Chinese he is also, at the time of the play, living as a Mongol or
Barbarian of high rank.

Ssu Lang after entering, walks across the stage with the
cheng pu, or normal pace of the *sheng* actor as described in the
chapter on technique. He walks over to *chiu lung k'ou*, nine
dragon's mouth, in front of the orchestra and standing to face the
audience performs *tou hsiu* (see p. 101) followed by *cheng kuan*.
The latter is a very characteristic gesture in which the actor
touches both temples with the fingers as though slightly
adjusting his hat. He then strokes his beard with the right hand,
i.e., *lü shu* (see p. 133). After this he holds the *tai tzu* lightly with
his left hand and walks slowly to the front centre of the stage
where he stands facing the audience and performs *tou hsiu* once
more with the right sleeve. He then recites the *yin tzu* which
consists of three sentences. After the first sentence the small gong
is beaten twice and after the second sentence there are two light
but quick taps on the drum. The words of the *yin tzu* follow.

> *Chin chin so wu t'ung,*
> *Ch'ang t'an sheng sui,*
> *I chen na feng.*

This might be translated as 'the wu t'ung tree locked in a golden
court yard, a long sigh carried away on the breeze'. The *wu t'ung*
is a tree famous in China where legend said that it was the only
one on which the sacred phoenix roosted. In this instance Ssu
Lang makes a rather poetic reference to himself as the tree. In
the *yin tzu* the first line is recited in the ordinary speaking voice
of the *sheng* actor but the second and third lines are half sung, the
last two words in the second line being drawn out while the
word *chen* in the third line is held for several syllables which rise
and fall. The *yin tzu* completed, there are two more beats on the
small gong, the actor places his right foot forward, turns left and
walks towards the chair at the centre of the stage in a line shaped
like an S. On arriving at the chair, he turns right face and seats
himself. He then recites the *tso ch'ang shih* (see p. 93) which

consists of four lines. The rhyming word at the end of each line should be noted.

> *Shih lo fan pang shih wu nien,*
> *Yen kuo heng yang ko i t'ien,*
> *Kao t'ang lao mu nan te chien,*
> *Tsen pu chao jen lui lien lien.*

The translation of this might read:

> 'Lost in a barbarian state for fifteen years,
> The wild geese come and go to other skies,
> It is difficult to meet my old mother,
> How can I not weep?'

After these words Ssu Lang lifts his sleeves to his eyes as though weeping, half rises in his seat, sits back and strokes his beard, then recites his name. This is the *t'ung ming* described on page 94.

> *Pen kung Ssu Lang Yen-hui.*

He lifts his hands in front of him, the knuckles of one clasped within the palm of the other and describes his father.

> *Wo fu Chin Tao Ling Kung.*

He raises his hands again then names his mother.

> *Wo mu She Shih T'ai Chün.*

> 'I am Ssu Lang Yen-hui
> M father is the honoured Chin Tao,
> My mother is the respected She Shih.'

It should be noted that the words *Ling Kung* and *T'ai Chün* are terms of rank and respect which find no exact equivalent in English.

He holds his *tai tzu* with both hands before continuing with his narrative.

> *Chih yin shih wu nien ch'ien,*
> *Sha T'an fu hui,*
> *Na i ch'ang hsüeh chan*
> *Chih sha te wo Yang chia ssu tsou t'ao wang,*
> *Pen kung pei ch'in.*

'Because of the meeting at Sha T'an fifteen years ago, that bloody battle, the Yang family suffered slaughter and those not killed, fled. I was taken prisoner.'

> *To meng T'ai Hou pu chan,*
> *Fan chang kung chu p'i p'ei.*
> *Tso jih shao fan pao tao,*

Hsiao T'en-tso tsai Chiu Lung Fei Ho Yu,
Pai hsia T'ien Men Ta Chen.

'I received many favours from the Empress Dowager who did not behead me, on the contrary she gave me the Princess as a wife. Yesterday a barbarian soldier reported General Hsiao T'ien Tso at Nine Dragons Flying Tiger Valley and he fought a battle at T'ien Men Ta Chen.'

Sung wang yü chia ch'in cheng,
Wo mu chieh ya liang ts'ao,
Yeh lai tao pei fang.

'The Sung Emperor himself was present, my mother was in charge of supplies and also came to this place . . .'

Wo yu hsin ch'ü tao Sung ying,
Chien mu i mien,
Tsen nai kuan chin tsu ke,
Ch'a chih yeh nan i fei kuo,
Ssu hsiang ch'i lai,
Hao pu shang kan,
Ai . . . . yen yeh.

'I yearn to visit the Sung camp and meet my mother face to face. How to cross the barrier which divides us, even if I had wings it would be difficult. When I think of it I am deeply moved. Ai . . . . . . (he gives a long drawn-out cry of anguish), alas for me.'

Ssu Lang then holds the right water sleeve with the left hand and lightly touches the right eye and then the left, symbolizing his weeping. The movement is performed neither too quickly not too slowly and the grace and timing of gestures such as these mark the accomplished actor. The *hu ch'in* now strikes up for the first time playing a *kuo men* passage in *hsi p'i man ban* tempo. During this interlude the actor may drink tea if he wishes, a characteristic scene on the *ching hsi* stage. The property man appears with a small teapot which in this case he offers from the left, the actor drinks from the spout but raises his right sleeve to conceal his face while drinking. Drinking tea by an actor during a performance is referred to in theatrical circles as *yin ch'ang*, literally 'watering the stage'. It is a time honoured custom which actors have adopted to ease the strain on their voices in much the same way as a speaker in the West will always have a carafe of water beside him. Ssu Lang then commences to sing in *hsi p'i man ban* style.

       Yang Yen-hui tso kung yuan.

Here there is a pause in the actor's song while a *hsiao kuo men* passage is played. The *hu ch'in* is accompanied by the *yueh ch'in*.

       Tzu ssu tzu t'an.

The word *t'an* at the end of this line is drawn out in a series of long syllables which rise and fall to the string accompaniment and at the end a *ta kuo men* passage is played before the actor proceeds with his song.

       Hsiang ch'i liao tang nien shih.

Another *hsiao kuo men* passage follows here.

       Hao pu ts'an jan.

Here follows a *ta kuo men* passage. The translation of the words of the song above reads:

       'Yang Yen-hui sits in the palace,
       And thinking to himself, sighs,
       Reflecting on the events of years ago,
       Sad and dispirited.'

His song continues.

       Wo hao pi lung chung niao,
       Yu chih nan chan.

A *ta kuo men* passage follows.

       Wo hao pi hu li shan,

A *hsiao kuo men* passage follows.

       Shou liao ku tan,

A *hsiao kuo men* passage follows.

       Wo hao pi nan lai yen,

The last word is drawn out at great length. A *hsiao kuo men* passage follows it.

       Shih ch'ün li san.
       Wo hao pi ch'ien shui lung,

A *hsiao kuo men* passage follows.

       K'un tsai sha t'an,
       Hsiang tang nien Sha T'an hui.

A *hsiao kuo men* passage follows this but the instruments change to *erh liu* timing. The translation of the continuation of the song above reads:

       'I am like a bird in a cage,
       I have wings but cannot stretch them,
       I am like a tiger forgotten in the mountains,

Alone and suffering.
I am like a wild goose come from the South
And lost from the flight.
I am like a dragon out of water
Surrounded by a sand bank.
I think of that year and the meeting at Sha T'an.'

All the time the actor has been singing this song he has been
seated: now, with the change in musical time, he rises and walks
to the front of the stage, the *t'ai k'ou*. Here he carries ou his
singing in *erh liu* style and the tempo quickens.

He begins to describe the slaughter on the battlefield beginning with the lines:

I ch'ang hsueh chan,
Chih sha te, hsueh ch'eng ho, shih ku tui shan, ...

'A bloody battle,
The fought, blood in rivers and the dead piled in a
mountain . . . . . '

It will be noted that the lines commence to use a rhyming
ending once more. The song continues and Ssu Lang tells how
he alone was captured from the fray and treated well by the
barbarian Empress Dowager who gave her pretty daughter in
marriage. He goes on to say that he has heard his mother is with
an attacking force in the neighbourhood after all these years and
laments the fact that he is unable to meet her and finally con-
cludes by walking back to his seat. The property man by this
time has placed a table in the centre of the stage with a chair at
either side and Ssu Lang sits to the left of the table, plunged in
melancholy thought. Then the voice of the Iron Mirror Princess
is heard calling backstage for her maid, in the high voice of the
tan actor.

Princess:

Ya t'ou! (The name for a maid).

Maid:·

Yu! (Here I am).

Princess:

Tai lu- a! (Come).

Maid:

Shih la! (I obey).

The *hsiao lo*, small gong, is beaten and the maid comes out on
the stage and stands at the side half facing the audience. She

carries a small doll in her arms to represent the child of Ssu Lang
and the Iron Mirror Princess. This is a common stage convention. Formerly the dolls used were Chinese style but in recent
years actors have thought nothing of using the flaxen-haired
western style article. The doll is only a symbol, what matter if it
is blonde or black-haired! Then the Princess of the Iron Mirror
comes out and walks to the front of the stage. She is wearing
ch'i chuang, or Manchu style costume with the *liang pa t'ou*
head-dress and *ch'i hsueh*, the special shoes used with this
costume. The shoes and head-dress have already been described
in a previous chapter. The costume consists of a long one-piece
robe which opens down the centre and has a high collar. It is
called *ch'i p'ao*. It is in crimson and richly embroidered with a
broad wave pattern round the hem. There are no *shui hsiu*,
water sleeves, with this costume. The sleeves proper have wide
cuffs which are cut just above the wrists. A large silk handkerchief is carried in the right hand while a long necklace of
wooden beads is worn hanging to the waist. The head-dress is
decorated with long hanging silk tassels and a huge peony in
the centre or alternatively a large phoenix ornament. Sometimes
a short waist-length, sleeveless jacket, the *k'an chien*, is worn
over this dress which is actually based on that worn by Manchu
ladies until the early years of the century. When the princess
reaches the front of the stage she touches her temple with the
right hand, the right sleeve being lightly held in the left fingers.
Then she adjusts her collar with both hands and commences to
sing in *hsi p'i man ban* time.

> Shao yao k'ai, mu tan fang, hua hung i p'ien
> Yen yang t'ien ch'un kuang hao pai niao sheng hsüan,

The singing is in the high falsetto style of the *tan* actor and it
takes an experienced ear to detect the separate syllables which
are run together or drawn out in time to the music. The two
lines translated read:

The peonies open, a mass of red blooms.
It is bright Spring weather and all the birds are singing. . .

After singing this the Princess places her right hand in front
of her breast and she continues her song.

Wo pen tang (she points towards Ssu Lang with her right arm
under her uplifted left sleeve) *yu fu ma, hsiao ch'ien yu.* She
drops both hands and goes slowly to the left and then very

slowly returns to the front stage singing as she goes and drawing out the last word *wan* in a long syllable. The meaning of the line being 'I ought to amuse my husband'. The small gong is then beaten and the *hu ch'in* plays *la ya ti*.

The Princess stands at the front of the stage and bends over as though to see what her husband is doing and lifts her left foot as though stepping over a threshold. Ssu Lang is by this time sitting and slowly shaking his head in despair and at the same time wiping his eyes. She steps back looking very surprised and exclaims '*Ya!*' She points at him once again under he sleeve and sings:

Tsan nai t'a chung jih li, ch'ou so mei chien.

'What is to be done, the whole day long, sorrow is written on his brow.' The whole of the time the Princess is speaking or singing she is using her handkerchief, changing it from hand to hand according to her movements, a very typical feature of the *tan's* technique in such a role. Her spoken words are in *ching pai*, that is to say the dialect of Peking, using the special inflections of the *tan* actor's vocal style.

From this point the plot of the play begins to unfold. After finding out what is wrong by a series of guesses the Iron Princess proceeds to secure the arrow of command from her mother to enable her husband to pass through the camp and reach the enemy lines where he is reunited with his family. There is a striking tableau on the stage when he is about to return, in order to keep his promise, his old mother, former wife and other relatives pleading with him to stay. It is a scene which offers a good opportunity for the singing and movements typical of the various roles. Ssu Lang is arrested as soon as he gets back by two Court officials who are also relatives of the Empress Dowager. The two men are played by *ch'ou* actors who are provided with ample scope for a great deal of humorous dialogue. In the final scene for instance they are all gathered before the angry Empress Dowager, Ssu Lang in chains and under penalty of execution. The Iron Mirror Princess has been asking the two officials for advice on how to get Ssu Lang reprieved. The two clowns tell her to use her small son Ah Ke in a ruse, as she used him originally to secure the arrow of command which has caused all the trouble. They advise her to toss the child to the Empress Dowager and pretend to cut her own throat, then, they say, the grandmother will pity her grandchild and reprieve his father. The Princess is dubious about using her child, however, and the following cross dialogue ensues.

First clown:

> *Ni yao shih shih she liao ti . . . . . .*
>
> If you don't give up the little one . . . . . .

Second clown:

> *Na ke chiu chiu pu liao lao ti . . . . . .*
>
> You can't have the big one . . . . . .

First clown:

> *Ni yao shih chiu liao lao ti . . . . . .*
>
> If you save the big one . . . . . .

Second clown:

> *Chiang lai yao to shao hsiao ti ma yu a . . . . . .*
>
> In the future there will be lots of new little ones . . . . . .

This kind of talk goes at a rollicking pace with the burr of the Peking dialect emphasized to its fullest extent. In the end, of course, the Empress Dowager relents and Ssu Lang is reprieved but ordered to take charge of a far Northern outpost where he will no longer be in danger of temptation. The play closes with Ssu Lang mounting his horse to set forth on this journey.

The reader will have been able to gather from the short excerpts given here the manner in which some of the various technical features discussed earlier in the book are incorporated in an actual stage performance. The passages used are taken from the play as it was performed by the actor T'an Hsin-p'ei and this is regarded as a classic version if a difficult one for modern actors. There are many variations in the dialogue as it is, or was, spoken by present day actors. The literary text of any play is never regarded as such hallowed material that it cannot be adapted to suit a particular artist.

CHAPTER VII

THE PLAYHOUSE

⌖

THE earliest permanent stages in China were those belonging to temples, made of stone and brick with ornate roofs. They were simple platforms with no curtain or proscenium built high above the ground and surrounded on three sides by the spectators. The performances were paid for by the wealthy men of the neighbourhood and the populace stood or sat in the open courtyard of the temple to see the performance. It was the temple stage which served as a prototype for that of the permanent playhouse of later centuries as well as the private stage used in Imperial palaces and noblemen's houses. The theatre early came under the patronage of the Court and it was the custom for companies of actors to entertain the officials and their high ranking guests in the main hall of palace or mansion. The tradition of private performances has only died out within very recent times and well to do people regularly invited actors to perform before their guests on special occasions such as weddings. In such cases if there was a stage at all it would be a temporary one although this was more often than not dispensed with. A well-known example of a private stage still in existence is that built for the Empress Dowager in the Summer Palace at Peking. This is somewhat more elaborate than most, being built in three stories with special devices which allowed evil spirits to appear on the stage from below and celestial beings from the second storey above. The building is in stone with glazed tile roofs and pillared supports.

The ordinary people were not admitted to performances such as those described above and after the temple stages by far the most common kind of public theatres were temporary structures of planks, bamboo poles and matting erected with in a few hours and dismantled as quickly. Travelling troupes went all over the country giving performances in country towns and villages in the festival seasons and were paid for their entertainment by popular subscription, there being no admission charges as such. These kinds of performances are still common in China today. Even in sophisticated Hong Kong and its outlying territory it is

still common to see the 'matshed' theatres, although Coca Cola
and patent medicine advertisements above the stage perhaps add
a slightly more modern touch and the plays are those of the local
Cantonese drama.

An interesting description of an open air theatre is given by
Robert Fortune in his book, 'A Residence among the Chinese',
published in 1857. His account is as apposite now as it was when
written. 'In the afternoon the play began and attracted its
thousands of happy spectators. As already stated, the subscribers,
or those who gave the play, had a raised platform placed about
twenty yards from the front of the stage, for themselves and their
friends. The public occupied the ground on the front and sides of
the stage, and to them the whole was free as their mountain air,
each man, however poor, had as good a right to be there as his
neighbour. And it is the same all over China, the actors are paid
by the rich, and the poor are not excluded from participating in
the enjoyments of the stage. The Chinese have a curious fancy
for erecting these temporary theatres in the dry beds of streams.
In travelling through the country I have frequently seen them in
such places. Sometimes when the thing is done in grand style, a
little tinsel town is erected at the same time, with its palaces,
pagodas, gardens and dwarf plants. These places rise and disappear as if by the magic of the enchanter's wand but they serve
the purposes for which they are designed and contribute largely
to the enjoyment and happiness of the mass of the people.' The
reference to the dry beds of streams might apply equally to
Japan for it was on the dry bed of the Kamo river in Kyoto that
the earliest Kabuki performance was staged by O Kuni in the early
years of the seventeenth century.

The permanent theatre of the cities had its origin in the
teahouse. During the Ch'ing dynasty (1616–1912) a type of
stage developed in the teahouses which remained the model for
the ordinary city theatre until the early part of this century. The
auditorium contained stools and tables at which the audience
sat and drank tea while the show went on. The tables were
placed endways on to the stage and people sat facing each other
across the tables not looking at the actors. A theatrical entertainment was a social occasion on which sipping tea, eating
dainties and conversing with one's friends were as important as
watching the play. There were no admission fees in such theatres,

the spectators paid for their tea when it was brought round, the fee being called *ch'a ch'ien* or tea money; in return the attendants provided a small slip of paper on which was printed the names of the plays for the day. Later the custom developed where a table in the auditorium could be sold in entirety rather like a box in the Western theatre, and guests were able to ask for special plays to be performed in which case an extra charge was made. In the old quarters of Fu Tzu Miao in Nanking, where the author was resident until 1949, there were still a number of small theatres which carried on the ancient system. The guest entered and took his seat at a table and attendants came round, served tea and collected a fee, and no doubt there were hundreds of such places scattered throughout the other large cities of China. Theatres always took the name of the tea house in which they were situated and in fact were referred to as *ch'a yüan*, tea gardens, and not as playhouses.

Probably the most famous old-style theatre in existence is the Kuang Ho Lo outside the Ch'ien Men in Peking which still retains its ancient stage although the auditorium now has Western style seating and lighting. It was built in the reign of K'ang Hsi (1661–1722) and stands as a symbol of days long since gone. The photograph on pl. III which was taken about 1898, gives a good idea of the theatre as it used to be. The stage was almost square and covered by a roof supported by lacquered pillars. It stood a few feet above the ground and was surrounded by a low wooden balustrade about two feet high. At the rear right and left of the stage were two doors hung with embroidered curtains, the *shang ch'ang men* and *hsia ch'ang men*, or entry and exit. Between these hung a large crimson embroidered curtain called the *ta chang*, or great canopy. The theatre was lit by oil lamps, later gas and finally electricity came to be used. Suspended from the roof of the stage was a horizontal bar which was used for acrobatic displays; a large lacquered sign board hung at the rear of the stage above the *ta chang* was inscribed with the name of the teahouse. The auditorium of a theatre of this kind was constructed on a regular plan. In addition to the tables and stools in the centre the ground floor was surrounded on either side by a verandah called the *liang lang* in which the audience sat on long benches. The verandah at the rear of the hall was called *san tso*. The spaces at the side of the stage were called *hsiao ch'ih tzu* and here tables were placed at which the true lovers of the theatre sat. Behind the *liang lang* there was a space described as *ta ch'iang* where there was a brick bench in a raised layer and for which one obtained cushions from attendants at the rear of the hall; there were the cheap seats. The second floor of the auditorium was reached by flights of steps at the entrance to the teahouse and consisted of a verandah running all the way round the theatre and directly above the *liang lang* and *san tso* on the ground floor. These verandahs were called *kuan tso* and were divided by partitions into boxes capable of seating twelve persons in each. Here sat the officials and wealthier classes and later, when women were admitted to the theatres but still kept strictly segregated, the second floor verandahs were for ladies' use only. The portion just above the stage on the second floor was called *tao kuan tso:* here it was possible to see only the backs of the actors whose relatives occupied these seats.

After the 1911 revolution the old theatre architecture began to change, the traditional stage was no longer used and the Western style proscenium was introduced. At first the stage was semicircular and protruded into the auditorium but later the frame type became common. The simple curtained background with no other accessories continued to be the basic stage setting but there were many experiments using scenery, and the Shanghai theatre in particular introduced a note of realism in this respect which was not always an artistic improvement on the dignified simplicity of the old stage. Electricity led to the use of footlights and effects but, until 1949 at any rate, they tended to be crude and harsh and the Chinese never seemed to achieve the happy blending of the new with the old as the Japanese have done in the Kabuki theatre in these matters.

The greenrooms in a theatre are situated behind the stage. Since the introduction of the star system during the past decades leading actors have individual rooms although often these are mere curtained enclosures in the one large room which, to most of the actors, serves as both dressing room and property department and is littered with make-up stands, costume chests and the beards, clothing, weapons and various accessories required for the performance. The ordinary greenroom of a *ching hsi* theatre presents an incredible kaleidoscope of colour and activity

Lung t'ao and the stage chair

in whose bustling confusion the layman might well be excused for wondering how it is possible to achieve the smooth precision associated with the entries and exists of the actor in other theatres, the Japanese included. It is achieved, however, for the informality of the greenroom is as deceptive as the informality of the musicians on the stage. Everybody knows what he is about.

The greenroom in the *ching hsi* theatre, as in others, is a world apart, with its own customs, slang and superstitions, although many of these are now obsolete. The members of a *pan*, or theatrical troupe, for instance, formed their own court to deal with delinquent players in former times. The leader of the orchestra acted as judge with the whole troupe in attendance. The highest penalty was dismissal from the troupe. No women were allowed on the stage before a performance nor was the *hua tan* actor until the time for his appearance. Every actor made an obeisance to the theatre shrine before he entered the green-rooms otherwise it was regarded as a bad omen for the performance to come. It was considered unlucky to open an umbrella backstage which was never referred to by its real name *san*, but as *yu kai*, or rain cover. The character for 'separate' has the same sound as *san* or umbrella and it was considered that it might indicate the breaking up of the troupe. If an actor was sick or unable for any reason to appear he had to report to the leader before the opening note of the orchestral overture on the brass otherwise he was compelled to appear whatever his trouble.

A custom of a different kind is described by Mei Lan-fang in his memoirs. He tells how during Ch'ing times it was the rule for all actors to cease appearing in public for one hundred days after the death of an Emperor, a period called *kuo sang*, or national mourning. Even at the end of that time they were only allowed to play in ordinary dress for another one hundred days, the *ch'ing i* with only a blue silk scarf round the head, the *ch'ou* with a dab of white paint on the face and so on. It was, needless to say, an etiquette which brought great hardship to theatrical people.

The change in the appearance of the playhouse during the last fifty years has symbolized the passing of the intimate style theatre known to an older generation and brought a more spectacular entertainment, at least in the larger city playhouses, which set the standard for the drama as a whole. In spite of this the old values have remained pre-eminent and the imaginative qualities of symbolism rather than the realism of imitation have continued to inspire it. Such scanty evidence as is available today from China appears to indicate that increasing emphasis may be laid on spectacle if not on realism, as against the more personal appreciation of the actor's art which has been prevalent in the past. When the new China produces a successor to a Mei Lan-fang, a Yang Hsiao-lou or a Yü Chen-fei, it may be conceded that the *ching hsi* is still a theatre which carries on a great artistic tradition.

GLOSSARY OF TECHNICAL TERMS

Cangue: Wooden device worn round the neck to secure the uplifted arms of a prisoner. Generally made of light metal on the stage, often in the shape of a fish.

Ch'a ch'ien: Tea money. Admission fee in old-style theatre.

Cha shang: Musical style used for actor's entry.

Ch'a yüan: Tea garden. Old name for a theatre.

Chan mao: Woollen hat worn by *ch'ou* actor.

Chan men sheng: Grouping used by actors on entry.

Ch'ang hsia: Special exit technique of actors.

Ch'ang mien: Stage orchestra.

Ch'ang shang: Entry of an actor singing.

Chang k'ao: Subdivision of *sheng* role. A general or high ranking warrior who wears the full regalia of stage armour.

Ch'ang pai: Vocal technique of the actor.

Chao pan: Actor's signal for the orchestra to accompany his singing.

Chao yuan ling hsia: Musical style used for actor's exits.

Ch'e ch'i: Flags used on the stage to symbolize a chariot.

Ch'e ssu men shang: Special entry movement for actors.

Ch'en: Term for officials in old Chinese society.

Cheng ching: Painted face roles for important personages of good character.

Cheng erh huang: Musical style used in the *ching hsi.*

Cheng hsi p'i: Musical style used in the *ching hsi.*

Cheng kung tiao: Singing style used by *ching hsi* actors.

Cheng lung: Dragon pattern on the front of a *mang.*

H

Cheng men i shang: Entry movement for supernatural characters.

Ch'eng p'ai: Singing style for *sheng* roles.

Cheng tan: Female role in *ch'uan ch'i* and *ching hsi.* A good and serious character.

Cheng tiao: Principal airs in theatre music.

Chi chi feng hsia. Musical style used in actor's exits.

Ch'i chuang: Manchu style costume for women.

Ch'i chuang t'ou: Manchu hair style.

Ch'i hsüeh: Shoes with short stilt soles worn with ch'i ch'uang.

Ch'i ku shang: Musical style used for actor's exits.

Ch'i pa: Series of postures and arm movements used by fighting characters on the stage, often when they make an entry. Said to be originally derived from the movements made by warriors when buckling on their armour.

Ch'i p'ao: Long robe worn by Manchu ladies.

Ch'i pa shang: Entry movements by military characters.

Chi san ch'iang hsia: Musical style used for actor's exits.

Ch'i yen hui hsia: Musical style used for actor's exits.

Cha jan: Long full beard worn by *ching* actors.

Cha tsui jan: Shorter version of *cha jan.*

Chia sha: Robe worn by important Buddhist dignitaries.

Chiang: Dark crimson colour.

Chiang yang: Rhyming group of characters in *ch'ang pai.*

Chiao: Foot movements.

Chien: Two edged sword.

Chien i: Long robe with tight cuffed sleeves worn with a stiff knotted sash. It symbolizes travelling or a fighter who does not wear armour. There are three styles.

Chien tzu: 'Sharp' character in actor's lines.

Ch'ih: Act of a *k'un ch'ü* play.

Ch'ih tzu tiao: Singing style used by *ching hsi* actors.

Chih wei sheng: Hsiao sheng actor who wears pheasant feathers in his head-dress.

Ch'in ma: Bamboo bridge used on *hu ch'in.*

Ch'in ping i: Style of *ma kua* worn in plays dealing with *Ch'in* dynasty times.

Ching: Classification for painted face roles in the *ching hsi.*

Ch'ing ch'iang yin hsia: Musical style used for actor's exits.

Ching chu ch'e k'ou: Rhyming formula of *ch'ang pai.*

Ching hsi: Peking classical drama.

Ch'ing i: Subdivision of *tan* role. The part of a faithful wife, lover or maiden in distress. A singing role.

Chiu ch'ui pan shang: Musical style used for actor's entries.

Ch'iu jan: Short curly beard worn by *ching* actors or fighting characters.

Chiu lung k'ou: Nine dragons mouth, a place on the *ching hsi* stage immediately opposite the drum player in the orchestra.

Ch'iung sheng: Hsiao sheng actor playing part of poor scholar or young man in distress.

Ch'ou: Classification for comic roles in the *ching hsi.*

Ch'ou san jan: Beard worn by *ch'ou* actor.

Chu chiao: Principal parts in *ch'uan ch'i.*

Chu nu erh hsia: Musical style used in actor's exits.

Ch'u tui tzu shang: Musical style used in actor's entry.

Ch'u tung chang: Backward entry of an actor.

Ch'uan ch'i: Important development of the *Nan ch'ü* or southern school of drama in Ming times.

Chiu hsia: Exit of people running.

Ch'ui ta shang: Musical style used in actor's entry.

Ch'un tzu: Skirt worn in female roles. Made in different styles and patterns.

Chung tung: Rhyming group of characters in *ch'ang pai.*

Chung yen: Term used in musical timing.

Erh hu: Two stringed instrument used as secondary accompaniment on the *ching hsi* stage.

Erh huang: Musical style used in *ching hsi.*

Erh hua lien: Painted face roles in which emphasis is laid on acrobatics and posturing.

Erh i hsiang: Second costume chest.

Erh liu: Special musical timing.

Erh lung ch'u shui shang: Entry grouping of actors.

Erh t'iao: Beard worn by *wu ch'ou* actors.

Fa hua: Rhyming group of character sin *ch'ang pai.*

Fa i: White cape worn by Taoist magician on stage.

Fa tien shang: Musical style used for actor's entry.

Fan erh huang: Musical style used on *ching hsi* stage.

Fan hsia: Cartwheel exit.

Fan hsi p'i: Musical style used on *ching hsi* stage.

Fan ssu p'ing: Musical style used on *ching hsi* stage.

Fang chih shao mao: Small oar blade shaped fins worn at the back of the *shao mao.*

Feng ch'i: Flags used to symbolize wind on the stage.

Feng huang: Phoenix.

Feng ju sung hsia: Musical style used for actor's exit.

Fu ching: Painted face roles portraying bad characters with vigorous action.

Fu kuei i: First garment in costume chest—indicates the wearer is in poor circumstances.

Fu mo: Secondary actor in the *ch'uan ch'i.*

Hai yen: Dramatic school which was a branch of the *Nan ch'ü.*

Hsi: Generic term for theatricals.

Hsi: Character for joy.

Hsi hsing hsia: Actor's exit movement.

Hsi p'i: Musical style used in the *ching hsi.*

Hsia: Secondary colours used for costume styles.

Hsia shou i: Costume worn by actors representing an army opposing Imperial forces.

Hsiang chin: Square-shaped hat worn informally by Prime Minister.

Hsiang tiao: Hard hat with square double crown worn by Prime Minister.

Hsiao chih tzu: Spaces at side of old style stage.

Hsiao chu erh hsia: Musical style used for actor's exits.

Hsiao hua lien: Another term for *wu ch'ou.*

Hsiao i: Stage costume for women in mourning.

Hsiao kuo men shang: Musical interlude in main action of play.

Hsiao ku: Another term for *tan p'i ku.*

Hsiao lo: Small gong.

Hsiao lo ch'ang szu t'ou shang: Musical style used for actor's entry.

Hsiao lo chi san ch'ang shang: Musical style used for actor's entry.

Hsiao lo feng ju sung ho t'ou shang: Musical style used for actor's entry.

Hsiao lo k'uai ch'ou t'ou shang: Musical style used for actor's entry.

Hsiao lo liu yao ling shang: Musical style used for actor's entry.

Hsiao lo man pan to t'ou shang: Musical style used for actor's entry.

Hsiao lo man ch'ou t'ou shang: Musical style used for actor's entry.

Hsiao lo mao erh t'ou shang: Musical style used for actor's entry.

Hsiao lo shui ti yü shang: Musical style used for actor's entry.

Hsiao lo ta shang: Musical style used for actor's entry.

Hsiao lo tso tso ts'ai shang: Musical style used for actor's entry.

Hsiao lo yuan pan to t'ou shang: Musical style used for actor's entry.

Hsiao sheng: Young scholar or lover role in *ch'uan ch'i, k'un ch'ü* and *ching hsi.*

Hsieh i tzu shang: Grouping used by actors on entry.

Hsieh i tzu hsia: Grouping used by actors on exit.

Hsieh men hsia: Special exit movement.

Hsieh men i shang: Entry movement for a spirit.

Hsieh men shang: Entry grouping for actors.

Hsien i tzu: Long strands of silk thread bound to a cord. Used in female hair styles.

Hsing: Musical instrument consisting of two small brass cups connected by a cord.

Hsing lung: Pattern on stage costume representing walking dragon.

Hsing t'ou: Stage costumes.

Hsiu hsia: Exit movement by *tan* actor.

Hsü sheng: Subdivision of *sheng* role. Middle aged statesman or scholar. Always bearded and singing is important in the role.

Hsüeh tzu: Stage costume. A general purpose robe made in a variety of styles and colours. Used as informal dress and as an undergarment.

Hu ch'in: Two stringed instrument used for song accompaniment on the *ching hsi* stage.

Hu hsu: Beards.

Hu kung: Bow of *hu ch'in.*

Hu ling: White silk stock worn beneath actor's outer robe.

Hu pan: Acting troupes from Anhui province.

Hu p'i p'i kua: Sleeveless tunic worn by 'ghost' soldier.

Hu tiao: Dramatic style originating in Hupeh province.

Hu wei: White fox tails on actor's head-dresses.

Hua lien: Lit. 'flower face'. Describes painted face roles.

Hua p'en ti: Shoe with convex curved sole worn with *ch'i chuang.*

Hua tan: Subdivision of *tan* role. A vivacious young woman, a coquette.

Hua ying hsiung i: Costume worn by brave and fearless fighters who are outlaws.

Huai ku: Drum similar to *tan p'i ku* but smaller. Used in *k'un ch'ü.*

Huai lai: Rhyming group of characters in *ch'ang pai.*

Hui chen shang: Entry movement for a general.

Hui lung ch'iang: Special musical style.

I ch'o: Rhyming group of characters in *ch'ang pai.*

I chiang feng hsia: Musical style used for actor's exits.

I ch'i jan: Small beard worn by *ch'ou* actors.

I fan chiang erh shui hsia: Musical style used for actor's exits.

I tzu chan man shang: Entry groupings for actors and officials.

I tzu hsia: Special exit movement.

I tzu jan: Beard worn by *ch'ou* actor.

I tzu shang: Special entry movement.

Jen ch'en: Rhyming group of characters in *ch'ang pai.*

Ju i: A form of sceptre.

Juan hsueh tzu: Hsueh tzu made of soft material.

Juan k'ao: Armour worn without pennants.

Jung ch'iu: Silk poms poms worn on actor's head-dress.

Ka pa shang: Musical style used for actor's entry.

Kabuki: Japanese classical drama.

K'an chien: Short sleeveless jacket worn by Manchu ladies.

K'ao: Stage armour worn with four triangular pennants at the back.

K'ao ch'i: Pennants on stage armour.

Kao fang chin: Hat of ordinary scholar.

Ke po: Arm movements of actor.

K'o pan: Theatrical training school.

K'o so shang: Special entry of actor.

K'u ao: Short tunic and wide trousers worn by *hua tan* actors.

Ku chuang t'ou: Coiffures based on historical models.

Ku jen erh mao: Two pointed tufts of hair worn above ears by *ching* actors.

K'ua men chien: Crossing the threshold. Actor's movement.

Kuai chang: Stuff carried by *lao tan* actors.

K'uai pan: Quick time in music.

Kuan hsueh: High black satin boots with thick soles worn by actors.

Kuan i: Stage costumes worn by officials. Made in several colours according to status.

Kuan Kung jan: Ling wide beard worn by actors portraying Kuan Kung.

Kuan sheng: Young lover or scholar role in *ch'uan ch'i.*

Kuan tso: Second floor balcony in old style theatre.

Kuan i hsiang jen: Men who look after stage costumes.

Kuei men tan: Young girl role in *ch'uan ch'i* and *ching hsi.*

Kuei tzu shou i: Costume worn by executioner.

K'uei p'ai: Song style developed by Chang Erh K'uei.

K'uei t'ou: Hats and head-dresses in stage costume.

Kumadori: Japanese *Kabuki* actors' painted face make up.

K'un ch'ü: Theatrical form which developed in the Ming dynasty and remained a national drama until mid 19th century when it was supplanted by the *ching hsi.*

K'un ch'iang: Music of the *k'un ch'ü* drama.

Kung: Term describing artisans in old Chinese society.

Kung ch'ih: Scale in traditional Chinese music.

Kung kan: Arm of *hu ch'in* bow.

Kung mao: Hair of *hu ch'in* bow.

Kuan tao: The green dragon blade, a weapon carried by Kuan Kung.

Kuo men: Preliminary and intermediate passages used in musical accompaniment.

Kuo sang: National mourning.

La hsia: Special exit movement.

La ma hsia: Exit leading off a horse.

Lao sheng: Subdivision of *sheng* role. Aged man.

Lao tan: Old woman role in *ch'uan ch'i*, *K'un ch'ü* and *ching hsi.*

Li hsien: Inner string of *hu ch'in.*

Li shui: Wave pattern.

Liang lang: Ground floor balcony in old style theatre auditorium.

Liang pa t'ou erh: Head-dress worn in Manchu hair style.

Lien p'u: Painted face make up of the *ching role.*

Ling chih: A fungus called the plant of immortality.

Ling hsia: Special exit grouping of actors.

Ling shang: Special entry movement.

Ling tzu: Pheasant feathers used in stage costume.

Liu shui pan: Special musical style.

Liu tzu tiao: Singing style used by actors.

Liu yao ling hsia: Musical style used for actor's exit.

Lo mao: Hat worn by fighting characters and retainers.

Luan tai: Stiff silk girdle with tasselled ends.

Lung t'ao i: Costume worn by the four stage auxiliaries who represent a general's forces.

Ma kua: Formal, short, wide-sleeved jacket worn when travelling and riding.

Ma pien: Switch with silk tassels used by actors to symbolize a horse.

Man jan: Long full beard.

Mang: Theatrical costume, an official robe. Made in several colours according to status.

Men tun tzu shang: Entry grouping used by actors.

Miao t'iao: Rhyming group of characters in *ch'ang pai.*

Mieh hsieh: Rhyming group of characters in *ch'ang pai.*

Mo: Secondary role in *ch'uan ch'i.*

Nan ch'ü: Southern dramatic school of Yuan times.

Nan lo shang: Musical style used for actor's entry.

Nan pang tzu: Musical style.

Nei pai shang: Special entry technique.

Nei ch'ang tso: The inner chair used as stage property.

Nien hsia: Special exit technique of actors.

Nien shih shang: Entry arrangement by group of actors.

Nü chien tsuan: Hair style worn by *ch'ou* actor representing elderly woman.

Nung: Term for farmers and agriculturists in old Chinese society.

Pa kua: Eight diagrams. Cabalistic signs used as pattern on stage costume.

Pa ta ts'ang shang: Musical style used for actor's entry.

Pa tzu: Moustache worn by *ch'ou* actors.

P'ai: General term for styles of singing peculiar to individual actors.

Pai hua: Everyday speech of Peking.

Pai tui hsiang ying hsia: Exit movement for host and guest.

Pai tui shang: Entry movement for a general.

Pan: Hard wood clappers used for time beating by the leader of the *ching hsi* orchestra.

Pan hsiang: Make-up.

Pan yen: Timing system used in the *kung ch'ih* scale.

P'ang ao: Padded sleeveless jacket worn as undergarment by *ching* and *wu cheng* actors.

Pang tzu: Dramatic form which originated in Shenshi province.

Pang tzu: Clapper used as a time beater, originally used in *pang tzu* style drama.

Pao chien: Two edged sword used in dances on the stage.

P'ao hsia: Running exit.

Pao pu: Blue cloth used as binding on body of *hu ch'in*.

Pao ti k'uai hsueh: Soft angle length boots with flat soles worn by fighting characters.

Pao t'ou ti: Assistants who specialize in making up the coiffures of actors.

Pao tsuan: Flat jade ornament worn with *ta feng kuan.*

Pei ch'i yen hui hsia: Musical style used for actor's exit.

Pei chiao: Secondary parts in *ch'uan ch'i.*

Pei ch'ü: Northern dramatic school of Yuan times.

Pei shao hsia: Exit to symbolize fire.

Pei hsin: Sleeveless knee length garment opening down the front. Worn by *hua tan* actors in various colours and patterns.

Pei huan hsia: Special exit movement.

Pei sha hsia: Special exit movement.

Peng tzu hsia: Special exit movement.

P'ei: Stage costume. An outdoor garment worn by people of higher rank. Made in several colours.

P'i huang: Musical style using both *hsi p'i* and *p'i huang* forms. The music of the *ching hsi* stage.

P'i p'a: Lute with pear-shaped body. Ancient instrument used as secondary accompaniment and occasionally solo on *ching hsi* stage.

P'i tzu: Snake skin used to cover face of *hu ch'in* body.

P'iao yu: Amateur.

P'ien shan: Grey robe of Buddhist priest.

P'ing chu: Dramatic entertainment originating in the countryside, not to be confused with *ching hsi.*

P'ing hsi: Another name for Peking drama.

P'ing pan to t'ou shang: Musical style used for actor's entry.

Po: Cymbals.

P'u tao: Short sword or scimitar.

San hsieh men i shang: Special entry movement of actors.

San hsien: Three-stringed instrument used for secondary accompaniment on *ching hsi* stage. Prototype of Japanese *samisen*.

San hua lien: Term used for *ch'ou* roles.

San i hsiang: Third costume chest.

San jan: Beard worn by *sheng* actors.

San pan: System of beats in musical timing.

San tso: Balcony at rear of old style theatre auditorium.

Seng pei hsin: Robe worn by high Buddhist dignitary.

Shan tzu sheng: Hsiao sheng actor who specializes in the play of his fan.

Shang: Pure colours. Term used in costume designs.

Shang: Term for merchants in old Chinese society.

Shang ch'ang: Entry of an actor.

Shang shou i: Costume worn by actors who symbolize an Emperor's army.

Shang tzu tiao: Singing style used by *ching hsi* actors.

Hsiao p'i kua: Sleeveless tunic worn by a 'ghost' soldier.

Sha mao: Hard double-crowned hat with two protruding fins at the back.

She t'ui p'i hsia: Special exit movement.

Shen chang erh hsia: Musical style used for actor's exit.

Shen shih: Term describing landed gentry in old Chinese society.

Sheng: Classification for male roles in the *ching hsi*.

Shih: Term describing scholars in old Chinese society.

Shih san p'eng lo shang: Musical style used for actor's entry.

Shou: Character for longevity.

Shu pan: Special rhyming form used in stage dialogue.

Shu pan hsia: Use of *shu pan* by actor making exit.

Shuai fa: Long plume of hair worn by actors playing the part of a prisoner or someone in distress.

Shuang hsieh i tzu shang: Grouping used by actors on entry.

Shui ch'i: Flags used on the stage to represent water.

Shui hsiu: Water sleeves, the white silk sleeves attached to the cuffs of actor's costumes.

Shui i: Under robe worn beneath all costumes with *shui hsiu.*

Shui mo tiao: Musical style of Ming times.

Shui sha: Fine gauze net used in basic hair styles.

So na: Wind instrument used on *ching hsi* stage.

So po: Rhyming group of characters in *ch'ang pai.*

Ssu chiao chan men shang: Entry grouping used by actors.

Ssu hsi jan: Beard worn by *ch'ou* actors.

Ssu pa men i shang: Entry grouping used by actors.

Ssu p'ing tiao: Musical style used in *ching hsi.*

Su pan: Acting troupes from Soochow.

Sun p'ai: Singing style developed by the actor Sun Chu-hsien.

Sung hsiang: Rosin.

Szu t'ao: Silk cords worn on the chest by *wu sheng* actors.

Ta chang: Curtain at rear of the old style stage.

Ta ch'ao shang: Musical style used for actor's entry.

Ta ch'iang: Cheap seats in old style theatre.

Ta ching shang: Musical style used for actor's entry.

Ta fa: Basic hair style in female roles.

Ta feng kuan: Phoenix head-dress worn by Empress.

Ta hsia: Musical style used for actor's exit.

Ta hua lien: All painted face roles in which singing is of prime importance.

Ta i hsiang: Principal costume chest.

Ta lao pan: Nickname for head of a theatrical troupe.

Ta lo: Large gong of the *ching hsi* orchestra.

Ta lo ch'ang chien shang: Musical style used for actor's entry.

Ta lo chi chi feng shang: Musical style used for actor's entry.

Ta lo chin ch'ien hua shang: Musical style used for actor's entry.

Ta lo ch'ou t'ou shang: Musical style used for actor's entry.

Ta lo ch'ung t'ou shang: Musical style used for actor's entry.

Ta lo fan ch'ang ch'ui shang: Musical style used for actor's entry.

Ta lo hui ts'ao shang: Musical style used for actor's entry.

Ta lo k'uai ch'ang ch'ui shang: Musical style used for actor's entry.

Ta lo luan ch'ui shang: Musical style used for actor's entry.

Ta lo man ch'ang ch'ui shang: Musical style used for actor's entry.

Ta lo niu ssu shang: Musical style used for actor's entry.

Ta lo shui ti yü shang: Musical style used for actor's entry.

Ta lo ssu chi t'ou shang: Musical style used for actor's entry.

Ta lo ssu pien chien chang shang: Musical style used for actor's entry.

Ta lo ssu pien shang: Musical style used for actor's entry.

Ta lo ta shang: Musical style used for actor's entry.

Ta lo tao pan shang: Musical style used for actor's entry.

Ta lo yin lo shang: Musical style used for actor's entry.

Ta lo yuan ch'ang shang: Musical style used for actor's entry.

Ta san t'ung: Prelude on the brass used before a *ching hsi* performance commences.

Ta ting: Plume of real hair used to make the chignon in female hair style.

Ta tsan: Metal hair ornament used to support a bun or chignon in female hair styles.

T'ai chi t'u: Mystic symbol of Taoism used on stage costume.

T'ai chiao shang: Entry grouping used by officials and generals.

Tan: Classification for female roles in the *ching hsi*.

Tan: Neck of the *hu ch'in*.

T'an p'ai: Singing style developed by T'an Hsin P'ei.

Tan p'i ku: Small drum used for beating time in the *ching hsi* orchestra.

T'ang ma hsia: Mounted exit.

T'ang ma shang: Actor's entry symbolizing a running horse.

T'ang mao: Head-dress of an Emperor.

Tao: Form of pike with large curled blade. Stage weapon.

T'ao hsia: Special exit movement.

Tao ma tan: Literally horse and sword *tan*. A variation of the *wu tan* role.

Tao pan: System of beats in musical timing.

Tao pan shang: Special entry singing of actor.

Tao pao: Informal garment worn by Taoist priest.

Ti tzu: Flute used in *ching hsi* orchestra.

T'iao shang: Entry movement for a god or spirit.

T'iao shui hsia: Suicide exit.

T'ieh tan: Secondary female role in the *ch'uan ch'i*.

Tien chiang ch'un shang: Entry used by military characters.

Ting hsia: Special exit movement.

T'o hsia: Special exit grouping.

To pan: System of beats in musical timing.

T'ou fa shui p'ien i fu: Coils of hair worn on the forehead and cheeks in female hair styles.

Tou p'eng: A wide sleeveless cape used on the stage.

T'ou yen: Term used in music for note accentuation.

Tsa chu: Dramatic entertainment of Yuan times which provided a model for future play construction.

Ts'ai tan: Woman of evil nature. Generally played by the *ch'ou* actor today.

Ts'ai hsüeh: Flat soled slippers in different patterns worn by women characters.

Ts'ai k'u: Trousers worn with high boots by male characters.

Ts'eng hsia: Exit of wounded person.

Tso ch'ang shih: Special narrative recited by actor on entry.

Tao t'o hsueh hsia: Special exit movement.

Tsou pien shang: Entry movement used by *wu ch'ou* and *wu sheng* actors.

Tsou yuan ch'ang shang: Special entry movement of *tan* actor.

Ts'ai ch'iao: False feet worn by female impersonators to represent bound feet of former times.

T'uan lung: Dragon pattern in roundels.

Tuan ta: Subdivision of *sheng* role. A fighter who is not an official military type.

T'uan tzu: Rounded characters in actor's lines.

Tui lien: Couplets recited by an actor on entry.

T'ung: Cylindrical body of the *hu ch'in.*

T'ung ch'ui: Alternative name for *ta hua lien* roles.

T'ung ming: A monologue which follows *tso ch'ang shih.*

Tung tso: Body movements and gestures of actors.

Tz'u ku yeh: Small prong shaped ornament worn on head-dress of fighting characters.

Tz'u sha: Female role in the *ch'uan ch'i.* A talkative, lively character.

Tzu wen hsia: Special exit movement.

Wai: Secondary role in the *ch'uan ch'i.*

Wai ch'ang tso: Outer seat, chair used as stage property.

Wai hsien: Outer string of *hu ch'in.*

Wan shou erh hsing hsia: Special exit movement of actors.

Wang p'ai: Singing style developed by Wang Kuei-fen.

Wang tzu: Skull cap worn as foundation for stage coiffures.

Wei sheng hsia: Musical style used for actor's exits.

Wei yen: Term used in music for note accentuation.

Wei tsui: Apron worn by *hua tan* and *ch'ing i* actors.

Wen ch'ou: Comic roles in which the characters are civilians.

Wen hsi: Plays dealing with aspects of domestic and social life.

Wen li: Literary style in speech and writing.

Wen sheng chin: Hat worn by *hsiao sheng* actors.

Wen sheng: Subdivision of *sheng* role. Civilian characters.

Wen wu sheng: Combines in one role *wu sheng* and *wen sheng* elements.

Wo hsia: Exit technique of an Emperor.

Wu ching: Painted face role in which fighting and gymnastics are predominant.

Wu ch'ou: Comic roles in which the characters represent minor military officials often performing stage acrobatics.

Wu hang: Acrobats.

Wu hsi: Plays with a military or fighting background.

Wu lao sheng: Subdivision of *sheng* role. An aged warrior who wears a white beard.

Wu ma chiang erh shiu hsia: Musical style used for actor's exit.

Wu pan men i shang: Entry grouping used for spirits.

Wu sheng: Subdivision of *sheng* role. A fighting or military character.

Wu tan: Subdivision of *tan* role. The part is one in which acrobatics and stage fighting are used by female characters.

Wu tsui jan: Beard worn by *ch'ou* actors.

Yao pan: System of beats in musical timing.

Yen ch'ien: Rhyming group of characters in *ch'ang pai.*

Yi yang: Dramatic school which was a branch of the *Nan ch'ü.*

Yin tzu: A *ch'ang pai* form used by actors on entering the stage.

Ying ch'en: White horse-hair fly switch carried by nuns, priests and Taoist magicians.

Ying hsueh tzu: Hsueh tzu costume made of stiff material.

Ying and yang: Symbolic Chinese motif representing origin of life.

Yu ch'iu: Rhyming group of characters in *ch'ang pai.*

Yu p'ai: Singing style developed by Yu San-sheng.

Yu tai: Lit. 'jade girdle'. A stiff loop-like girdle worn with the *mang.*

Yu yao: Dramatic school which was a branch of the *Nan ch'ü.*

Yuan ch'ih sha mao: Rounded fins worn at the back of the *shar mar.*

Yüeh ch'in: Four-stringed instrument with a circular body. Used for secondary accompaniment on the *ching hsi* stage.

Yun lo: Musical instrument which consists of a chime of ten small gongs.

Yung tzu ma chia: Variation of *shao p'i kua.*

INDEX

中文索引